POWER
LINES

SOUTH AFRICA

20°E · 30°E

ZIMBABWE

NAMIBIA

BOTSWANA

Kalahari

Gaborone ⊛

Desert

NORTHERN
PROVINCE
Tzaneen
Nkowakowa

Kangwane

Limpopo

MOZAMBIQUE

—25°S

Soshanguve
Administrative capital PRETORIA ⊛
JOHANNESBURG
Soweto

N1

Tembisa
Middelburg
N17
Ermelo

Nelspruit
Kromdraad
2

MAPUTO ⊛
Mbabane

SWAZILAND

25°S—

NORTH WEST

FREE STATE

N1

N3

KWAZULU-
NATAL

Lochiel

N2

Kimberley

Bloemfontein ⊛
Judicial capital

Maseru ⊛
LESOTHO

3

DURBAN

NORTHERN

CAPE

Orange

Other Provinces
1 GAUTENG
2 MPUMALANGA
3 EASTERN CAPE

Atlantic
Ocean

EASTERN CAPE

Robben
Island

WESTERN CAPE
George

N1

N2

East London

CAPE TOWN
*Legislative
capital*

N2

Port Elizabeth

Cape of Good Hope

Indian Ocean

—35°S

35°S—

0   miles   300

0   kilometers   400

AFRICA

Capital
⊛ Capital
• Other city or town
⌒ Selected former
Homeland

---- International boundary
········· Provincial boundary
═N1═ Highway
—·—· Intermittent river

20°E

SOUTH
AFRICA

POWER

TWO YEARS ON SOUTH AFRICA'S BORDERS

LINES

Jason Carter

INTRODUCTION BY JIMMY CARTER

NATIONAL GEOGRAPHIC

WASHINGTON, D.C.

Published by the National Geographic Society

Printed in the U.S.A.
Interior design by Melissa Farris

Library of Congress Cataloging-in-Publication Data

Carter, Jason.
    Power lines : two years on South Africa's borders / Jason Carter ; introduction by
Jimmy Carter.
        p. cm.
    ISBN 0-7922-8012-1
    1. South Africa--Description and travel. 2. South Africa--Social conditions--1994- 3.
Carter, Jason. 4. Peace Corps (U.S.)--Biography. I. Title.

DT1738.C36 2002
968.06'5--dc21

                                                            2002022370

One of the world's largest nonprofit scientific and educational organizations, the National Geographic Society was founded in 1888 "for the increase and diffusion of geographic knowledge." Fulfilling this mission, the Society educates and inspires millions every day through its magazines, books, television programs, videos, maps and atlases, research grants, the National Geographic Bee, teacher workshops, and innovative classroom materials. The Society is supported through membership dues, charitable gifts, and income from the sale of its educational products. This support is vital to National Geographic's mission to increase global understanding and promote conservation of our planet through exploration, research, and education.

For more information, please call 1-800-NGS LINE (647-5463) or write to the following address:

National Geographic Society
1145 17th Street N.W.
Washington, D.C. 20036-4688 U.S.A.

Visit the Society's Web site at www.nationalgeographic.com.

For Nombhuso, Andiswa, Twana, Sicelo, Sesi, and Nomfundo
May you grow up in a truly new South Africa.

An Issue of Knowing

I could try, and I could try
all night and after all day
to the putting of myself in black man's shoes.
And I could.
But to the putting of myself in black man's feet
is an another issue.
An other issue entirely.

–J. Clayton L. Jones
Calhoun, Georgia, March 18, 1998

CONTENTS

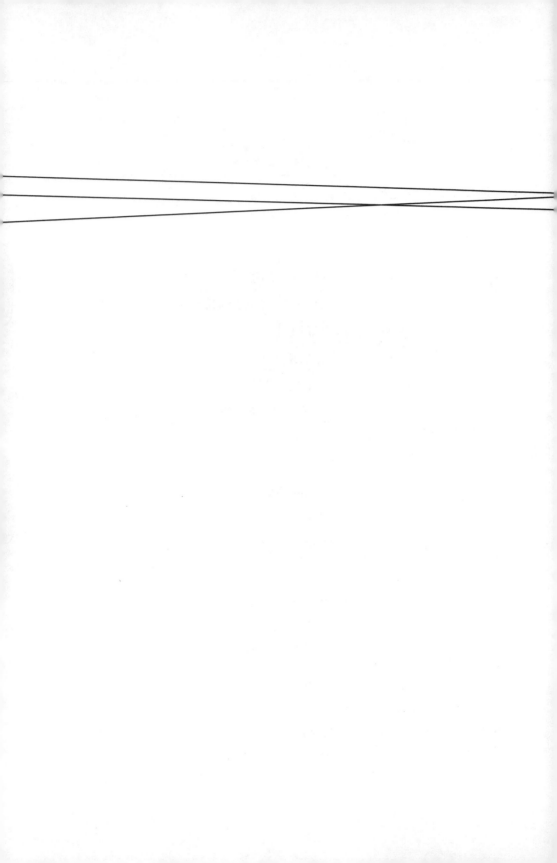

INTRODUCTION

JIMMY CARTER

THIS BOOK IS JASON'S INTRIGUING ACCOUNT OF HIS EXPERIENCES in the Peace Corps. It is especially meaningful to me because he is my grandson and in many ways has followed in the footsteps of my mother, Lillian, who served 30 years earlier.

Since the Peace Corps was founded in 1961, 162,000 volunteers have brought great personal benefits to millions of people in 135 different nations. Participation in and financial support for the organization have varied over the years, with the number of volunteers ranging from more than 15,000 in 1966 to a low of 5,400 in 1982. About 7,000 volunteers are currently serving in 77 countries. Fortunately, unchanging ideals have inspired generations of volunteers who still come forward to offer a part of their lives in service to others.

The basic character of the Peace Corps is represented in the experiences of my 70-year-old mother, who served in India, and of my 22-year-old grandson, who went to South Africa. It is intriguing to consider the differences and common themes of her tour in Vikhroli, a village near Bombay, and his in Lochiel, a small community just north of Swaziland.

The reader will soon share Jason's fascinating story of a young man using his natural ability to absorb the native languages to immerse himself as deeply as possible among people who are struggling to outgrow the ravages of apartheid. Jason lived and worked in an isolated and poverty-stricken community, but he was always just a few miles or computer strokes away from an advanced and prosperous First World society. Sometimes, with feelings of guilt, he escaped on a few occasions from his Peace Corps assignment into the modern era of airplanes, luxury resorts, and the Internet. But there was always a natural attraction that drew him back to Lochiel, among the students, teachers, and the host family who adopted him as their own.

Jason grew up near Chicago, was educated in a fine university, visited several African countries as a boy and young man, and saw his Peace Corps service as an interesting and worthy challenge. He tells us about modern youth, clashing cultures, racism and oppression, personal courage, severe challenges, and shared hope for the future.

Jason's experiences were remarkably similar to those of a mature woman from a small town in southwest Georgia who had been an exceptional holdout within a legally accepted culture of strict racial segregation. Lillian Carter felt that she had completed her life's work as a mother and a highly trained registered nurse, but became bored and impatient with her relatively idle days as a well-to-do widow. She responded to a television recruitment call for Peace Corps volunteers, with "Age is no limit!" flashing across the screen, and decided to seek a final opportunity for challenge and adventure. She asked to go where people had dark skin, were poor, and needed medical care.

When her Peace Corps application was accepted and the time came for her to leave Plains, Lillian packed a single suitcase, voted an absentee ballot, and walked out of her house leaving the doors unlocked, as they were to remain for the next two years. During that time, she wrote home at least once a week, and my sister Gloria collected all the letters and published many of them in a book, *Away From Home: Letters to My Family*.

There seems to have been an exceptional response to the recruitment drive to which she responded, and a concerted effort was made to de-select as many volunteers as possible. Everyone was required to single out five others in the class who should be sent back home—something like the modern television show, *Survivor*. Mama was desperate to remain in the class, and she volunteered to perform extra tasks, once claiming that she could type and offering to address a stack of envelopes during her spare time on Sunday.

She wrote: "Well, after everybody else left, I locked the door and looked at the typewriter—then I looked out the window to see how far it was to the ground. (I didn't want to mess myself up too bad if I decided to jump.) I finally figured out how to put the paper in, and after fooling with it 30 minutes, mashed the right button to make a capital letter. It took me another hour to find out that long thing on the bottom made the space between words. I worked all day to address 40 envelopes, and I'm afraid they'll think I did such a good job they might ask me to do this every time!" The Peace Corps psychiatrist finally told her that she was trying to be too friendly.

Mama was finally selected as a volunteer and made the long trip to India. Her monthly stipend was $30. She was assigned to work in a factory town about 20 miles from Bombay, which was owned in its entirety by the extremely rich Godrej family. Because of the nature of her intimate personal contact with the workers and their families, she was treated as one of the lower caste. She washed her own clothes, walked four miles a day up and down the hillside where most of the laborers lived, and went into their homes to promulgate a family planning program that Prime Minister Indira Gandhi had adopted as a national goal.

She braved the changing seasons along with all the other workers and made the best of difficult times. Once, she caught a ride during a monsoon, the truck drowned out under a railroad bridge, the driver left her while he went for help, and she waited until the water rose above her knees. Then, she said, "I tucked my dress around my waist and waded a city block with swirling water waist deep."

She wrote to us regularly, describing her mostly losing struggles with Hindi, Marathi, and Gujarati, and her attempts to control tears and nausea as she immersed herself in the lives of the Vikhroli people. Mail was slow, requiring two or three weeks for an exchange, so we had to be careful not to write her about transient illnesses or personal problems that would cause her to worry long after we had forgotten about them.

On a few occasions she had some limited success, like Jason.

"I had tea with a Hindu couple yesterday. He and I sat on pots and watched while the wife made tea. She squatted on the floor, where she had a towel that she picked up with her toes (she used all ten), then she pitched it in the air and caught it to wipe cups and saucers, floor, and vessel. I watched with awe, getting more unhungry by the minute. The table was about six inches high, made of cow dung, and the floors were paved with the same. When she fixed our tea, she didn't have any for herself, and I refused to eat without her—so, for the first time, she ate with her husband. When I left, they promised me that from now on they would eat together, unless someone else was there!"

Mama's primary problem was becoming too personally involved with some of her patients as she grew to know the families of factory workers. She shared with Jason a struggle against excessive emotional attachments to suffering people, while acknowledging the impossibility of changing the basic circumstances of their lives. For weeks, she was tortured by the suffering and slow death of a leprous woman who lay beside the path that Mama had to walk twice a day. The doctor and others ordered that the dying woman be left alone and not treated in any way.

"That woman is still by the side of the road, still starving, drinking water from a mud puddle—and something in me dies every time I see her.... I bought two loaves of bread today, and on my way home, she was dragging herself across the road to drink that muddy water. Her fingers are nearly all gone (leprosy). She's a solid sore, and was diarrheaing all over the place. I put the bread down beside her, but I couldn't look her in the eyes." She was afraid they would leave the cadaver for vultures, but 20 days later she wrote: "Oh, everything is rosy, and I feel so good. The woman finally died, and they did move her instead of leaving her there to rot."

Mama described in vivid terms learning to do without toilet paper, to clean herself with her left hand, to eat and touch others with her right fingers, and to drink from a shared bottle while holding it six inches from her open mouth. She learned to appreciate the serviceability of dried cow dung and the value of an empty tin can or a discarded plastic container.

When we developed a roll of film she sent home at the end of her first year, we were startled to see how gaunt she had become, and we all noticed that her succeeding letters were filled with thoughts of food.

"Have you seen a hungry hound looking at a hog killing? That's how I feel. I'm not starving hungry, just protein hungry. I'd rather have a chunk of cheese than diamonds."

"Everything smells like chitlings."

"When it's so hot, I remember my freezer to make me feel cooler, but try not to think of the food inside."

Still with months to go, she wrote: "When I get home, I want a t-bone steak, tossed salad, a biscuit, a good drink, some grits, peach ice cream, a drink, some butterbeans, flowers on the table, and a drink...."

Although the practice was discouraged, we began to send her some food parcels, and her response was ecstatic. "Excuse me while I have a fit! I just had to open one package, and it was a can of TURNIP GREENS! I was starving, but I just didn't know what I was so hungry for—it was something green. I can hardly wait for dinnertime, this will be my very best meal in months."

When her shoes wore out, she found that all the *chappals* (sandals) were too wide for her narrow feet, so she finally decided to walk her four miles a day barefoot.

MY MOTHER'S HINDI TEACHER INSISTED ON LEARNING ENGLISH SO he could read her King James Bible and insisted that they concentrate on the proper use of "thee," "thou," "thy," and "thine." She finally lent him her Bible, found that his daughter had smallpox, and insisted on changing her loan to a permanent gift.

She learned to ease her pent-up frustrations by loudly cursing drivers who passed without giving her a ride and by smiling and calling supercilious people vile names—always in English that they couldn't understand.

Mama had begun working in a family planning center, teaching families about the advantages of having few children, distributing condoms, and offering opportunities for extra schooling for children or factory job promotions to parents who had vasectomies. They averaged 20 of the operations per day. She devised every means of escaping from this unpleasant chore and spent all her off-duty hours helping Doctor Bhatia in the factory clinic. She used her salary to buy medicine, and we children supplemented this effort with antibiotics, aspirin, and some vaccines that could be shipped without refrigeration. Eventually, she became too valuable for Dr. Bhatia to spare, and her request for reassignment to his clinic was finally approved.

Mama was euphoric with her new mission, even when exhausted after 12 hours on duty. "I could use a little rest, as we saw three hundred and sixty patients, besides the regular injections, so I haven't had a chance to sit down all day. Never have I worked as hard, nor loved it more."

A voracious reader, my mother constantly urged us to send her books and magazines and to wrap all her packages in recent newspapers. She prodded us by inserting strong hints in her letters:

"Woe is me! I've run out of something to read again. I'm reading Voltaire and other French short novels, but, honestly, just to exercise my eyes. They are horrible."

"Actually, I find that books are better the third and fourth time, so I'm reading Anna Karenina again."

She also read the Bible, studied Hindu texts, and attended lectures along with 30,000 others by the famous Swami Sadhanalaya, who visited the Vikhroli community. She was intrigued with his teachings and her other studies, but finally concluded: "Religion, as such, means so little to me. Now, just people, and their problems—hunger, housing, clothes. Oh, God, I have seen it all. I can never again take bread or warmth for granted."

She went to Goa for a regional Peace Corps meeting and splurged on a beautiful cashmere shawl. A few weeks later she wrote: "The weather here is colder than ever in history, so I wore my shawl to the Clinic today. One of the patients came in with pneumonia, and since we have no blankets I wrapped my shawl around him, and let him wear it on home. Material things have lost all meaning for me."

On August 25, 1968, she wrote: "This will be the last letter, because I will arrive in Atlanta Monday evening at 9:30. Please be at the airport by six, and wait for me; don't dare leave until I get there." When she changed planes in London, she had only ten cents and tried to drag her bag across the floor as she changed terminal gates. A porter came to help her, discovered where she had been, and refused to accept the only tip she could offer him. Mama had lost 35 pounds, and at the Atlanta airport we forced her to travel to her new Oldsmobile in a wheelchair.

Mama didn't realize that she would come home to live 15 more years, campaign aggressively to help her son be elected governor and President, and make more than 500 speeches about the wonders of the Peace Corps and how her audiences should not let their lives be constricted by advancing age. She never dreamed that, after ten years, she would return to Vikhroli and be greeted by a cheering crowd of thousands, this time as leader of the official delegation of the United States to the funeral of India's president.

In a letter written on her birthday, August 15, she wrote:

"I am seventy years old today, and I think of where I am, and what I'm doing, and why. When Earl died, my life lost its meaning and direction. For the first time, I lost my will to live. Since that time, I've tried to make my life have some significance.

"I didn't dream that in this remote corner of the world, so far away from the people and material things that I had always considered so necessary, I would discover what Life is really all about. Sharing yourself with others, and accepting their love for you, is the most precious gift of all."

Despite the many distinctions caused by a half-century difference in age, three decades in time, and the geographical and cultural chasm between Vikhroli, India, and Lochiel, South Africa, my mother in her letters and Jason in this book have expressed the essence of service in the Peace Corps.

PROLOGUE

AS NHLANHLA NDLOVU WAS LEAVING SCHOOL ONE FRIDAY IN THE southern winter of 1998, he invited me to his brother's exchange of *lobola* in Potchefstroom. Lobola is bridewealth—traditionally cattle given by the groom's family to the bride's in exchange for the right to marry their daughter. I agreed to go. He said he would pick me up at 4 a.m. because it was a long drive and the family had to be there in the morning. "Fine," I said. I had no idea what to expect.

I didn't know if we were going to a farm near Potchefstroom, to Potchefstroom the town, or to the black township outside. I didn't know if the family lived in a tiny mud hut on a farm or in a nice house in town like Nhlanhla's mother. I didn't know what language they would speak, or if there would be a hundred people or seven. Nhlanhla's brother was going to pay his new in-laws for the right to marry their daughter. Would they be wearing traditional Zulu attire, animal skin loincloths and headdresses? Or would they be wearing suits and ties? Would they slaughter a goat and serve me cooked blood and gallbladder?

Standing in the freezing cold at four in the morning at the gas station under the single light, I waited for Nhlanhla. He drove up in jeans and a button-down shirt.

Pulling the tie out of my collar, I said, "Can I put this jacket back in my room?"

Nhlanhla laughed. "You thought you had to wear a tie? Come on, man, this is lobola."

"Of course," I thought as I went back to my room to change, "lobola."

I lived in a small rural village in South Africa as a Peace Corps volunteer. The Peace Corps was helping Nelson Mandela's government implement a new educational curriculum designed for the new post-apartheid South Africa. I worked at three schools in the area with teachers like Nhlanhla, who taught math and science at Lochiel Primary.

I was the only white person for miles. But the Peace Corps trains all of its members to speak the local language, and the grounding I received in Siswati and Zulu allowed me to put black South Africans at ease and to participate in their lives to an extent unheard of for most of white South Africa.

I had been in the country for more than a year, and in his car on the way to Potchefstroom Nhlanhla and I talked comfortably as he offered his thoughts on our destination.

Potchefstroom is a very conservative town west of Johannesburg. Frederik W. de Klerk, the last white president of South Africa, was born there. It is "full of Boers," Nhlanhla said as we drove. The black people speak Sotho. *"Watsiba seSotho?"* Nhlanhla asked in Sotho.

"What?" I said, surprised.

"Ha-ha. Do you speak Sotho?" he said in English, knowing I did not.

We talked about urban South Africa and people from Gauteng, the tiny province that contains Johannesburg and Pretoria. "You know," Nhlanhla told me, "I met this girl; she says she is from Gauteng. And when you hear someone say they are from Gauteng, you think she is somebody. But I went to this place in Gauteng two weeks ago, not the girl's place, but another place." He spoke mostly in English, but he would switch to Zulu for emphasis. "And this place, it was the same as this farmland here. *Beyifanana*, exactly the same. People think that if you speak Sotho, you come from Gauteng, you must know Soweto or Jo-burg. They look at eLukwatini or Ermelo and they say, '*Bahlala emaplasini*—They live on the farm,' but there are farms in Gauteng. You'll see, Jason, some of the people are just the same."

Still in rural South Africa, we picked up several members of his family, including his mother, Ma'am Ndlovu, her two brothers, Nhlanhla's brother, and his sister. His sister, Carol, in her mid-20s, was dressed in an Adidas sweat suit, presumably because she was going to be around people from Gauteng and wanted to look her coolest. Ma'am Ndlovu's brothers started drinking in the car (it was seven in the morning), and we ended up talking for a few hours. I hadn't met them before, and they were excited that I spoke a little Zulu.

We drove through Johannesburg and exited the highway onto a smaller road that cut out through a stretch of farmland. Nhlanhla said to me in Zulu, "You see, Jason, just like I told you. There are farms in Gauteng. Don't think that that all the people who speak Sotho and come from Gauteng live in the location. They don't all stay there." It was the first I had heard of this insecurity. I had not been in South Africa long enough to have picked up this widespread stereotype, but his country-boy nervousness as we passed through the city was not a surprise.

The cities of South Africa, with their complex mix of white neighborhoods; black, Coloured, and Indian townships or "locations"; First-World banking and industry; and developing world poverty, were very different from the tiny rural village of Lochiel, where Nhlanhla and I spent most of our time.

We arrived in Potchefstroom around ten o'clock in the morning. We drove straight through town, between rows of trees lining the streets, under several arches that spanned the road welcoming us to Potchefstroom in Afrikaans, and entered the location, where the vast majority of black people still lived. The beautiful, tree-lined, paved roads of the white town instantly became the brown, dusty roads of the black township.

The bride's family had a nice concrete-block home with maybe six rooms. Surrounded by a short fence, with a dirt yard in the back and a small porch extending in front of the main door, this simple home could have been in any township in South Africa. But because their daughter was attending medical school in Soweto, I knew the family had at least enough money to pay for her education. This made them extremely wealthy by South African standards. A short fence with a gate surrounded each house on the street. The family had set up a tent to cover the concrete porch in front of the house. We found the groom, Bafana, and three of his friends from Soweto on the grass across the street from the bride's house. The four men sat there next to the open trunk of their car, drinking beer. We pulled up, and Nhlanhla backed his car alongside them. The women and the older men got out of Nhlanhla's car and went immediately to the house to greet the new in-laws. Nhlanhla introduced me to his friends, all of whom spoke perfect English. Then we walked across the street to the house.

The bride was beautiful: tall and thin with long hair and delicate features. Her family spoke English to me, and they went out of their way to make me feel welcome. I was the first white person ever to visit their house. All around, the in-laws were meeting and greeting. Both sides understood each other, but I often heard two people having a conversation in different languages.

Sotho: "How are you?"

Zulu: "Fine, and you?"

Sotho: "Fine. How was your trip?"

Zulu: "Good. We left in the morning when it was still dark, but we made it OK."

Sotho: "Isn't it a beautiful day?" And so on.

The slang and the common words changed markedly fr[o]m place in South Africa. People from neighboring townships used different words to say the same thing. The people in Lochiel, where I lived, were greatly influenced by traditional Swazi words, and few spoke English. Many people in Ermelo, including Mrs. Ndlovu's brothers, conducted their business in Afrikaans, the European-based language of the whites in town, and their Zulu had incorporated many Afrikaans words. In Gauteng, there were Sotho words that Zulu speakers used. With so many languages, the regional differences were often vast, but most black South Africans understand several languages.

Nhlanhla and I returned to the cars across the street to sit with the groom. I began to better understand Nhlanhla's insecurity about people from Gauteng, whom he regarded as more cosmopolitan and confident. Bafana had met his wife in medical school in Soweto. His three friends sitting on their car had jobs unlike any imagined by schoolchildren in rural Lochiel. One was a stockbroker, another taught computer programming at a technical college, and the third was a marketing specialist for South African Broadcasting Corporation (SABC) sports. They spoke Zulu, and I could follow easily because they used so many English words. When I responded to questions, or offered anything to the conversation, I spoke in English. Black South Africans are so unused to white people speaking Zulu that I could always impress them, but with this group, each of whom spoke English all day at work, I felt comfortable speaking in my native tongue.

Two speakers positioned under the tent in the bride's yard blasted music into the street. People passing by stopped to ask what was happening and congratulated Bafana when they found that it was a lobola party. The two families mingled and talked. Every once in a while an older person from one of the families would come over and talk to us. The five of us young men sat in the grass on the sunny afternoon on the township street, drinking beer and talking.

I asked question after question about modern South African lifestyles. Who does the chores? If both you and your wife are doctors, will you still expect her to cook every night?

"Oh, no," Bafana said. "We will negotiate that. Some nights I will do it, some nights she will. Is that strange to you? Isn't that how they do it in America?"

"That is basically how we do it in America," I said, "but that is very different from the way they do it in Lochiel."

At some time, signaled somehow in secret, Bafana left our group and put on a robe. It was not traditional Zulu attire, but a long, flowing, Nigerian-style batik robe in fashion in Soweto. The lobola ceremony began.

Bafana's family and friends gathered in the street. The group sang a traditional lobola song, and we walked through the gate of the bride's house, the women carrying blankets and other gifts for the family of the bride. All of the neighbors on the crowded street came into their yards to sing and cheer. Across the street a father stood in his yard pointing and explaining to his son the ancient tradition.

I suppose in the past Bafana's family would have brought cows to lobola, but on that day they just brought a check and handed it over. I did not see any transaction, but at one point they told me the ceremony was complete and they turned the music back on. As a matter of custom, the men might have all performed a *gita,* the traditional Zulu dance, but this day we simply stood in a circle and danced to *kwaito,* South Africa's hip-hop.

After we danced in celebration, the families and friends sat down under the tent to eat. The bride's family served the meal, and as tradition demands, the groom's family had to keep saying they were hungry. We ate for an hour, as the music played, drinking beer with the in-laws. I learned how to say hello and how are you in Sotho and had wonderful conversations with several people.

They had welcomed me, a white man, into their traditional celebration. We had sat together, shared in an ancient custom, and spoken our many languages.

That, I thought as I got in the car, is the future of South Africa.

AFRICAN FIRSTS

CHAPTER ONE

IN THE YEARS BEFORE I SERVED IN THE PEACE CORPS, SOUTH AFRICA made history, capping a glorious struggle against apartheid with a successful election and a jubilant celebration of the inauguration of Nelson Mandela, their first black president.

From its inception in 1948, South Africa's apartheid government paddled furiously against the tide of world opinion and resisted multiculturalism and the ideal of racial equality. "Separate development," as apartheid was officially known, was brutally imposed. People were removed from their homes, separated from their families, and stripped of their dignity in one of the most terrible social engineering projects in history. Archbishop Desmond Tutu said of the system, "It is intrinsically, categorically, evil—without remainder."

The opponents of apartheid within South Africa were violently repressed until after more than 40 years the government was forced to admit failure. On February 2, 1990, the white president F. W. de Klerk announced in Parliament that the African National Congress (ANC), the Pan Africanist Conference (PAC), and the South African Communist Party (SACP), all formerly banned antiapartheid organizations, were now legal. They would be allowed the rights normally allowed to political groups in a democracy. The periodic states of emergency under which South Africans had lived for years were at an end. Nine days later, Nelson Mandela, the symbol of the struggle against apartheid, the president of the ANC, and perhaps the most famous prisoner in the world, walked out of Pollsmoor Prison in Cape Town a free man. He cast the first electoral ballot of his life on April 27, 1994.

The four years between February 1990 and April 1994 are testaments to how much work was accomplished in the negotiations for a peaceful end to white supremacy. When you ask someone in South Africa about the date of "independence" or "liberation" they say, "de Klerk's speech was February 2, 1990, and we voted April 27, 1994." Today, South Africans celebrate April 27 as Freedom Day and remember exactly where they were when they heard the news on February 2. These are the dates that South African children memorize in school.

When I left for South Africa in January 1998, I thought I had arrived too late to participate in the revolution in any meaningful way. I was there for the inauguration of Thabo Mbeki, as the second black president of South Africa, which occurred in June 1999 in the middle of my Peace Corps service. On that day South Africa's official political transition period ended. The Interim Constitution expired and the new constitution came into effect; the transitional "Government of National Unity," whose job had been to oversee the transition to democracy, was replaced by a government whose structure was now enshrined in the permanent constitution.

My fellow volunteers and I would soon see that this changeover to black rule, which had been labeled a "miracle," was perhaps the easiest of the countless transformations wrenching South African society. We were dropped into black South Africa as a diverse group of Americans, at a time when all of the rules were changing. As black South Africa began to emerge from apartheid, many saw for the first time just how strong that system's grip was. As Americans participating in this process, with no real relationship to white South Africa, our perspectives were unique.

But before we could understand anything in this complex country, we had to learn the basics of life in Africa. As I sat on the airplane to Johannesburg, I thought I was lucky because I had been to Africa before and had some idea what the continent offered.

I FIRST TRAVELED TO AFRICA IN 1988, WHEN I WAS 13. NINE MEMBERS of my family spent three weeks in East Africa, accompanying my grandfather Jimmy Carter on a business trip. We began in Tanzania with a climb up Mount Kilimanjaro and concluded with a whirlwind tour of several countries. I still have vivid memories from that trip.

I remember thinking that the first people who arrived at the Ngorongoro Crater must have thought they had found the Garden of Eden. The crater is a stunning walled paradise almost half a mile deep and three and a half miles across. Inside the crater the horizon slopes toward the sky on all sides.

I remember the children in a Masai village nowhere near a paved road, sitting in their mother's arms without flinching or swatting at the flies that swarmed under their noses and around their eyes.

I remember walking into a dung house, bending under the very small doorway, and secretly touching the walls even though I knew what they were made of.

More than anything else, though, I remember two other 13-year-olds I saw in Uganda. We arrived there less than two years after President Yoweri Museveni had come to power. He had fought a five-year protracted liberation war from central Uganda into the capital, Kampala, overthrowing the dictator Milton Obote. Obote had succeeded Idi Amin, one of the most infamous leaders in Africa's often violent history. Museveni was intelligent and well respected, and many people in the war-weary country were hopeful.

My grandfather had come on behalf of the Carter Center. He and my grandmother founded the center in 1982 to continue part of the work that they had begun while in the White House. They traveled continuously in the Third World to promote the center's efforts in agriculture, disease prevention, democratization, and conflict resolution. On this trip my grandfather was meeting with Museveni on behalf of the center's Global 2000 program to negotiate an agricultural project in Uganda.

We stepped off the airplane and were greeted by a row of dancers and two rows of armed escorts. I saw a boy my age holding a machine gun. His chin was slightly raised, and he was looking straight at me. When I made eye contact, he might have tipped his chin a little so he could look down at me. He didn't blink.

He looked at me with a self-confidence that I could not have mustered at that age, and I felt embarrassed. I know now that his childhood ended when he was thrust into war, and I have often pitied these child soldiers. But that day I took in the look of strength in that 13-year-old's eyes and I envied his pride.

We were lodged in the Nile Hotel in Kampala, the first guests after its recent refurbishing. My father let me read an article from a news magazine that had been circulated among the family. The article chronicled the atrocities that had occurred at the Nile Hotel when it served as the headquarters of the secret police under Amin. There were reports of torture in the rooms and in the basement. People were thrown down elevator shafts after interrogations. And high-ranking police and government officials reportedly fulfilled their sadistic fantasies on the roof of the hotel. Taking women randomly from the street and bringing them to the roof, they tied the women's wrists to their ankles, raped them, and threw them off the edge as the women begged for their lives.

We found bullet holes in the walls of our balcony. We couldn't use the elevators, and we were told that they were having problems getting them to go down past the third floor. Outside the dining area was a patio stained with streaks of black and dark red. Surrounding the patio in the yard were 15 or 20 marabou storks.

President Museveni and his family welcomed us at the conference center in Kampala. I was introduced to the president's son, Muhoozi Museveni. In the typical wild swings of 13-year-olds he was a foot taller than I was. If he lived in America, he could surely start for the Nichols Middle School basketball team. But I wondered if he had ever seen a hoop.

Muhoozi and I said hello and then sat on the floor with my cousin and my sister while the rest of the families exchanged greetings and talked politics. I wasn't really sure what to talk about. My father worked at a bank in Chicago; Muhoozi's dad had been a guerrilla leader in central Africa who fought his way to power a few years ago.

He asked where I lived. I said, "In the middle of the country, in the North, near a really big lake called Lake Michigan, in the second largest city in the United States, called Chicago."

"Oh," he said. "Do you know Michael Jordan?"

I was shocked. Perhaps, I thought, the gap between Africa and America is not as huge as I guessed.

MY SECOND TRIP TO AFRICA CAME ONLY MONTHS BEFORE I LEFT FOR THE

Peace Corps. Between these two trips I graduated from high school in Illinois and then college in Durham, North Carolina. During that time I talked and thought about Africa quite a bit. I took a course in African history at my high school and read books and saw movies about Africa when I could. I listened to reggae musicians sing about Zimbabwe, Nelson Mandela, and "Botha the Mosquito." My memories of Africa remained vivid, even though my experiences there seemed so removed from my life in America.

The summer after my junior year in college, I went to work at the Carter Center as an intern to research and write about conflicts and wars, mostly in Africa. I was assigned to monitor on a daily basis the conflicts in Sudan, Uganda, Ethiopia, Liberia, Sri Lanka, and Gaza and the West Bank. One day a human rights report would chronicle the genocide in southern Sudan. The next day "Heart Men" would raid a town in Liberia, reportedly removing the coveted organs and eating them. Thousands of children in northern Uganda, some as young as eight, were abducted by a rebel group; the boys forced into the soldier corps, the girls into sexual slavery. After intense "training," the first assignment for these new "recruits" was to go back to their villages and kill their families.

The next year, my grandfather delivered the graduation address at my school. He said, among other things, that all of us sitting in that stadium were rich. "I'm not talking about bank accounts," he said. "A rich person is someone who has a decent home, a modicum of usable education, and access to reasonable health care. Rich people like us feel that the police and the judicial system are on our side and think that if we make a decision, it'll make a difference, at least in our own lives." And then he went on to ask how many of the rich people in that stadium knew a poor family well enough to invite them over for dinner, or go to their house and have a cup of coffee. He suspected it was very few. "Why is that?" he asked. "I think the natural thing is for all human beings to believe we are somehow superior, and that the way we live— mostly in an encapsulated world, quite secure—is adequate.... We tend to live in an isolated environment which we create, and we rarely look toward other people as equal or deserving." He then told stories about several of his friends, "rich in every way, who decided to live their lives among the poorest people on Earth."

After graduation, I felt a need to go back to Africa, and I volunteered for a Carter Center trip to Liberia to help with the center's election-monitoring mission. They agreed to let me go because I had worked on

Liberia as an intern and knew something about the Carter Center's policy—and also because Liberia was a dangerous place. The Carter Center knew they could send me anywhere, and no matter what happened, my family wouldn't sue.

I left for Liberia in July 1997. In my three weeks there, in addition to the work, I was going to decide if I wanted to spend more time in Africa. I got on the plane unsure of what lay ahead.

Liberia, in West Africa, was founded in the early 1800s by freed American slaves. The capital, Monrovia, is named after James Monroe, the U.S. President at the time of the ex-slaves' transatlantic voyage. Other major towns up and down the coast have the names Robertsport, Buchanan, Greenville, and Harper. The cultural descendents of the American slaves colonized the tiny piece of land in West Africa and dominated the social and political life of the country for the next 150 years. A list of the famous past presidents of Liberia reads like a list of governors from South Carolina: Joseph J. Roberts, Edward James Roye, Charles D. B. King, William V. S. Tubman, William R. Tolbert, Jr., Samuel K. Doe, and Charles G. Taylor.

Not until William Tubman came to power in the 1940s did the interior of Liberia truly come under government control. Liberia has 16 different ethnic groups in a country the size of Alabama. It was controlled only through the shrewd and sometimes brutal leadership of Tubman, who ruled for 27 years. During that time very little was done to stimulate the economy, and virtually nothing was done to educate children. The extremely dense jungle that blankets the countryside makes it very difficult to build infrastructure and communications.

When President Tubman died in the 1970s, William Tolbert—one of Tubman's lieutenants in his True Whig Party—came to power. In 1980, Samuel Doe, an army officer, led a group of men into Tolbert's house and assassinated him. Doe's seizure of power was followed by a civil war that began in 1989. The conflict destroyed the meager progress that had been made in Liberia's economic development, and it devastated the image and self-confidence of the Liberian people.

Eventually, Charles Taylor, the leader of the National Patriotic Front of Liberia (NPFL), was able to gain control over most of the country; his "Operation Octopus" became the most famous campaign of the war. He set up a parallel government, and the places under his rule enjoyed a relatively high level of stability.

ECOMOG, the Nigerian-dominated peacekeeping force, eventually fought back the NPFL and the other factions and restored some semblance of order. The ensuing standoff between the factions led to a negotiation in which the parties eventually agreed to hold an election. The Carter Center would monitor the election to ensure that it was free and fair and that the will of the people was expressed.

Aboard the creaky, old, Soviet-era Russian plane en route to Liberia, the row of seats in front of the bulkhead was used for baggage storage. On one side were crates of live chickens, and on the other side, stacks of HP Laserjet printers being brought in by various aid agencies.

We touched down in Liberia, the pilot dodging potholes on the runway, and met with several Carter Center staff. I spent the next few days traveling the Liberian countryside, ensuring that there would be satisfactory accommodations for our observers, who included many prominent academics and election experts, as well as the president of Benin, my grandfather, and former U.S. Senator Paul Simon.

I was basically a gofer, but I traveled all over the country. Liberia was almost entirely controlled by ECOMOG forces, with ubiquitous checkpoints manned by soldiers. Looking out at the countryside, it was almost impossible to imagine how people lived there. The jungle was so dense that you could not see into it. Flying over the tightly packed forests in a helicopter, you saw vegetation that looked like a sea of moss.

After the election, won in a landslide by Charles Taylor, my grandfather asked my uncle Chip and me to stay for another three weeks to represent him at Taylor's inauguration. My uncle and I spent a lot of that time traveling, trying to find out what was going on outside the walls of the compounds where most diplomats and international bureaucrats lived.

One night we found ourselves sitting in a bar on a two-foot-wide street. The bar consisted solely of a bench and a stool on a tiny porch. A window opened into a store where a man named Mike sold necessities to people who could afford them. A gas lamp inside shot light out into the pitch-blackness so the store glowed from within. The store stocked several kinds of canned food, matches, candles, beer, and cigarettes sold one at time. We had been led to the place by Joe, a political organizer for the United Democratic Movement, one of the many political parties.

My uncle and I were the first white people to ever visit Mike's bar, according to Joe, even though it was just around the corner from several foreign compounds. There was no easy way to find the bar in the maze of tiny streets, and even if any white people had stumbled across it, they would have never known that it was a bar.

People heard about us and came to see if the report was true. Kids filled the streets and the building across the way, which, of course, had no doors or windows. There were bullet holes in the walls, and the barroom furniture—the bench and the stool—had clearly been made by hand from scraps left behind by the looters.

We sat there and talked. We answered questions about America and asked questions about Liberia. We went back most nights for two weeks, and the crowd inside grew to as many as seven people, although that stretched the capacity of the bar to its limit.

One night one of the Nigerian soldiers from the checkpoint up at the main road strolled in. He had tribal markings on his face like many Nigerians. They called them "whiskas" because the markings looked like cat whiskers. His scars began at the sides of his mouth, three or four lines, an inch long, and fanned out across his cheek, inscribed permanently by a knife when the boy had become a man. Nothing made Nigerian soldiers look more menacing than the scars on their faces.

He sat down and we started talking. He had heard of us, but just wanted to make sure. "Let me buy you a beer," he said.

"No," I said. "We'll take care of it."

"No, really, I insist. I'll buy one for each of you."

"No, it's fine," I said. "Here are three dollars. We'll each get one." I was giving my money to Mike in the store window when the soldier grabbed my hand.

"I know that you are rich and white and from America," he said. "And I know that I am poor and black and from Africa. But I can buy you a beer. I know that you are rich, and that I am poor. I knew that when I offered to buy your beer. I know how much money I have, and I know that I have enough to buy you a beer. Do not disrespect me. Allow me to pay for it because I want to. Because I want to sit here as equals and share our beer."

He spoke with a thick Nigerian accent, and we had to listen closely to make out exactly what he was saying. But in the end his message could not have been more clear. Africa's is not only a story of war and famine and disease. It is also a story of triumph and self-respect in the face of those hardships.

WHEN I RETURNED HOME, I CALLED MY RECRUITER AND ACTIVATED A Peace Corps application that I had filed before leaving for Liberia. At the time I had been unsure of my interest in making a two-year commitment to Africa, but my experience in Liberia decided me. It took months to complete all of the requirements and interviews, but they finally called back. "You can leave for South Africa on January 17."

My heart sank a little. When the American media covered Africa, it was usually South Africa, the most westernized country on the continent. The country had good roads, rental cars, phone systems, hotels, airports, and restaurants. Some of us at the Carter Center called it "Africa Lite." This was not the Africa I wanted.

My great-grandmother, Miss Lillian Carter, had braved the hardships of rural India as a Peace Corps volunteer when she was 70 years old. She had been miles from any contact with the First World, had gotten ill on several occasions, and had lost 35 pounds. My Peace Corps experience would not test my physical well-being like hers did. And for letting my great-grandmother take the tougher job, I was slightly embarrassed.

But she was also from Plains, Georgia, and her family had lived through the South's desegregation battles. My grandfather's first public position was on the Plains school board, to which he was elected in the 1960s promising to integrate the schools. This battle, and these hardships, I could perhaps tackle in South Africa.

And I also had little choice. This was the assignment the Peace Corps had offered. I could accept it or wait months for something else.

As it turned out, I cannot imagine having gone anywhere but South Africa. I lived and worked in the tiny, and poor, community of Lochiel and witnessed the post-apartheid struggle. In that place, in the face of overwhelming problems and difficult issues, the people still took pride in their projects, like that young soldier in Uganda and the Nigerian soldier in Liberia. And very much like people in poor, tiny communities in south Georgia.

NEW RULES ABOUT RACE

CHAPTER TWO

WHEN I WOKE UP ON JANUARY 18, 1998, WE WERE TOUCHING DOWN in Johannesburg. I was not a tourist. I had moved to Africa to live. I looked out the window of the airplane on that first morning and saw the red dirt of central South Africa. My ancestors had been trying to make a living out of red dirt since they moved to Georgia in 1769. I had been in Africa for seconds, and I could already see how similar it was to home.

I knew South Africa would be different from Liberia or Uganda, but I knew little for sure about life there. I thought I knew, however, how to tell the oppressed from the oppressors, the good guys from the bad. When that plane touched down, I believed that every Afrikaner was a brutal policeman, and every black person a freedom fighter. Granted, the revolution was over, but in my mind the roles were still the same, and I knew whose side I wanted to be on.

I approached the immigration booth, where two white men sat in uniform. I thought about the fact that these people instituted apartheid. They were direct descendants of Dutch settlers who arrived in the 1600s and then spread out over the country for the next 300 years, subjugating the black populations. As World War II was winding down and as the rest of the world was moving away from colonialism, the National Party, made up of Afrikaner nationalists, was institutionalizing the white supremacy of the past. They created a society based solely on their desire to keep power in white hands. The system's brutality would eventually lead the United Nations to declare apartheid a "crime against humanity."

Like Nelson Mandela, I was going to make sure I looked the man in the eye as he checked my passport. He took my passport without looking at me and muttered something to his partner in Afrikaans.

I couldn't believe that these men were still speaking the language of the oppressors. It was this language that had triggered the Soweto uprisings of 1976, the event that marked the resurrection of the antiapartheid struggle. The students who marched then were protesting the government's plan to teach classes in Afrikaans.

The language was dark and harsh, with the scraping guttural tones of the "g" rumbling from deep inside like an old man snoring in his chair. The immigration officers spoke back and forth, in short almost grunting bursts—clearly, I thought, having a problem with my passport. What was wrong? I looked around for help, but everyone was busy.

Before I knew it, one of the officials stamped my passport, said "Thank you," smiled, and sent me on my way.

I caught up with some other members of my group. "Wow," I said to Nicole, an African-American woman. "I felt like I was being singled out. I mean those Afrikaners weren't on my side at all."

"Yeah," she said, smirking. "I feel like that at home."

She smiled. Red dirt, I thought, just like Georgia.

OUR FIRST DAYS WERE SPENT AT A HOTEL IN PRETORIA WITH A PEACE Corps medical officer and her syringes full of various vaccines and boosters. Looking out the hotel window over the skyline, I could have been in any city in the Western world. The buildings, roads, cars, parks, and the edge of the city giving way to the tree-lined suburban streets were all familiar. Was the Peace Corps really needed here?

We went out at night in a big group, like a herd of college freshmen. Every bar in downtown Pretoria looked as if it could have been in Athens, Georgia, or on any main street in any American college town. Every Afrikaner, it seemed, was jovial and wanted to make sure we all enjoyed ourselves. The fashion on the street was European—supershort skirts and too-tall shoes—but the people were familiar. We saw few, if any, black people.

Our daytime experience was very different. As part of our orientation, we took a tour of Soweto and visited several townships in the Pretoria area. Atteridgeville, along with Mamelodi and Soshanguve, is on the outskirts of Pretoria on the other side of the hills, out of sight from downtown and the suburbs. Coming from Liberia, I had been skeptical about the nature of poverty in affluent South Africa. But when we arrived in the township, we found squatter camps with dirt streets two feet wide, lined with houses made from sheet metal held together with mattress springs. Kids were running around in the mud near the single water spigot that served dozens of households, while their mothers or sisters or brothers stood in line with buckets and containers to collect water to wash and cook. In houses no bigger than a hotel bathroom, people lounged on stacks of flattened cardboard they used for beds.

It is one thing to go to the Third World and see poverty. But in South Africa you see, first and foremost, luxurious First World living. There is no trace of poverty in the malls or the cafés of Pretoria. The beautiful purple jacarandas and the huge palm trees lining the streets convey a sense of comfort and security. Yet down the road an amazingly short distance, there is poverty that rivals any in the Third World. The proximity makes South Africa's poverty more difficult to excuse. There are no palms lining the township streets.

In addition to the squatter camps, where people build houses themselves, Atteridgeville and Soweto have houses built by the apartheid government. These "matchbox houses" are identical. Rows and rows of them cover entire sections of the townships as if they had been churned out in a factory and laid down by a big farm machine. There is the four-room variety, the three-room variety, and the two-room variety. To many, the rows of identical houses symbolized the oppression of apartheid.

A small portion of the black population is made up of middle- and upper-middle-class people who made money as teachers, doctors, or small-business owners during apartheid. They still live in the townships, but they live in elaborate brick houses. The number of bricks in a house is apparently a status symbol, for we often saw large, unnecessary appendages extending well above the roof, faux walls, and elaborate carports, fences, or garden walls. These sand-colored brick houses are right next to the squatter camps, sometimes just across the street. The schoolchildren who go home to the squatter camps have classmates who live behind brick and wrought iron fences that cost more than entire blocks of squatter camp accommodations.

Seeing the township's different divisions drove home the point that apartheid was, above all else, inflexible and systematic. Like a machine with an input and an output, you plugged in your skin color and were told where to live. You plugged in your income, and you got one of the three kinds of houses. If you were black, you chose from a list of maybe 30 occupations that were reserved for you. There were no other options. White people lived their lives basically as Americans did, albeit with much more concern for their security. But, as our tour guide said, "Black people lived according to the system. There were no exceptions."

We had been told very little about our jobs. Where were we going to start? Were we going to work on the jobs that we often heard about in other Peace Corps countries—digging latrines, building fish ponds, forestry work, teaching English? Pretoria certainly did not need any of these things.

The Peace Corps had been invited by the South African government to send volunteers to help with the educational system, and we began intensive technical training in South Africa's new curriculum.

The Peace Corps brought in speakers to tell us about the history of the educational system in South Africa. Education had been an integral part of apartheid's plan. The official policy was to educate people "in accordance with their opportunities in life." For black people this meant their schools were designed to teach them how to follow rules, how to respect authority, and how to prevent ambition from clouding their minds. Bantu Education, as the government policy was called, was designed to ensure that black South Africans lived within the system.

Science and math were purposely limited, because there would be no need for them. There was no career planning or vocational education. History was taught as an unending stream of European victories over the savage black tribes. Learning how to listen in English and in Afrikaans was given high priority, while learning how to speak and write was neglected as less necessary.

The teaching methodology did not encourage teachers to become freethinkers or creative educators. Its focus was on discipline and knowledge of basic facts. The curriculum was tightly controlled by inspectors who ensured that teachers were not straying from the government's policies.

Long before apartheid ended, South Africa needed to drastically change its educational system. To compete in the global economy, or even to expand the economy at home and create desperately needed jobs, the country needed problem-solving entrepreneurs, and their schools were not producing them. One of the first tasks of Mandela's government was to create an education task force to draft a new curriculum for students of the "New South Africa." This new curriculum would follow the Outcomes-Based Education model. The Department of Education knew what kinds of thinkers they needed to produce, so they focused on results.

As long as the schools were able to get those results, little else mattered. The curriculum would be flexible in its prescriptions for everyday lesson planning, and creativity among the teachers would be encouraged. The curriculum focused more on long-term goals and less on inspecting the everyday work of the teachers.

While the old curriculum would have given specific instructions, and an exact lesson plan for what to do on the third day of second grade, the new curriculum would simply tell the teacher what the children should be able to do at the end of the year. In theory, this allowed the teachers to tailor their lessons to the needs of their particular students and to vary the subject matter from region to region to make it more familiar to children who lived in widely varying environments.

But the curriculum was complex, with 65 outcomes to be furthered each year and a methodology that was utterly foreign to teachers trained in the old system. It required new and creative ideas and radically different classroom environments. Perhaps more important, it freed teachers from the top-down regulation of the old system. When they arrived in class on the first day, however, most teachers saw this not as freedom but as a lack of guidance. How were they supposed to proceed?

Our job as volunteers was to work with teachers in rural areas to help them implement the new curriculum and reform other parts of their school organization and teaching practices to better fit the new educational environment. It was a well-designed project, and we all felt as though we were on the front lines of one of the most important battles of the post-apartheid struggle.

Our technical training was run with great aplomb by Yvonne Hubbard, an intelligent and witty woman whom we all respected immensely. Yvonne, an African American from North Carolina, had been in the Peace Corps in Sierra Leone in the 1970s and had lived in Indonesia for years. Her dress reflected these influences, with flowing robes, big earrings, and intricate hairstyles that changed, it seemed, every day. She is a truly wonderful woman who was later named the Peace Corps's country director in South Africa.

When she first introduced us to our job, we were overwhelmed, but our first experience in school got us moving. While still in Pretoria, we were split into smaller groups that were then sent to different schools in the area. My group went to Atteridgeville, to a school that consisted of several buildings set in a dusty schoolyard. When we arrived, the children were lined up for the morning assembly, all dressed identically in their black and white uniforms, standing in rows like the matchbox houses. We stood there as the principal went through her morning announcements and introduced us as American visitors. Then, as they do every morning, they sang. One of the older girls led with a powerful voice stored somewhere inside her tiny body, the older boys sang the bass part, and the rest split up according to their classes and harmonized in a slow, soft melody:

> *God is so good.*
> *He's so good*
> *to me.*
> *God is so good.*
> *He's so good*
> *to me.*

Each of us visited a different classroom and observed for an hour or so. Then we all met for tea with the principal and several other teachers. We had been instructed by Yvonne to report what we had seen to the rest of our training group. We noted that the school was doing a good job implementing the new curriculum and that the principal was an impressive woman with a number of solid ideas for involving the community in her school.

While all of this was true, what struck me most in the second-grade classroom I visited was the mobile hanging from the ceiling. Made from a few wire hangers, it had cards hanging on different lengths of yarn. The children in the class were seven or eight years old, which meant that they were born in 1990 or 1991—just after Nelson Mandela's release from prison. The cards were labeled "Freedom," "Celebration," "Gift," "Happiness," "Nelson," and "Hero." I asked what the mobile represented. They had one in every room, the teacher said. Each card was the English translation of a student's name.

IN PRETORIA, WE ATE MOST OF OUR MEALS AT THE HOTEL RESTAURANT. It featured a big buffet, and we could eat outside on the patio or inside in the pink-and-purple dining hall. On the third day, one of the waiters came up as I was standing outside, having just finished dinner. "I really like Americans," he said. "You guys are really cool."

"Thanks. Y'all have taken good care of us."

"You really like to have fun, and it's really cool that you all stick together. I mean, racially."

"Yeah, well, that's something we're all working on."

"I guess it's easier for you guys, though, because your blacks are so much more civilized than our blacks."

How do you begin to respond?

It quickly became clear that one of the most difficult parts of moving to South Africa was learning to live with white people. And we weren't even going to live with them. The last thing I expected when I left for Africa was that rich white people would play such a prominent role in my experience. But in South Africa, the white people had defined the society.

THE DUTCH FOUNDED A PERMANENT COLONY IN WHAT IS NOW CAPE TOWN, South Africa, in 1652. Along with German and French Huguenot colonists, they came to the Cape to begin new lives, and during the next 150 years they spread gradually east, claiming enormous tracts of land, studying their Bibles, and creating a new language based on the Dutch they had brought with them from Europe. By the time the British arrived to take over the colony in the late 1700s, an entirely new society had evolved. The Afrikaners had their own language, a slave-owning farm lifestyle, a Calvinist-based Christian religion, and a fierce belief in individualism.

Over the next century, those elements of their identity would be forged into a quasi-religious Afrikaner nationalism that would eventually propel apartheid's political party to power in 1948 and provide the ideological basis for the racist system of "separate development." This nationalism was a powerful mixture of religion and a pride in their heritage that convinced the Afrikaner people that they were chosen by God to inherit the land of South Africa.

The centerpiece of this legacy was the Great Trek, a mass migration of Boers, the Afrikaans word for "farmers," who moved out across the northern and eastern parts of South Africa in the 1830s to escape British rule. In many ways these "trekboers" were pioneers, but unlike those in America, they were not fortune seekers. Instead, they were simply trying to preserve their way of life, in which every family lived in almost complete isolation on enormous estates and raised and educated their children solely on the Bible and the ways of the farm. The Boers who moved farthest away from the British in Cape Town were those most intent on preserving their way of life. Their descendents, who still populate the most northern inland areas of South Africa, remain the most conservative.

According to apartheid's historians, the "Vow of the Covenant" was sworn on the eastern end of the Great Trek. In 1838, Piet Retief, one of the Trekboers' most famous leaders, was betrayed and killed by the Zulu chief Dingane. Dingane told Retief that he would agree to a treaty, but in reality Dingane, who had heard how the Boers had overrun other African groups, decided to act preemptively to avoid similar humiliation. When Retief and his small group of Trekboers arrived at Dingane's headquarters, Zulu warriors killed him, his colleagues, and their families.

Feeling betrayed, the remaining Trekboers vowed revenge and, though terribly outnumbered, organized a commando raid against the Zulu. They marched into the heart of Zululand, in the far eastern part of today's South Africa, and arranged a circle of wagons on a hill above a now famous river.

Within this laager of ox wagons, they are said to have prayed for days. On the eve of the battle, the Trekboers made a final promise to the Almighty: If God would deliver the enemy into their hands, the Afrikaners and their descendents would forever celebrate his name and the date of the battle as the greatest victory God had yet given to his chosen people.

The next morning, December 16, 1838, the Zulu army attacked. Thousands of warriors rushed the hill only to be shot down by the 530 Boers sitting in their circle of wagons armed with rifles. While the Afrikaners sustained virtually no injuries, the river below ran red with the blood of thousands of Zulu. The battle became known as the Battle of Blood River, and it was eventually celebrated under apartheid as a day of national thanksgiving.

Between 1838 and the National Party victory 110 years later, the quasi-religious nationalism had grown to include the tenets of apartheid. At the end of the Great Trek, the Afrikaners established two inland Boer republics, the Orange Free State and the Transvaal, to shield themselves from imperial British rule.

They were content to live simple agrarian lives, but history intervened. Diamonds were discovered in 1867, and a few years later mining began on a neighboring farm owned by a pair of Afrikaner brothers named Nicolaas and Diederik de Beer. Their land contained the world's richest deposit of "blue diamond–bearing kimberlite." Within months British and other foreign speculators and entrepreneurs arrived, and thousands of people were working in the mining industry in Kimberley, the new town that sprang up to support the mines. (The de Beers eventually sold their farm to a speculator, and he started a mining syndicate that today controls a vast majority of the world's diamond production.)

Two decades later, in 1886, gold was discovered in the Transvaal on the Witwatersrand, a ridge near Johannesburg. Many of the same speculators who had developed Kimberley expanded to Johannesburg, and in less than 40 years it became South Africa's biggest city, with a population of more than 300,000.

The Afrikaners who controlled the undeveloped states where these discoveries were made had little time to adjust. The mining industries imported technology from Europe and America, and South Africa industrialized more quickly, perhaps, than any country in history. The Afrikaner governments, still intent on preserving their rural way of life, were ill prepared to handle the new technology and were disinclined to participate in the rampant capitalism spawned in the new cities. This, coupled with the enormous wealth from gold and diamond deposits and the overwhelming British inclination toward imperialism, created tension between the British colonies and the Boer republics. The Anglo-Boer War erupted in 1899.

The British eventually defeated the Afrikaners in a brutal conflict that devastated the land, reduced many Afrikaners to abject poverty, and—because of tactics employed by the British (including the introduction of the term "concentration camp" to the language of modern warfare)—fueled Afrikaner nationalism and caused a public outcry in Britain.

After the war the Union of South Africa consisted of the Cape Colony, the British colony of Natal, and the two Boer republics. In this new country Afrikaners found themselves trudging to the cities as poor, uneducated workers forced to compete with black Africans, Indians, and others they had long considered inferior.

The resentment spurred by this competition was harnessed by the planners of apartheid and incorporated into Afrikaner nationalism.

The political leaders, ministers of the Dutch Reformed Church, and other Afrikaner intellectuals began to preach adherence to strict, biblically based ideas about racial purity. One of the leading intellectuals put it this way: "The Afrikaner believes that it is the will of God that there should be a diversity of races and nations and that obedience to the will of God therefore requires the acknowledgement and maintenance of that diversity."

This struck a chord among the poor Afrikaner population, and when the incumbent United Party was equivocal on race relations, the National Party won the election of 1948 with apartheid as its platform. Almost immediately they set about drafting legislation to make their ideas on racial purity the law of the land; the supremacy of the Afrikaner was their primary goal.

This was hardly the beginning of racism in South Africa. Nelson Mandela himself had marched for the first time five years earlier, and the African National Congress (ANC), the organization that would become the primary opponent of apartheid, was founded in 1912. In 1944, when Mandela, Walter Sisulu, and others founded the Youth League, they were able to cite 40 years of legislation that they opposed.

But the arrival of apartheid was still a catastrophe. The National Party legalized the racist customs that had previously been observed merely as social convention. Common racism was replaced with a codified, systematic racism backed by the entire force of the national government. As Mandela explained, "The often haphazard segregation of the past three hundred years was to be consolidated into a monolithic system that was diabolical in its detail, inescapable in its reach and overwhelming in its power."

Among the flood of legislation passed by the new government were the cornerstones of apartheid. The Population Registration Act required each person to register according to his or her race. And the Group Areas Act demarcated certain land for certain races, providing the basis for the famous "forced removals" of entire communities.

The government insisted on perfecting the existing segregation and thus decided that certain areas inhabited by blacks—"black spots"—needed to be cleaned up so that whites could live there. The most famous of these removals occurred in Sophiatown, a vibrant black community and one of the first cultural centers of urban South Africa. The government ordered the people to move to a preexisting black area known only as the South West Townships. They then arrived with bulldozers and flattened the community, including the homes of those who would not move. The South West Townships of Johannesburg became the ultimate destination for many of those removed and was later known by the acronym Soweto.

Job reservation laws made it illegal for people of certain races to perform certain jobs and served as an aggressive affirmative-action program for the down-trodden Afrikaners. The Bantu Education Act was designed to restrict educational opportunities and systematically undereducate black South Africans. Other laws segregated every aspect of daily life from the buses to the bathrooms.

Over the next 50 years, living under the strict laws of apartheid, South Africa became the most race-obsessed society in the world. It was into this society that we ventured as a diverse group of American volunteers.

WE LEFT PRETORIA AND WENT TO THE TRAINING SITE IN NKOWAKOWA, A black community outside the Northern Province town of Tzaneen. The countryside around Tzaneen is breathtakingly beautiful. Lush tea and mango plantations spread over rolling hills all the way to the horizon. One of the most famous luxury hotels in southern Africa is nestled in these hills, and part of its fame stems from the views of the countryside in which we would be staying. The town itself is crisscrossed by quaint, well-manicured boulevards and shaded streets lined with impressive homes.

But Tzaneen is one of the most conservative areas in an extremely conservative country. The white people there were proud of their lifestyle and customs, not apologetic for them.

Everywhere I went, race dominated everyday life in South Africa to an extent that I had never experienced. I was, for the first time, a member of a minority and was constantly conscious of my race. But compared to others in my training group, I had it easy. Both black and white South Africans would talk to John, an African American whose mother is white, in Afrikaans. "I am American," he would say. "I don't speak that language."

"But aren't you Coloured?"

In those first days, nothing better illustrated South Africa's racial obsession for me than learning about the concept of "Coloured people." Apartheid created a separate classification for people who were not black or white, but fell somewhere in the middle. The descendants of parents of different races, some Coloured people traced their roots to Malay slaves brought over by Dutch colonists as craftsmen, some to the Khoi or "Hottentots" that worked on white people's farms in the early days of European settlement, and some to slaves imported from other parts of Africa. In the settlers' early days, there were few women in the new colony, and white men often stole away to the slave quarters, which of course means that Coloured people in South Africa have as much claim as the whites to being the descendants of the first European settlers in Africa.

The Coloured people shared cultural and language bonds with the Afrikaners. Because Coloured people tended houses for many settlers, many Afrikaners were raised almost exclusively by Coloured nannies. The families lived together and grew up together. The traditional food that is now served in Afrikaner households was served first by Coloureds. A compelling argument can be made that the language of Afrikaans—the distinctness of which is a major source of pride for the Afrikaner people and a cornerstone of their nationalism—was created as much by the Coloured nannies, as they spoke to the babies of Afrikaner families, as it was by the Dutch-speaking parents themselves.

Even today, Coloured people speak Afrikaans as their first language, and among them are some of the most well-known and revered Afrikaans writers and poets.

It is easy to see how Coloured people did not fit within apartheid's strict interpretations of race. Once the Afrikaner Nationalists, the National Party, came to power in 1948, they created a separate class that had special privileges and special constraints. Certain jobs were reserved for white people, and certain others were reserved for Coloureds. They were more privileged than the blacks, but their rights were still circumscribed. In 1952, the National Party government passed the Immorality Act, making sex across racial lines illegal. As Allister Sparks put it, the law "was a statutory declaration that the Coloured people should never have existed, that their procreation was a sin and a crime which should have been prevented."

For us, just hearing the word "Coloured" was offensive. Most foreign journalists when writing about Coloured people in South Africa have problems with the word and often add "so-called." After talking to Coloured people, though, I learned some of them had a different view. They considered themselves Coloured, and they shared a common history and common identity with other Coloured people. To call them "so-called" was to deny that they had a legitimate identity as a group.

White supremacists in Tzaneen had ideas on racial purity that were so strong that they would almost arrange marriages for their children so that their grandchildren would be full-blooded Afrikaners. Imagine their surprise when two prominent families in Tzaneen had their children marry, and the children gave birth to a beautiful grandchild with a wide nose, kinky hair, and big lips.

WE HAD A VERY DIVERSE GROUP OF VOLUNTEERS. WE HAILED FROM all over the United States and from all different backgrounds. I was the only white southern frat boy in the group. There were seven African-

American women, two over 50 and five younger; ten white women from varied backgrounds; one middle-aged white married couple; a middle-aged white man; two Filipino Americans; a Laotian American; a Japanese American; and a Dominican American who spoke English as his second language. Our interactions with South African society were going to force us to learn about each other and our unspoken assumptions about America.

We all had a good idea of the racial distinctions in America, and some of us were able to talk about the way we were going to attack the problems we would face in South Africa. Nicole, who was from south-central Los Angeles and had brought only high-heeled shoes, was not going to take grief from anyone. John, a black man seen in South Africa as Coloured, was going to reason everyone's racism into the ground. Clemenceau, a 70-year-old black woman from Alabama, had seen it all before and wasn't going to let it affect her. Most of us white people were going to fight prejudice, but mostly because we had never fought it before. Now that we were able to point fingers at other oppressors, we were ready to hold high the banner of justice.

A black male Peace Corps volunteer from the first group in South Africa, which had been in the country for about a year when we arrived as the second group, told how he made sure he was respected. He went into Tzaneen regularly because he was stationed in the area and bought his food there. In the stores he would look white people in the eye, make them speak to him in English, and stand at the counter until they picked up the money they had thrown at him and placed it in his hand.

We were one of the first groups of outsiders ever to be dropped into black South Africa without having any experience living in white South Africa. Our starting point was among black South Africans. Our homes would be located in the townships and homelands of the black population. When we went to town, when we participated in white South

African life, we were just visiting. When journalists and others who lived in South Africa went into the townships, they were out of their element and often uncomfortable. For us, on the other hand, these were the places where we would soon belong.

SWAZI HILLS

CHAPTER THREE

THE MOST INFLUENTIAL PERSON IN MY TRAINING WAS ZAKHELE
Ndisimane. Our training group of 42 was split into six different language groups, which corresponded to our eventual placement in the country. My group spent two hours every day in Siswati class with our teachers, Zakhele and Lindiwe Langa. Zakhele, or Zakes, and Lindiwe were both in their early 20s. They had been hired because of their command of English and their ability to articulate their cultural practices, which included not just Swazi traditions but, perhaps more important, modern South African life. A great teacher, Lindiwe told us all about what it was like being a young, intelligent black woman in South Africa—a formidable challenge because sexism, as they say, is the only tradition in South Africa that truly crosses racial boundaries. As for Zakes, he was my best friend during training.

I learned as much playing pool with Zakes as I did in any class. Zakes was six feet four, which must have made him one of the tallest black men in South Africa. I saw many tall white South Africans, but when I was among black people, at five feet nine, I normally towered over the group. Zakes's mother's brother is Mathews Phosa, the premier of Mpumalanga, where we were living. Zakes always had the fanciest shoes, the best cologne, and the smallest cell phone. But most of us decided he was cool because he was curious and well informed. Even though it was not required, he spent most of his time-off sitting in on our group discussions. He was always interested in educating himself, trying to find new ways to look at the world.

In the beginning, however, I was much more concerned with Zakes's ability to teach me the language. There are 11 official languages in South Africa. English and Afrikaans are spoken throughout the country. Pedi, Tswana, Sotho, Venda, Tsonga, Xhosa, Siswati, Ndebele, and Zulu are spoken to varying degrees in certain regions. Throughout the townships of Johannesburg and Pretoria, all 11 of these languages are spoken. Growing up in Tembisa, it is not uncommon to find someone who speaks seven languages by the time he or she finishes school. Soshanguve, the name of the largest township outside Pretoria, stands for "Sotho, Shangaan, Nguni, and Venda," representing all of the language groups spoken there.

Zakhele and Lindiwe taught me Siswati, one of the four Nguni languages. Within that group, the languages of Siswati, Zulu, Ndebele, and Xhosa are much more closely related than, say, Spanish and Italian. Speakers of the different languages can understand each other perfectly. In the town of Lochiel, where I would live, about 40 percent of the schoolchildren speak Zulu at home, and 60 percent speak Siswati.

These Nguni languages, the most distantly related to the original Bantu, are unique in the world because they contain clicking consonants that were absorbed into their original language from the nomadic Khoi. The Khoi people, made famous in the movie *The Gods Must Be Crazy*, traveled the mountains and valleys of southern Africa for millennia. Variously called Bushmen, Hottentots, Khokhoi, or San, the Khoi developed a distinctive language using several different clicking sounds. As black Bantu-speaking people from the north arrived, some adopted parts of the San language, so that now some South African languages contain the clicking consonants. The Zulu and Swazi children in Lochiel learn a little about the Khoi in grade school history, but the only real remnant of the Khoi is the clicking of Lochiel conversations.

Zakhele, like virtually every other person I met, can recite his ancestral lineage, based on his clan name, back ten or twelve generations. He could do it on the spot, at any moment, in the pool hall or in the classroom. This Swazi oral tradition provides the backbone of all we know about them and their heritage.

It begins with the famous Swazi king Ngwane, who brought his people, the Dlamini, from the coastal lowlands of what is now Mozambique to the valleys of present-day Swaziland in the mid-1700s. They settled just above the coastal plain in a valley known as Ezulwini, or "heaven." To this day, two and a half centuries later, Ezulwini is still home to the Swazi king, the Dlamini are still the ruling clan of the entire Swazi kingdom, and Swaziland itself is known to local people as KaNgwane, or "the place of Ngwane." When I went to live at Lochiel, I visited Ezulwini, and the valley certainly lives up to its name. Surrounded by blue-green mountains with huge dark sheets of exposed rock, it is a stunning place. Waterberry trees, Australian eucalyptus, and other gum trees dot the horizon, and pockets of denser forests enclose small corners of the valley. The game parks in the south end of Ezulwini are home to all manner of African game and hundreds of species of birds.

There is something enchanting about Swaziland, and this piece in particular. The people know that Ezulwini is the center of their life as Swazi people and it has been for as long as they have been a people. This sense of history pervades the atmosphere and can be felt as soon as one enters the valley. It is a powerful feeling. Swazi heritage, Swazi language, and Swazi culture are all tied strongly to the land.

Our assistant training director was a man named Tsimanga, who is also from Swaziland. An expert in Swazi culture and tradition, he took great pride in his language and loved explaining many of the traditional terms for practices that changed drastically when white people arrived. On our first day in South Africa, Tsimanga told us that his name meant "surprise" and that we should expect the unexpected. He also talked to us about how to tell time. His grandfather, he said, used to tell him that they needed to meet when he was "this tall"—holding his hand down around his waist. That referred to the size of his grandfather's shadow. "But today," he said, "we say be there at 11:30, and if you're late we start without you."

WE CONTINUED TO LEARN ABOUT THE HISTORY OF BLACK SOUTH Africa, and this part Zakes knew well. In the early 1800s, the cultural, military, and political landscape of southern Africa was constantly changing. The region was home to many different ancestral groups, sharing a name and lineage, and other more loosely defined tribes, groups, and subgroups. Very similar to feudal Europe, there were alliances and deceptions; daughters married into other groups at the kings' request; there were major battles and shifts of power occurred. When one group controlled another, the dominant group would attempt to assimilate people into their culture so they would permanently identify themselves as members of that community.

The greatest of these conquests was led by Shaka Zulu in the early 1800s. The upheaval came to be known as the *mfecane*, and its effects are still being felt today. Despite his sometimes brutal tactics, Zulu and other South Africans still regard Shaka as one of their most revered heroes.

According to the history books used at the local high school, Shaka was born out of wedlock to a mother impregnated by the king of the Zulu. The king denied that Shaka was his son, and even denied that the woman was pregnant. The name "Shaka" comes from the word for stomach worm, which is what the king claimed was at issue.

Shaka distinguished himself as a warrior under the Mtetwa, a neighboring group that had gained a degree of sovereignty over the Zulu. When the leader of the Zulu—Shaka's father—died, Shaka seized control of the Zulu clan, and later of the Mtetwa.

Shaka quickly put his position as the head of his ancestral group to use. At the time there were only a few thousand Zulu, but that number grew rapidly. It may have quadrupled in the first year of Shaka's rule as he conquered and assimilated neighboring groups. Shaka expanded the Zulu sphere of influence so greatly that today nearly ten million people consider themselves Zulu. Sixteen of the other trainees in my group learned Zulu—by far the largest number.

At that time Zakhele's ancestors, the Swazi, were struggling to remain independent. Shaka's headquarters was south of Ezulwini Valley, in what is today northern KwaZulu-Natal. The Swazi were in extremely close proximity and survived as a distinct people because they were blessed with great leadership, a strong identity, and a homeland that was easy to defend. King Sobhuza of the Swazi organized his army along Shakan lines, but he pursued a different political tack. He made peace with the Zulu to the south and west and with the Shangaan to the north, providing a buffer state for both.

After Shaka's death, Sobhuza and his son and successor, Mswati, from their base in Ezulwini, reclaimed much of the land and many of the groups to the north and west, creating a powerful, far-reaching kingdom. It was at this time that the people under his rule began to consider themselves "Swati," after their king, Mswati. The Zulu pronunciation of that word is "Swazi," and that is where the country of Swaziland gets its name. We would soon be living on the very soil where this slice of history took place.

In the third week of our training, our group was split in two, based on the languages we were learning. The Zulu- and Swazi-speaking groups, along with our instructors, left Tzaneen to stay for eight weeks in a small community in the mountains of eastern Mpumalanga, near the Swaziland border. This land would have been spared apartheid had that border been drawn farther west, placing the valley safely in Swaziland.

Today, Kromdraai, or eKulindeni, is situated in a green valley on the eastern edge of South Africa. At the time I did not know it, but just below the ridge is where I would spend my two years in the Peace Corps.

At the end of a long dirt road, we stepped off the bus in a little town ringed by mountains. The houses were laid out on a grid with ten hundred-foot streetlights to discourage crime and, during apartheid, to ensure that everything would be seen. It reminded me in an odd way of a baseball stadium. The houses were tightly packed, and most were built of concrete blocks or brick, though some homesteads still had outbuildings made from sticks and mud. In the distance we could see a mine with its huge gray-and-white slag dump, lit up at night, standing in contrast to the dark green of the mountains.

We got off the bus at a school, which we would use as a training center. Sithuthukile Primary School, consisting of three brick buildings, is painted with murals by schoolchildren, and in the yard it has a multi-level garden surrounded by carefully placed rocks. The principal, Nicolas Dlamini—from the name, a descendant of the inner clan of Swazi royalty—was a dapper, intelligent, and impressive man who welcomed us along with the teachers from the community.

We were each assigned to a family who had agreed to accommodate an American volunteer for eight weeks. Twenty families had sent representatives to come pick up their Americans. Mothers, sisters, and little children, older brothers, grandmothers, and grandfathers were all sitting in a classroom, pointing and laughing and hoping that they would get the best one. As they spoke in foreign tongues that we couldn't understand, popping and clicking, we were sure they were saying, "I wonder if that one is ours?" "We want that one!" "I hope we don't get stuck with that one."

We looked around nervously, wondering who we would live with. "That person looks pretty cool," I said to my pool-playing, beer-drinking buddy, Radhames. I pointed to a guy with gold-rimmed MC Hammer–style glasses, a gold tooth, and a white tank top.

They called names, and all of us met up with our families. We shuffled with our brand-new, bright backpacks with straps and buckles and clips and places for our water bottles over to the little groups of people waiting for us. MC Hammer and a short, wide girl, barefoot in a pink dress, had come to pick me up. I asked about their names. Hers was Zanele. MC Hammer said, "My name is Doctor Magagula."

"Are you a doctor?" I asked, not having any idea what to expect.

They laughed and laughed, but I did not understand and was uncomfortable. Zanele reached for my bag and the box of food that the Peace Corps had given us for the family. She put the box on her head and picked up my bag. "Wait," I said, thinking about my manners and what my grandfather would say about me letting a young lady carry my bag. "I'll carry the bag."

"No," she said, smiling. "You can't. It's too far."

"No, really, it's OK," I said, taking the bag and putting it on my back. "I can carry it."

She turned and walked off with the box on her head. Doctor and I followed, but soon lost sight of her as she hurried home. I wondered if I had failed my first test. I did not know what was polite or what was rude. I wondered if I had offended her. I had no idea. And when the other volunteers walked away, I was left on my own to make these determinations. I could no longer use other Americans to insulate me when I made a mistake.

Doctor and I walked down the hill on the dirt streets past some of the huge lights, a health clinic, and men playing chess under a tree, one of whom was wearing a red South African Communist Party T-shirt, complete with a yellow hammer and sickle. We walked up to the house where I would be living for eight weeks.

Three men sat in the shade to the side of a mechanic's garage. The sign above the garage door said "Cool Runnings Tuck Shop" in black letters painted over a rainbow. I would soon learn that a tuck shop was a small store that sold household items, but that this one had not operated in some time. In the yard were two major remnants of cars, rusted out with no wheels, and a minibus that probably still worked sometimes.

We went around back. In the small yard was a full-size porcelain bathtub, a metal clothesline apparatus, a small pen for chickens, and a tap where the family drew their water. The house, which was separated from the garage by a two-foot concrete walkway, was a typical four-room matchbox-style house. I could see through the door that Zanele was in the kitchen putting away the groceries that the Peace Corps had given them. I still didn't know if she was mad. She told me I was supposed to sleep in a room attached to the garage that opened to the backyard.

I was excited. It was a perfect arrangement because I would be separate from the family and would have some privacy, but my door was only a few feet from the kitchen so I would still be close.

Zanele said her mother would be coming home soon. Doctor said he was leaving because he had to go home. "Home?" I said, thinking he had used the wrong English word. "Don't you live here?"

He chuckled and yelled something to Zanele in Zulu, and they both laughed. "No, my friend," he said. "I have my own house. I do not live here. I am only a friend to them. Do not worry. I will come back and visit you later."

He left and I unpacked in my gray concrete-block room. I put my clothes in a wooden chest in the corner, slid my backpack under the bed, and stared up at the tin roof. There was nothing else in the room, but I was happy. I laughed at my mistake. Doctor, the family representative who came to pick me up, was not a doctor or even a member of the family. I was a little afraid to talk to Zanele, so I stayed in my room.

Soon everyone returned. Two young boys, Nkululeko and Sibusiso, whose names mean "Freedom" and "Blessing," returned from primary school in the blue shirt, gray shorts, and black shoes of their uniforms. Thokozo, in tenth grade, returned from the secondary school with Manzini, the oldest son, who was in his final year of high school. The last child also surfaced at this time. She was a three-year-old named Nombulelo, who had been in the house with Zanele all day but had refused to talk to me.

All of these kids belonged to Mrs. Busisiwe Khoza and her husband, known to everyone by his nickname, "Bra Sphiwe" (pronounced Spee-Way). Manzini and Zanele were not biological children of theirs, but belonged to a family member who was close enough that Zanele and Manzini called the Khozas mother and father. Westerners would call them nieces and nephews. None of these relationships were explained to me, and I did not find out this fact until six months later, when I came back to visit the Khozas, and Zanele had gone to live with her parents.

Busisiwe, or Busi, is a third-grade science teacher. Her husband works as a sometime mechanic, sometime garbage man, and full-time political organizer. Well known and well regarded throughout the town, he is a Rastafarian and a guitar player. I had met him around front with Doctor when I had arrived. When I realized that he was the father, I immediately wished that I had greeted him more formally. I had basically ignored him because he was part of the group of mechanics out front. Had I already shown him disrespect?

I wanted to examine the house. Where did they put all these people? The three younger boys and three-year-old Nombulelo slept in one bedroom, and Busi and Bra Sphiwe slept in the other. There was also a kitchen and a living room. Manzini, the oldest son, stayed in another room connected to the garage that opened out to the front, and Zanele, it turned out, was staying with a friend. I felt guilty taking a room, though I told myself that I was paying rent and bringing food and that they were clearly accustomed to close quarters.

Because Busi was a teacher with a regular income and her husband also earned some money, they were a wealthy family. Because they had the money, they filled the house with furniture. I had to squeeze between the two couches in the living room to sit down to watch a TV that was maybe eight feet away. And I had to keep my legs right in front of me or they pressed up against the coffee table. In the kitchen they had a table, a stove, a countertop sink (with no faucet), and a refrigerator. It was an extremely tight fit.

For the first few days I was very shy. I spoke virtually no Siswati, and the family members were all embarrassed to speak English. I was checking them out to see what they were like, and they were watching me in return. The Peace Corps had given us explicit instructions on how to behave. We were never to wear a hat indoors. We were never to drink alcohol or do anything to disrespect the family. We were to be culturally sensitive at all times; these people had welcomed us into their homes, and we needed to ensure that they would not be disappointed with us. I walked on eggshells for the first few days, having a hard time making the transition to an entirely alien culture. We had been with Zakhele and the other trainers, but at the training center in Tzaneen we were still Americans in an American environment. Here, in rural South Africa for the first time, everything was different.

I wanted to go and shoot pool and relax and have a beer with Zakhele and Radhames. Instead I went to bed at seven every night because my room was my only refuge. The family was as nervous as I was, and none of us knew how to bridge the gap. My presence was paralyzing for both sides. When I was there, no one could move without fear of offending. So I went to bed early and read and wrote in my journal until late.

I was lying in bed late on the fourth night, starting to go to sleep, when I heard something from Manzini's room. Two people walked in, and one let out a high-pitched giggle. "Shhhhhh," Manzini said. And then he whispered something in Siswati and seconds later turned on his tape player. I heard: "Gimme the beat, boys, and free my so-oul, I wanna get lost in your rock and roll, and drift away-ay...."

I laughed out loud. "Loosen up," I told myself. "Apparently, 20-year-old boys are the same everywhere. Sometimes they even listen to the same old seventies rock." I rolled over and went to sleep, laughing at the conversation I planned to have with Manzini in the morning.

I had that conversation, laughed with him for a while, and went to play pool that night. As I was playing, two of the teachers from the school came in, and then Bra Sphiwe. He smiled at me and said how great it was to see me there. He had snuck around the back way so I wouldn't see him leave the house, because he had been nervous that I would disapprove. And then Thokozo, the tenth grader, came in with some of his friends.

From then on everyone was much more relaxed. There were no problems with our different cultures, no issues of disrespect. When I did something offensive, such as drink from the hose, or eat with my left hand, they told me. When I was uncomfortable, I said so and they respected that. I had created culture shock all by myself out of imagined differences that didn't really exist.

Bra Sphiwe would get out his guitar and play in the backyard all afternoon, and then all night in the garage. We borrowed a tape player, and I played American music for them. Bra Sphiwe loved Jimi Hendrix and could tolerate some of my extensive country music collection. (When I left, the only tape he asked me for was the Grateful Dead's *Reckoning*.) Different people came by all the time, and sometimes we would sit in the backyard listening to Bra Sphiwe's favorite song, "Fire on the Mountain," while he, dreadlocks and all, played along, fumbling a little, on his guitar. The kids from the four neighboring houses ran under the laundry on the clothesline and around and around the spigot in the yard. Sometimes, Busi would put the three younger kids and two or three neighbors in the bathtub in the backyard and bathe them.

Again and again, the cultural similarities were more striking than the differences. The two young boys had to write in a journal every day for their English class. On March 8, 1998, Sibusiso, who was eight years old at the time, wrote this:

> *I like to sit when I write.*
> *I like to eat bread and tea.*
> *I close the door when it is cold.*
> *I like to eat peanut butter.*
> *I like to light with a torch when it is dark.*
> *I like to lie on a shadow when the sun is hot.*
> *I like to play with my ball.*
> *I like to drink Coke.*

We were instructed by the Peace Corps to find out as much as we could about the history of Kromdraai. More recently, in addition to the Swazi and the Zulu, the rolling hills and steep cliffs were overtaken by white people.

By pure chance, the first white people arrived in the area fast on the heels of the mfecane. Shaka's ten years of conquests set off waves of refugees wandering all over southern Africa in search of a place to continue their way of life, without being subsumed by the Zulu vortex. Shaka and his major military opponents, Mzilikazi and Soshangaan, fought mercilessly. They tried to convince potential subjects that surrendering without a fight was better than the alternative: annihilation. These armies ransacked, burned, and destroyed not just homes but massive swaths of land. Mzilikazi led his group of Ndebele-speaking people north to what is now Zimbabwe, scattering the groups of today's northern South Africa in his path. Soshangaan worked his way east and created an enormous empire of his own in what is today Mozambique. People moved as far north as present-day Tanzania to escape the wars, and thousands were displaced into what are now the countries of Malawi, Zambia, Botswana, Mozambique, and Zimbabwe.

When British missionaries and Afrikaner pioneers arrived, the desolate land and stories of brutality colored the whites' first impressions of the people. Plus, the war-ravaged state of the black population made it easy for the new arrivals to take over. If they had arrived earlier, or later, there is no telling how the history of South Africa would have unfolded.

Mswati first met with white people in 1846, and his successors entered into a series of deals and concessions that allowed the English and Afrikaners to progressively gain more and more control over mining and other resources under Swazi rule. Eventually, to protect themselves from the encroaching Boer republics, the Swazi kingdom asked to be named a British dependency in the late 1800s. In the negotiations that followed the Boer War between the Afrikaners and the British in 1902, the European combatants redrew the borders of Swaziland to their present locations. This finalized the map of South Africa, giving the Swazi and Sotho small parcels of land under British protection—Swaziland and Lesotho—while all of the other black African groups were placed officially under the rule of white people in South Africa proper.

Kromdraai was placed within South Africa, but it was almost entirely uninhabited. Before the 1970s white farmers owned the land, and very few black people lived there. Today there is a substantial population, and all the people are black. Townspeople say that many of the original inhabitants came from a place near Pretoria called Kromdraai, Afrikaans for "bent road," and that is where this small village got its name.

They were displaced by the apartheid government, which forcibly removed many black people from regions that had been deemed white areas by the system. In the mid-1970s the Zulu- and Swazi-speaking people near Pretoria represented a "black spot" in a white area and were sent to this place in the hills west of Swaziland. They were told to wait there. eKulindeni, the official name of the town, means "place of waiting," and 25 years later the Khozas and their neighbors are still there, waiting.

Many of the older people I talked to remember coming to this place and not knowing why. They worried about how they would make money, where they would find food, and what their lives would be like in this strange place. Then they discovered that an asbestos mine had just opened a few miles away. The white mine owners and managers came to the new community to recruit labor, because there was no other major settlement anywhere within a 20-mile radius. The combination was serendipitous as far as the government was concerned, yet another example of the twisted politics and economics of apartheid.

Once the carcinogenic properties of asbestos were known, the demand for it dropped sharply. The mine was no longer profitable, and it closed down in the late 1990s, relegating most of Kromdraai's population to unemployment. When we arrived, and indeed when I left the area more than two years later, the community was still half an hour from the nearest paved road. The little town's economy is now based on government jobs: teachers, police, sanitation workers, and other local officials, plus elderly people who receive a government pension check every month. Some people living in Johannesburg or the major towns of Mpumalanga, such as Nelspruit and Barberton, send money back home to their families.

Because the area's hills and streams make the landscape incredibly beautiful, the government is developing the ecotourism industry, and the nature reserve near Kromdraai, run by the National Park Service, brings new hope to the community. The Songimvelo Nature Reserve has elephants, zebras, and other wild game, a host of birds and fish, and even a few leopards. You also have a better chance of seeing white rhinos in Songimvelo than in most other places on the planet. The reserve's impact on the quality of life for the people of Kromdraai will clearly be positive. Still, in terms of job creation, it is difficult for conservation to take the place of mining, one of the most labor-intensive industries in history. After I left Kromdraai, Bra Sphiwe was lucky enough to get one of the jobs working on the reserve, and I saw him a few times in a Songimvelo Nature Reserve pickup truck. But few other people in Kromdraai would benefit directly.

WE CONTINUED OUR TECHNICAL AND LANGUAGE TRAINING EVERY DAY

at the school. Representatives of South African nongovernmental organizations who had experience working with teachers came and talked to us about conducting workshops, approaching the new curriculum, improving school management, and doing demonstration lessons. Zakes and Lindiwe continued to teach language class twice a day, although it became more of a question-and-answer period about the community and their local dialect. The immersion in community life was a great way to learn the language, especially with our teachers as guides.

Among my initial cultural experiences, I learned to eat *phuto* and *amasi*. Phuto is a dry maize meal porridge, almost like crumbled cornbread, and amasi is sour milk—some would say spoiled milk, but I liked it fine and would eat plenty of amasi mixed with phuto over the next two years.

I learned to enjoy watching soccer on television. South Africa's national team, Bafana Bafana, was playing in the African Cup of Nations—the African championships. I had fun sitting with the family in the tiny living room with all the furniture, while up and down the street everyone was watching the same game. Because of the construction of the houses, we could often hear the people next door and across the street celebrating along with us when South Africa scored a goal.

I also learned that we in the developed world have been spoiled by shoes. The children would take off their shoes the minute they got home from school. Most of the time their mother did, too. It was always blazing hot, and I would sit sometimes in the shade of my doorway with the door open so I could look out at the backyard and the circle of mountains in the distance. The kids would sit around and talk and laugh and teach me Siswati. What they found strangest of all, and the biggest difference between us by far, was the bottoms of our feet. They would stare at and touch the bottoms of my feet and scream and laugh and run away and go get their friends, all the while running on the gravel and glass and rough rocks of the dirt roads and yards. My soft, wrinkly white soles were worthless by comparison.

I bathed in my room in a small basin, with water drawn from the tap in the yard and heated in a kettle on the stove in the kitchen; I never did find a way to get completely clean. The hardest transition to life in rural South Africa, though, was using the toilets. The latrines operated on a bucket system. In the little tin shack in the yard, there was a bucket on the floor with a small seat on top of it. The community sanitation workers picked up and emptied the buckets every few weeks—people claim that the removal was not that rare, but I don't believe them. There were nine people living in our house. The bucket was surprisingly small, and it would get very full by the end of the time period between removals. Once early on, I went to the latrine at night and decided, stupidly, to take a flashlight. I went in and inadvertently shined the flashlight into the bucket. It was full almost to overflowing. If I had touched it with my foot, some would have spilled out. Inside the bucket, making up the entire top layer, were thousands of white worms or maggots of some kind. They were crawling all over each other like bees on a honeycomb. I turned outside and vomited twice. For the rest of my stay in Kromdraai, I used only the facilities at the school, where they at least had a proper pit latrine with a very deep hole.

I also had my first experience with the rural South African health system. On a day off, several of my friends and I were in the nature reserve visiting the trainers, who were staying in cabins there. While a few of us were swimming in the nature reserve's pool, I slammed my shoulder against the brick of the poolside. Through the two-inch gash I saw muscle and bone. I found Yvonne and told her I needed stitches. We took a Peace Corps vehicle back to Kromdraai to go to the clinic. When we arrived, the doctor was nowhere to be found. We asked around and eventually found him walking down the street near his home, having just returned from a trip to Barberton. He was a young man with glasses, and his name was Justice. I knew by now that his name meant no more than Doctor's. Doctor, I found out, raises chickens for a living and is a friend of the family who was sent to get me because everyone else was busy.

"Excuse me," I said, holding my shirt to my shoulder as blood trickled down my chest and arm. "Do you think you could help me out with some stitches?"

"Actually, it's my day off," he said. "Can you wait until tomorrow?"

"Well," Yvonne said, giving him one of her looks, "can we just borrow your needle and thread?" He laughed nervously and said he thought he could do it if we gave him a ride to the clinic. Then he proceeded to put three stitches in my shoulder from a perfectly sterile suture kit with the utmost competence.

JUST AS I WAS SETTLING IN AND BECOMING COMFORTABLE IN MY NEW rural environment, South Africa's racial reality reared its head. Because the Khozas were rich, they were able to send their children to the Diepgezet Primary School. The school, set up to educate the children of white managers at the Diepgezet Mine, was forced to integrate when apartheid ended, so it accepted children from the Kromdraai community. The level of education was very high, especially in English and Afrikaans—the first languages of the white teachers. Most of the black teachers and principals from the Kromdraai community schools paid the higher school fees and sent their own children to the mine school.

One day Nkululeko wrote in his journal about the American that was staying with them. The principal of the mine school, Mr. Boschoff, a middle-aged Afrikaner, found out about us, and invited three of us to his house for dinner. Ned was a fun person from Oregon who wore purple socks and did not have a TV until he went to college. Nikki was an African-American woman from Miami who was in my Siswati language group and would become one of my best friends in the Peace Corps.

By now all three of us had grown accustomed to our lives in our respective families. Ned had the whole town talking because he liked to cook, and that went against generations and generations of gender dynamics. "Oh, Ned?" people would say. "Yes, I know Ned. He is very tall and skinny, and he is a man who likes to cook."

Nikki was staying with a well-respected school principal. Nikki enjoyed her family and the rest of the community so much that she requested to be placed in Kromdraai for her permanent assignment. She had visited Africa before, but moving there to live was an emotional experience. For black women who are used to being treated as they are in the United States, the attitudes toward race and gender in South Africa are especially difficult to accept. Nikki received a lot of harassment from men, including marriage proposals and rude comments, but took it all in stride. I was excited to go to the dinner with both of them.

Mr. Boschoff and his wife picked us up in a fancy little pickup truck and drove us across the strange one-mile divide to the area around the mine. His house was set on a hill in the midst of a perfectly manicured garden overlooking a cliff across the river. The house itself was spacious and reminded me of any number of American homes built in the 1960s. The meal, served by Mrs. Boschoff, was enormous: baked chicken, sweet potato casserole, broccoli, scalloped potatoes, and wine.

The Boschoffs were genial hosts, and we sat, mere minutes from where I had bathed in a bucket for six weeks, drinking scotch and being asked if we wanted to play golf or go horseback riding in the morning. It was a bizarre feeling that left us confused, and with aching bellies because we had eaten too much. Their hospitality was genuine, but it was disconcerting to see such wealth in close proximity to the poverty we'd experienced. "If there is anything we can do to help, please let us know," they said sincerely.

They were teaching black students, helping to fight against the belief that black people were inferior to whites, but did not interact with the black people in their community in any meaningful way. And there is no doubt that the families with whom we stayed could find no way to relate to the Boschoffs either. That is the legacy of apartheid.

AT THE KHOZAS' I BEGAN TO WATCH THE NEWS RELIGIOUSLY.

The reports about the ongoing transition were fascinating. The South African government was transforming from a massive organization designed to maintain white power and strengthen apartheid into a government that would create jobs and provide services to the millions of black families that had been neglected for so long. It was a daunting task.

We were intimately involved in the grassroots transformation of the educational curriculum, and we discussed it every day in training. But other political and cultural transitions that the country faced were just as complex and far-reaching. When Thabo Mbeki, Mandela's deputy president, was asked about the most surprising aspect of coming to power, he said, "We just had no idea how much we had to do."

Every aspect of government was being overhauled. The police force had been designed to protect white communities and to suppress antiapartheid activity in black ones. At the top levels it was controlled and staffed by whites. It would now need to protect much larger, poorer communities, and the leadership would have to be changed to reflect the country and the country's new policymakers. The armed forces of South Africa—also controlled exclusively by whites—were slowly incorporating the leadership and soldiers of the Mkhonto weSizwe, the armed wing of the ANC. Sworn enemies were being joined together under racially mixed command.

The ANC had promised to build a million new homes, and so the housing ministry was, while restructuring its management to end the whites-only control, also embarking on the largest housing project in its history. The finance ministry, throughout all of its own changes, was trying to maintain the confidence of international capital markets so that they could fund the massive antipoverty projects that the other parts of the government had undertaken.

The very foundation of the government was changing. Mandela's government was technically a "Transitional Government of National Unity," and its first task had been to draft a new constitution for South Africa. When I arrived in Kromdraai, the Constitutional Convention had ended, and the new document had been ratified. But the government was still educating people about their new rights and the structure of their new government. The permanent constitution was to take effect after the June 1999 elections.

Everyone in Kromdraai was politically astute and supported the ANC. One of the elected town councilors lived across the street. Bra Sphiwe had been an organizer, and ANC posters hung in our garage. It seemed every third T-shirt on the street was from a political rally. I was surprised by how well informed and how committed people were to political activism. Anyone could tell you the ANC party line on a number of issues, and most claimed to have marched or rallied during the first election. I had the same conversation about exchange rates at least ten times—why did it take five South African rand to get one American dollar? And how could a loaf of bread cost two dollars in America but only two rand in South Africa?

The Truth and Reconciliation Commission dominated the news. Chaired by Archbishop Desmond Tutu, the commission was set up to examine the crimes of apartheid. Perpetrators of crimes applied to the commission and then testified before them. If they gave a complete and honest account of their crimes, they were granted amnesty. Victims could also apply to the commission and tell their stories. Since it was completed, the commission has been the subject of at least two wonderful books, *Country of My Skull* by Antjie Krog, and *No Future*

Without Forgiveness by Archbishop Tutu. During its work the commission was celebrated throughout the world for the creative and productive way it dealt with the crimes of the past.

The commission steered a course between the inappropriate "collective amnesia" that would have resulted from ignoring the crimes, and the equally negative results of a vindictive prosecution of all the perpetrators who committed crimes in what amounted to a full-scale war between the apartheid government and the liberation movements. But in Kromdraai it raised some controversy. Many people on my street thought the perpetrators, who were mostly white, should be punished severely. Among them was Busi Khoza. She was very shy, and didn't like to speak in English—an odd trait for a teacher—but when I brought up the subject of the commission, she became animated. She thought it was not doing enough for victims.

"Musa," she said, using the name they had given me because they had trouble pronouncing Jason, "we had put so many things behind us. And now, with this, they asked us to bring all those things back." She had high expectations when she applied to the commission that they would investigate the disappearance of her brother. "He disappeared, Musa, a long time ago, and all of us were OK and we had stopped hurting. But we thought we could know once and for all what happened, so we applied. But this thing is not for us. They said he was not involved in politics, but I know he was."

"They said, Musa, that we would not be able to know. Even today we do not know. And we had to go through it again, and we cried, Musa, me and my sisters, we cried." They denied her family's request to examine his case because they said there was not enough evidence to prove the disappearance was politically motivated.

Talking to her there in her cramped living room in rural South Africa opened my eyes. I still thought the Truth and Reconciliation Commission was a noble effort, but I could see the personal side as well. I was no longer studying or watching a transformation from afar. I was living in it.

THE MAN

CHAPTER FOUR

AT THE END OF OUR TIME IN KROMDRAAI WE WERE EACH assigned to a site where we would live for two years. The government of South Africa chose the sites, and the Peace Corps tried to match volunteers to the communities. I was assigned to live in Lochiel, a small community in the mountains above Kromdraai. I knew only two things about Lochiel: The Peace Corps told me I would be living with a practicing minister, so I would need to be respectful, and the high school boys in Kromdraai laughed and told me that it was a very poor place with no electricity and nothing to do.

Before going to Lochiel, I returned with the rest of my training group to the training center near Tzaneen. We had to complete a few more days of paperwork and medical training before we could be sworn in as Peace Corps volunteers.

It so happened that my grandparents were on their way to Mozambique to conduct Carter Center business: an economic policy project and the beginnings of an election-observation mission. My grandfather was then traveling on to Kenya for meetings with two groups fighting a war in the region. Because they were going to be so close, they wanted to come and see me. At the same time, they decided also to pay a courtesy call to President Mandela. Because they wanted to see both of us in the short time they had, and because I was significantly less busy than President Mandela, we decided that the meeting should be at his place instead of mine.

We were to visit with Mandela early in the morning for tea, before he went to a press conference. I was to travel down to Pretoria the night before and ride with my grandparents to the president's house in Johannesburg. I was excited, but having been out of town for weeks I had little advance notice. All of a sudden I had to get to Pretoria.

Simon, one of the Peace Corps staff, agreed to take me to the taxi rank. Simon, who spoke all 11 South African languages, spoke with a taxi driver, pointed me to the Pretoria taxi, and left after I assured him I would be all right.

The taxi rank in Tzaneen has several rows of minibus taxis, each row headed for a different destination. They fill up the first taxi in the line, and then the next, and so on. People come from all over the region, and the taxi rank serves the same function as a regional airport. All the people are in transit, most traveling alone, some mothers with children. I had been to only a few ranks, but they have them in every town, and these hubs represent the fundamental means of transport for most of the black population.

I was lucky that there was a taxi straight from Tzaneen to Pretoria. On my previous trip by taxi, from Kromdraai to Tzaneen as part of a training exercise, I had to make several connections: Kromdraai to Nhlazatje, Nhlazatje to Nelspruit, Nelspruit to Hazyview, Hazyview to Bushbuck Ridge, Bushbuck Ridge to Acornhoek, and finally Acornhoek to Tzaneen. That trip took an entire day and went off without a hitch, but the prospect of blazing a trail through unfamiliar towns was intimidating. This time I was going directly to Gauteng, the famous province that contains Jo-burg and Pretoria.

I climbed into the taxi and sat in the fourth and last row of seats. The first three rows could hold three people each; my row held four. A decal sign pasted on the inside of the door said that the van was "certified to carry 15 passengers." Two people sat up front with the driver.

The van was a typical *koombi* taxi. As best I could glean, the word "koombi" is an Africanization of "combi," an acronym for Consolidated Mini Bus Industries. This koombi, like most others, was not even close to the size of an American 15-passenger van. The original three rows had been removed and four had been added in their place. The rearmost seat, where I was sitting, was pressed up against the back door and window. The other seats were so close together that my knees were bent up and jammed into the back of the seat in front of me. The vinyl backing of that seat was ripped where other knees had been pressed into it.

The taxi had only four passengers so far. I sat for 20 minutes, but no one else came. I knew that the taxis did not leave until they were full, and after an hour I began to worry. I had ridden in koombis once before, but I had never traveled into Gauteng. The province had a fearsome reputation. In Kromdraai, many of the cars had Gauteng plates, which all had the letters GP. The first five people I asked said it stood for Gangsters' Paradise. In the four days we spent in Pretoria at the beginning of training, three different groups of my friends were mugged. The province, renowned for producing 80 percent of the nation's economy, produced almost that much of the nation's crime. We had heard on the news, and in different training sessions, that the townships in Gauteng had the highest rate of violent crime in the world.

People say that in Tzaneen, it gets so hot the chickens faint. Sitting in a hot koombi, with a bag of clothes on my lap, I had no doubt this was true. Women and children were walking around the taxi rank selling snacks and "cold drinks," so I bought a Sprite. It was hot, and as I drank it, I could feel it immediately sweat out through the pores on my face. I don't think any of it made it to my stomach. My hair was soaked, as were several patches of my shirt and pants.

A man jumped into the taxi and started speaking quickly in Sotho. As the other passengers began gathering their belongings, he looked at me. "Come. We are combining with the Jo-burg taxi. They will drop you in Pretoria." I got off and followed him to another van. Maybe ten people were sitting in it, and the last row had one open seat. I made my way, bent in half at the waist, shuffling across the other people to the back. I squeezed myself into the seat. My sweaty shirt pressed into the hot skin of the person next to me. I felt a trickle of sweat rush down my spine into the back of my pants.

Then I became aware of an odor that I associate most closely with koombi taxis. It was a distinctly African body odor, and it was over-powering. People who bathe not in showers but in buckets of river water, people who eat certain foods—cheap, dried soups full of MSG and minimal meat from questionable sources and mounds of maize meal por-ridge—people who wash their clothes with bar soap and with no flow-ery fabric softeners, people who sit in stifling, non-air-conditioned koombis, only those people smell like this. To some, this scent would be offensive and gross, and maybe the first time I smelled it, I thought the same. This time I lifted an arm so that I wouldn't be as wide, and as I was putting my arm in front of me to sit slightly sideways, I caught a whiff and realized I was generating my own share of the koombi smell.

We sat and sweated for a few more minutes. The man next to me was clearly trying not to touch me. I think it was because I am white, but I didn't ask. I smiled and said hello to everyone. No one spoke Siswati or Zulu, so English was my only option.

Eventually, a mother and two children arrived to fill the taxi. We each paid 50 rand (about 10 dollars) and received our appropriate change. The driver climbed in and we were off—across the street and straight into a gas station. The koombi had been sitting at the taxi rank for three hours or more, and yet the driver waited until 15 people were packed into it before he filled it up with gas. We sweated and waited. I asked why they didn't fill it up before, but got no response.

Over the next two years, I would ask that question a hundred times. I had friends who owned taxis and friends who drove them. The taxi industry was one of the largest in black South Africa. It represented the only economy at all in Lochiel, the town where I would be living. Yet the drivers had to collect money for the trip before they could fill up the tank.

We left and drove for hours. It was dark when I saw the sign for Mamelodi, an infamous township outside Pretoria. The driver pulled onto the shoulder of the highway. "You're going to Pretoria?"

"Yes, I am," I said.

"Well, it is very late, so everyone who is going to Pretoria must get off here."

Some of the others complained in Sotho, and the driver apparently gave in and agreed to give us all five rand for the taxi to town or to the township. After he reluctantly disbursed the money, he left four of us on the highway between Pretoria and Mamelodi in the dark.

Two of the men were young and well dressed and spoke to me in English: "Where are you going?"

"To Sunnyside," I said, mentioning the neighborhood near the Peace Corps office. It was the only part of Pretoria I knew. I had heard of Mamelodi because one of the leading South African soccer teams was the Mamelodi Sundowns, and the township was prominent in the crime reports on the news. But I knew no one, and didn't particularly want to go there. I am sure that I was the only white person for five miles.

"You need to get a taxi into town," one of them said.

"How do I do that?" I asked, giving up my feeble attempt to look as if I knew what I was doing.

"You just go over there, and when you see a taxi, you point your finger up in the air." He looked at his friend, no doubt noticing how utterly inexperienced I was in this endeavor. The friend nodded. "OK," he said. "We'll come with you."

We walked down the exit ramp and across the street. Sure enough, a taxi came by, and when we raised our hands and pointed in the air, it stopped.

"See you," my new friends said. "Go well." Those two men were the first in an as yet unbroken chain of kind, helpful people that I managed to meet whenever I needed them.

When I climbed into the taxi, with my bag and my baseball cap, looking like a typical American tourist, everyone stared. The driver started talking to me in Afrikaans. I said in Zulu that I did not speak Afrikaans and that I was from America. The driver smiled and the four passengers laughed. I felt more at ease.

Most of the local koombis are "local" because they are unable to withstand the rigors of long-distance travel. We drove 15 minutes into town, the tires, windows, and doors rattling, cracking, and popping. The driver stopped and pointed down a long, dark street. "Sunnyside is down that way. Bye-bye."

"Bye," I said. "*Ngiyabonga*—Thank you." And they all laughed again.

As I headed down the street, the tall buildings, the beautiful parks, the wide streets all seemed more foreign than they had when I arrived from America. Other aspects that I hadn't considered absurd when I first arrived were utterly out of place in my new view of South Africa. Bushes, curbs, sidewalks, lines on the roads, and traffic lights did not exist in Nkowakowa or Kromdraai. I saw up ahead an array of lights and glass, a Holiday Inn Crowne Plaza. I realized that I had been almost running.

My demeanor changed completely. No longer nervous or even disoriented, I strolled up to the reception desk and asked the woman if she had a phone that guests could use to make local calls.

Without hesitation she gave me a phone from behind the counter. I made two calls and got a taxi. The driver put my bag in the trunk, and I sat in the backseat of a traditional taxicab. The driver turned on the meter, and I paid 22 rand to go from one neighborhood in Pretoria to another just down the road. In six minutes on a dark street in Pretoria, I had walked out of the Third World of black South Africa and into the First World of white South Africa.

The taxi stopped at a small hotel across the street from the U.S. ambassador's residence in Waterkloof. It could have been in Beverly Hills. The views of Pretoria's hills dotted with lights were stunning, the walls were mahogany, and a mosaic of a mermaid lay at the bottom of a pool fed by two fountains. There was an unused room, and the manager, apparently very excited to have my grandparents staying in his hotel, agreed to let me use the extra room for free. I gave my things to the bellman and went down to see my grandparents.

I shook hands and hugged my aunt and uncle and my grandmother and grandfather. I was overflowing with stories to tell them. I had been living in Africa for three months, and we hadn't communicated at all. "This place is amazing! You won't believe how different it is where I am going to be living. The transportation system is really interesting. They have these minibus taxis called koombis...."

My grandmother choked back a cough. My grandfather put his hand on my shoulder. "Well, Jason," he said, "we are very proud of you. Why don't you go take a shower and then come back and tell us about it?"

My grandmother had tears in her eyes. I really didn't think I smelled that bad.

AFTER TALKING LATE INTO THE NIGHT, I WOKE UP BETWEEN BEAUTIFUL sheets in an immaculate room. At seven we left to see the president. I put on a tie, and in the car I tried to plan what I was going to say to him. What did I know about him?

As I was growing up, Mandela was the subject of songs and even albums by reggae singers and rappers. *Free Nelson Mandela* was the title of one album and the subject of many reggae songs.

My aunt Amy was arrested while a student at Brown University for protesting against apartheid in front of the South African embassy.

When I picked up Mandela's autobiography, *Long Walk to Freedom*, in December 1997, less than a month before I was to leave, I felt a little silly knowing nothing about the country that would be my new home. I knew only Mandela as the international symbol and cultural icon.

In South Africa, Mandela's impact was overwhelming. He had been a successful attorney in the 1950s, assisting black people whose rights were so limited that it became almost impossible to avoid breaking the law. As one of the ANC's top leaders he was watched intently by the authorities and was often "banned" from making public appearances or participating in meetings of any kind. Tried for treason and acquitted along with a host of his colleagues, he quit his law practice and spent more than a year underground as the head of Mkhonto weSizwe (MK), the ANC's military wing. He became legendary for avoiding capture and became apartheid's most wanted enemy and one of the heroes of black South Africa.

In 1962 he was apprehended by the government. His subsequent trials and imprisonment made him an international figure and the symbol of the antiapartheid struggle. He was first tried alone and convicted of both "inciting Africans to strike" and "leaving the country without valid travel papers." But soon after he went to prison for these offenses, the government raided a farm in the Johannesburg suburbs that MK had used as a headquarters. They uncovered enough evidence to retry Mandela, with several of his closest colleagues, for sabotage, a crime punishable by death.

During this trial Mandela made perhaps his most famous statement. He spoke in his defense before the court for four hours and concluded:

> *During my lifetime I have dedicated myself to this struggle of the African people. I have fought against white domination, and I have fought against black domination. I have cherished the ideal of a democratic and free society in which all persons*

live together in harmony and with equal opportunities. It is an
ideal which I hope to live for and to achieve. But if needs be,
it is an ideal for which I am prepared to die.

Mandela and his colleagues were convicted and sentenced to life in prison. They were sent to serve their sentences in the infamous prison on Robben Island. Oliver Tambo, Mandela's best friend and former law partner, went into exile as the ANC's leader.

While in prison on Robben Island, Mandela became the symbol of antiapartheid. He smuggled *The Struggle Is My Life* out of the prison and, along with other leaders of the liberation movement, he developed a plan to seduce the Afrikaners, the other whites, as well as the blacks, to come together peacefully to create a new, nonracial South Africa. When he emerged in 1990, after 27 years in prison, he was a legend and a symbol much larger than any man.

Mandela's mission, from the moment he was released, was reconciliation and peaceful transition. Today, everywhere you look in South Africa, you see what he has done. Everyone you talk to was touched by him. Conversations about the "New South Africa" with black people, white people, Indians, and Americans include the phrase, "Well, if not for Mandela...[who knows what might have happened]." The publication of a controversial, pessimistic book, *After Mandela,* showed that even conservatives had to give Mandela his due. Most people called him by his clan name, Madiba—a sign of both intimacy and extreme respect, as one would call a father or grandfather.

My Peace Corps group went on a tour of Soweto run by a group called Jimmy's Face to Face Tours. On the way back to Pretoria, a few of us sat in the back with Jimmy, who talked about the new South Africa. He kept saying, "since independence." I asked him what "independence" was. He said, "Mandela was released in 1990, and he was elected in 1994." I asked if anything had changed. "Oh yes, " he said. "I used to live in

Soweto. Now I live in the suburbs with the Joneses and drink orange juice and eat lettuce." Jimmy was typical in his views about Mandela: The man embodied the transformation.

Of course, the complete abolition of apartheid was and is a more complicated process. During the transition period between his release and his election, Mandela had walked a tightrope. He could not afford to alienate either the black majority, restless after years of oppression and burgeoning with the enormous expectation of imminent liberation, or the white minority, who still controlled the government, economy, and formidable military of South Africa. Factions split off on both sides of the ensuing negotiations. Violence erupted on several occasions and many people were killed. Civil war, it seemed, simmered just below the surface throughout the four years of negotiations that led to the elections of 1994. But Mandela, having displaced President F. W. de Klerk as the true leader of South Africa, was able to keep the tension and hostility from bubbling over. He steered the ANC and the country through a maze of obstacles and came out with a fair election and a smooth transition to power.

I had seen firsthand much of what Mandela had done, the many manifestations of his leadership, but there was one thing I could not get out of my head. Mandela was so persuasive with the public that his vision of a unified, multiracial South Africa permeated all aspects of South African society. I had seen proof on a napkin in Nando's Spicy Chicken, a South African chain restaurant in Tzaneen: "One Nation. One Chicken. Nando's." I smiled to myself. Mandela had truly changed the world.

WE PASSED THROUGH A TEN-FOOT GATE TOPPED WITH RAZOR WIRE AND stepped out of the car into Mandela's huge front yard. The house was beautiful and secure, but it did not appear to be any different from the other houses on the block, in the rich Johannesburg suburb of Houghton. Wealthy white South Africans were so security conscious that not even their president could outdo them.

We were escorted into a room with two couches and two chairs. My grandfather sat in one chair, and the rest of his entourage—my grandmother and I, my aunt and uncle, the associate executive director of the Carter Center, and the United States ambassador to South Africa—sat down on the couches. The protocol officer who greeted us said that President Mandela would be a few moments late.

Mandela quickly arrived, limping slightly down the stairs. He apologized "with all humility" for being late, but his physical therapist had detained him. Mandela's knee had been permanently damaged by prison guards in an incident on Robben Island. He told us that he had been in Mozambique the night before and was late getting in. At the time he was very publicly courting Graça Machel, the widow of the former president of Mozambique, Samora Machel. They were married the next year in a celebration that coincided with Mandela's 80th birthday.

He shook hands with everyone, and we all sat back down. Mandela was wearing one of his signature Madiba shirts: silk, with an elaborate, intricate flowered print, buttoned to the top. He and my grandfather asked each other about their businesses and their families. "What brings you to Africa?" My grandfather told him about some of the Carter Center's work in the 35 African nations where it has programs. "How are things here?" Mandela said they were good, but that he was still confronted with a lot of the old ways. That day he was going to a press conference to announce the retirement of a key general in the army.

"My grandson is here in the United States Peace Corps."

"Oh, that's wonderful. What exactly are you working on?"

"We are working with groups of teachers in rural schools to help them cope with the new curriculum," I said. "As you know, Curriculum 2005 is really complex and difficult for some of them."

"Oh," he said. "Have you met Thabo Mbeki?"

"No," I smiled. Thabo Mbeki was the deputy president. Mandela had made no secret of the fact that Mbeki, who had been Oliver Tambo's top lieutenant in the exiled ANC, was running the show while Mandela was announcing decisions and acting as a symbolic figurehead. Mandela was old and did not need to deal with the day-to-day operations of the government.

"He speaks fluent Zulu," my grandfather said, pointing to me.

"Oh, *uyasithetha siZulu?*"

"Uh, um, *yebo,* um, *ngiyasikuluma kancane,*" I said, haltingly.

"*Oh, uyasikuluma! Uzosebenza kuphi?*"

"Uh, *eMpumalanga.*"

We continued for about 30 more seconds in my extremely broken, stumbling Zulu. If he had said, hello how are you, I would have been fine. If he had wanted to talk about shooting pool, I would have been in great shape. But I was ill equipped for talking to the president, and I guess I was a little nervous. He asked me if I knew the premier of Mpumalanga, Mathews Phosa. I said no, and smiled again at his desire to bring his friends into the conversation.

Then, just like every other person I had met in Kromdraai, he showed his low expectations for the language skills of white people. "Wow, he speaks better than me. How did you master the language so quickly?"

I loved him. He and my grandfather talked for a few more minutes about traveling in Africa and chuckled about how difficult it is to get Castro on the phone. Mandela talked about his grandkids and his children. I could not help smiling. Here were two men who had reached the pinnacle of political life without compromising their morals or their beliefs. These two men proved it is possible to be a good person and a successful politician.

Mandela had to go to work. He and my grandfather exchanged gifts, and I asked the president to sign my copy of his autobiography. We then went outside and took a few pictures. Mandela reminded everyone that we couldn't use a flash camera—his eyes are permanently damaged because of the glare from the white stone in the quarry where he had worked every day on Robben Island. His physical scars from his time in prison still affected him, but emotionally and spiritually he seemed untouched. In his public life he even seemed inspired by his experience.

My grandfather insisted that we get a photo of just Mandela and me. He had only his Polaroid camera, and he couldn't figure out how to turn off the flash, so he put his hand over the bulb and snapped the picture.

We all said good-bye. Mandela went to his press conference, and my grandparents went on to another event. I told Mandela that I was going to be the first person to leave his house and go straight to the taxi rank. He thought I was joking. Luckily, the embassy staff knew that I wasn't, and they gave me a ride back to Pretoria, dropping me off at the Peace Corps office.

As I rode on the highway from Johannesburg to Pretoria, I chuckled to myself. I had just seen one of the greatest living human beings, one of the pillars of our age, and he was a tall, 80-year-old man with a slight limp who was late because he had been out too long the night before at his girlfriend's house in Mozambique. He had talked about his family and his friends, had shared some jokes, and I had stood with him while the former President of the United States took our picture with a cheap Polaroid camera. "Look! Here it comes. It's developing!"

I had been prepared to meet a legend, a man much larger than life. But this experience drove home the point that all people, regardless of what they have accomplished, are still people. I have seen others approach my grandfather that way. In a McDonald's in Cordele, Georgia, a woman once ran up to him and screamed, "Oh, my God! Do you know who you are?"

"Yes," he said, calmly.

I began my official Peace Corps service days later with this image of these two men. Just two plain old men concerned about their retirement and their grandchildren, their lives the same size as everyone else's. I was inspired by the impact that one person can have. That thought would sustain me for the next two years.

THE NDZUKULUS

CHAPTER FIVE

THE TOWN OF LOCHIEL IS SITUATED ON A RIDGE OF MOUNTAINS
along one of the main highways to Swaziland about 15 miles from the
border. From the top of that ridge to the north, the land drops off steeply
into a valley, and the view goes on for miles to the next ridge of green
mountains that is now part of the Songimvelo Nature Reserve. In the
summer the mountains and valleys are a bright blue-green, with large
pools of blond and brown rocks that seem to have bubbled up out of the
grass and make sometimes towering domes and spires.

During the mfecane, and other battles for power, many of the look-
out points along this ridge were used by soldiers, and the hills served as
camps for regiments on their way to battle or for people defending the
passes that crisscrossed the area. Before and after those wars, though, the
families on the small homesteads dotting these mountains on the western side of the Swazi empire were, like every small collection of families
in history, less concerned with politics than with raising their crops and
their cattle and their children. These families identified with their small,

local ancestral clan and listened to their local leaders. After the mfecane and Shaka's single-minded reconstruction of his conquered peoples' lives, they came to respect their kings, Sobhuza and Mswati, and appreciated the stability afforded them. Even today, the older, more traditional people living in the communities around Lochiel still listen intently to the discussions of the local traditional leaders and speak with pride and reverence for the more distant Swazi king.

When the white settlers came, they surveyed the vast green valleys and the waterfalls gushing off the mountains in the distance and believed that God had sent them to this enchanting place for a reason. Some of the small communities in the valley and up on the mountaintops still retain the names given to them by Afrikaner or English settlers. Yet today no white people live here, and the valley is overpopulated and poverty-stricken. Where a scattering of families once lived off the land, the valley north of Lochiel contains more than 150,000 people, and the valley to the south has almost as many. In an urban area with a viable economy these numbers do not seem so large. But there is very little economic activity here. When I arrived, none of the communities had a grocery store or a bank. The high rates of unemployment, alcoholism, and poverty make the region seem all the more crowded.

The large settlements in the valleys, with their streets set on a grid, have a township-like feel. But the communities along the ridge where I worked, while still densely populated, make up a small percentage of the local population and are true rural African villages where people carry their water from the river and build their houses out of sticks and mud.

The Zulu words for town or city or township do not apply to Lochiel and its surroundings. The word they use to say "out in the country" is *emakhaya*—literally translated, it means just "homes."

"Where do you stay? In town?"

"No, not in town. I stay out there, where there are homes."

In Lochiel, these homes are homemade, made from wood and mud, with metal roofs held down by heavy rocks or logs placed around the edge. These homes dot the mountainside not according to any planning, but from a simple natural progression and an individual preference for being closer or farther from one's neighbors. The mud crumbles, and houses get rebuilt every few years. They build the new houses right next to the old ones. Everyone needs enough land to have two houses, so they can live in the old one while the other is being built. The floor plans grow or shrink as children come and go.

The 200 families of Lochiel live on two lightly inclined hills shaped like an amphitheater. The two sides slope down to a small stream, which runs between them, and opens out to the road—Highway 17, the main connector between Johannesburg and Mbabane, the capital of Swaziland. From that road you can see every house in Lochiel except those on the far ridge.

As you walk through the town, it is impossible to keep a straight path. Instead you crisscross from house to house on paths that exist only for that purpose—passing from house to house. It is not an efficient means of getting to a destination, and for the five or six people who have cars, the going is slow. But it is also nice to pass by the neighbors every time you go for a walk.

Women are out hanging the laundry, carrying water, chopping wood, or sweeping their dirt yards so that the yards look nice and the snakes will stay away. The men sit outside the little stores drinking beer from quart bottles. There is always a teenage boy trying to look cool, standing and talking to one or another teenage girl in her school uniform who bobs back and forth nervously on her bare feet. The kids play in the paths and yards with toy cars they made from old wire and aluminum cans, or with soccer balls made from plastic bags tied together real tight. When I walked up to the ridge, they would always stop what they were doing and say, "Hey, Musa! Where are you going?"

"I'm just walking around, going to see the view at the top of the ridge."

"Hah! He's going to watch the mountains again!" They would laugh and run away.

Some families in Lochiel had livestock: cows, goats, chickens, maybe a sheep or two; one family had a few ducks and another had some geese. No one had all of those animals, and only the richest had more than just a scrawny dog and a few chickens. Cows are the symbol of wealth. Everyone who has them is proud of their cattle, even though each is usually just skin and bones. The livestock wander around town grazing in whoever's yard has grass. Everyone just knows which cows belong to which family. My family, I think, had more cows than anyone. They were rich. And they lived at the hotel.

The hotel was built in the 1940s as a combination rest stop, resort, and gathering place for the white farmers in the region. A Scottish family built the structure after they settled there and gave Lochiel its name. In its heyday, the hotel must have been splendid. Its brick and plaster main building originally housed the reception area, the dining hall, and the bar/lounge. In front is a courtyard, and a garden with several types of acacias, green bushes with red berries that someone informed me were nana berry trees, a beautiful wild pear tree that explodes in white and yellow blossoms in the spring, several ferns, thorny bushes around the edges, and, as a centerpiece, a seven-foot succulent that in the spring sprouts huge yellow flowers. A long arbor-covered walkway extends into the garden surrounded by various trees and flowers. The guests used to stay in the individual cottages that surround the garden. There is one private cottage, with its own bathroom, and two two-room suites that each share a bathroom.

At some point the Scottish family sold the hotel to a man from the Netherlands. According to the current owner, that man was a relative of the king, and when the king came to visit, he stayed at this quaint hotel in the mountains near the Swazi border. There is a swimming pool in the garden, tennis courts out back, and a 20-foot-round brick rondavel that was built for the king of Holland.

A few times I met white people who talked about the good old days in Lochiel. While hitchhiking, I met a man who had lived nearby. He said he'd lived on his father's farm in a mud house "just like that one" (he pointed) until he made enough money to buy a new farm closer to town.

On Christmas Day I met a man in the township outside Carolina, a small all-white town west of Lochiel. He pulled up to a house to drop off some gifts for one of his workers, and he recognized Ned, a Peace Corps friend of mine whom I was visiting. The man asked where I lived, and when I told him, he became nostalgic. He had grown up out there on his father's farm near Mooiplaas. The hills are the most beautiful in the country, he said, and he wished he still lived in the valley. The government bought the land from his family and told them to move to town, but he still remembered the old hotel out there, and good times at the bar. "Is it still a hotel?"

"No. Not really anymore."

"Well, it figures," he said. "That's too bad."

An Afrikaner woman who works at the Oshock border post just east of Lochiel grew up in a farmhouse that she can almost see out her office window. She talked about the magnificent mountains and about all of the stories that she heard and the fun she had at the hotel bar in Lochiel.

"It really is a shame that we can't even go there anymore. It looks so dangerous, I wouldn't even stop there now. It's too bad what they have done to it. It used to be a beautiful little place where you could go and spend the night and have a nice meal. And lots of really nice people passed through. *Ag, shame,*" she said, shaking her head.

When I arrived in 1998, the hotel and its surrounding buildings were run-down but bustling. The tennis courts had grown over beyond recognition, the swimming pool was full of rotting green slime and had to be fenced because of the health hazard, and the rooms were shells of their former selves. But the complex had grown to include a large general store, spaces for smaller stores, a gas station serving the highway, a mechanic's garage, and a few unused stables. Since 1975 Elias Langa Ndzukulu has owned it all.

Mr. Ndzukulu is a short man with a big stomach that is almost always covered with a cardigan or a vest from a three-piece suit. He speaks with his hands like a preacher, swinging them out and in, alternately welcoming you and everyone else in the world, and then singling you out with both index fingers as the person who most needs to hear what he is saying. When the Peace Corps arrived in Lochiel to determine if it was a suitable place for a volunteer to live, he gave them a three-hour lecture on the Bible, his belief in our Lord Jesus Christ, and the extent to which all he owned was given by the grace of God. Would he allow a volunteer to stay on his property? Yes, but would the volunteer be respectful? And would he or she pay rent?

He is a high official of the regional Methodist Church and never loses an opportunity to give all the credit to God. He is also a shrewd and successful businessman, and has been for his entire life.

Mr. Ndzukulu hails originally from the township outside Carolina, just west of Lochiel. He considers himself a Swazi, although he has members of his family who consider themselves Zulu, and Zulu is his first language. Before taking over the land in Lochiel, Mr. Ndzukulu was a shoe salesman based in Soshanguve, a township near Pretoria. He traveled all over the former Transvaal, the northern part of South Africa between Swaziland and Botswana. In that single region he learned to speak Sotho, Tswana, and Pedi, as well as Tsonga and the rare Venda.

At that time, Afrikaners controlled most of the smaller segments of the economy, such as retail and wholesale shoes. Mr. Ndzukulu claims that his Afrikaans is better than his English, which is flawless if somewhat formal.

While Mr. Ndzukulu was selling shoes in the sixties and early seventies, the National Party's apartheid government began to consolidate its political power. Hendrik Verwoerd came to power in 1958, when Prime Minister Strijdom died in office. Verwoerd's previous position had been minister of Native Affairs. This meant not only that Verwoerd's area of expertise was in government policy toward black Africans, but that this issue was important enough in the eyes of the National Party to elevate him to the head of the government. Verwoerd is known as the "Architect of Apartheid," and under his leadership South Africa's commitment to separate development grew according to a plan he called "Grand Apartheid."

The plan was to allow all of the cultures in South Africa to develop separately, without interference from others. The country would be divided using the same theory that the great powers of the Western world used after World War II: Each ethnic group would have a separate nation—*bantustans* or homelands. Each nation would then be able to raise its children in accordance with its particular customs, which would be preserved rather than swallowed up by the amalgamation taking place in South Africa. The plan was designed to prevent the "dominant" European cultures from overtaking the "primitive" black South African cultures. But more important to the government, the plan would preserve Afrikaner culture and entrench their power and legitimacy in South Africa.

During the political process that led to the creation of the homelands, the apartheid government approached Mr. Ndzukulu and asked him to participate on the Swazi National Council, the organization that oversaw the creation of the Kangwane homeland for Swazi people. Members were to work with the National Party government to create a constitution and a government for the new homeland.

The government had decided that there would be nine homelands, and they recruited some traditional leaders as well as people such as Mr. Ndzukulu to participate. The political process was complicated, requiring the government to make many arbitrary decisions. All of these were made with no legitimate representation of the black population. Still, some people had high hopes that the policy would be beneficial.

Once the government released maps showing how land had been allocated, however, any thinking person would have realized that the idea of homelands was a cruel joke with no hope of success. They were not at all geographically coherent. Instead, each was a noncontiguous smattering of worthless land. In all, 13 percent of the land was allocated for 70 percent of the people, and much of it was the driest, least productive land in all of South Africa. In Kromdraai, for example, the border of the homeland was drawn so that the lucrative mine remained in South Africa while the laborers lived in the homeland with no claim to the wealth.

In addition to creating the absurd borders, which provided for countless little islands of homeland spread around in the sea of South Africa, the government had to assign people their ethnicity and relocate them to their appropriate homeland. In urban South Africa different ethnic groups had been mixing for years. The apartheid government had to therefore decide arbitrarily who was a Swazi and who was a Xhosa.

The government forcibly removed people from their homes and sent them to places they had never seen. All of the current inhabitants of the area around Lochiel were moved there during this process. As they arrived, the people were given a choice. They could settle on one side of the valley or the other. A small number established an informal settlement at the crossroads, across from the hotel.

Mr. Ndzukulu's position on the Swazi National Council allowed him to land one of the best pieces of real estate in the region: the gas station and hotel complex at Lochiel. He got a jump on building contracts in the major resettlement camps in the valleys and became for a time the sole distributor of soft drinks for the entire southern part of the Kangwane homeland.

As he tells it, he had no other option. You either lost the opportunity or you helped people out. Thousands were being forced to live in the area whether he liked it or not, and these new arrivals had nothing: no homes, no building materials, no water, no toilets, not even holes for pit latrines or trees to cut down for wood poles, and many of them had no idea what to do. "We had to provide concrete blocks, tin for roofs, cement—everything. We had to get these people homes in almost no time at all. We had teams of people digging pit latrines and helping with construction. If we were not there, some of these people would have had no place to live for months at a time." If there was to be any hope for them, he contended, they needed people like him to provide services and jobs in their economy.

Mr. Ndzukulu did what the apartheid government wanted him to do and benefited greatly from it. As it turns out, he was on the wrong side of history. Steve Biko, a liberation hero and one of the great minds in the history of South Africa, said this at the time about black people participating in the system:

> We have some men in these bantustans who would make extremely fine leaders if they had not decided to throw in their lot with the oppressors. A few of them argue that they are not selling out but are carrying on the fight from within. . . . {But} no matter how one views it, the ultimate truth is that participation in the bantustan set-up is dangerously misleading to the black population. . . .
>
> The argument runs that all other forms of protest, disagreement and opposition are closed to black people and that we can call the bluff of the government by accepting what they give and using it to get what we want. What most people miss is the fact that what we want is well known to the enemy and that the bantustan theory was designed precisely to prevent us from getting what we want. . . . When they created these dummy platforms, these phoney telephones, they knew that some opportunists might want to use them to advance the black cause and hence they made all the arrangements to be able to control such "ambitious natives."

Mantanzima and Buthelezi {the leaders of the Transkei and KwaZulu homelands} can shout their lungs out trying to speak to Pretoria through the phoney telephone. No one is listening in Pretoria because the telephone is a toy.

Nelson Mandela never supported the homeland policy. He remained in jail rather than go free and be forced to live in his "homeland" of the Transkei. But I suppose it is possible to understand why Mr. Ndzukulu acted as he did.

Powerful leaders participated in the new regime. Chief Mangosuthu Buthelezi represented the internal wing of the banned ANC, the chief opposition to the apartheid government, but he was also the leader of the KwaZulu homeland. Much to the chagrin of the apartheid government, Buthelezi flew the ANC flag above the KwaZulu statehouse (until eventually, personal issues between Buthelezi and the ANC leadership in exile caused a split). Both the United States government and the British government supported the homeland policy to some extent, and they recognized leaders such as Buthelezi. Enos Mabuza, the chief executive of the Kangwane homeland, was widely considered a great leader and was one of the first homeland leaders to meet with the ANC in exile.

Moreover, the people deported to the homelands were in dire need of certain services. As Mr. Ndzukulu says, the trucks dropped people off in the middle of nowhere, and the government was not going to provide much assistance. There are famous pictures of the "houses" that the government provided in the "relocation camps." They look like rows and rows of outhouses, or cube-shaped pens, with five sides of corrugated iron and a dirt floor.

In any case, Mr. Ndzukulu was a busy man. He had other properties, including a store in a township outside Pretoria and another house in Mayflower, one of the major communities in the southern valley. In fact, he spent almost all of his time there and visited Lochiel rarely, leaving his local dealings to his wife, Selina Ndzukulu.

Mrs. Ndzukulu would play a larger role in my life over the next two years than anyone else. She is a short, wide, somewhat light-skinned woman whose dresses hang straight down from her chest to the ground. In the two years I lived in her house, I never saw her without a hat or a headcloth covering her head. Inside the family we all called her "Gogo," the word for old woman or grandmother. Outside, she was known only as Ma'am Ndzukulu, for she was one of the most influential members of the community. She was involved in everything that went on in Lochiel.

Before completing the final two weeks of our training, we visited our final placement site for a week to ensure that the living arrangements were satisfactory. Peace Corps regulations stated that we must have a door that locks and a concrete floor, and Gogo's hotel was the only option in Lochiel. Another of our tasks was to meet with several of the people who held key community positions.

After I moved into Gogo's house, the list of people I needed to meet shrank considerably. She was the chairman of the School Governing Body, the postmaster, the head of the Lochiel branch of the Methodist Church, the landlord for the entire commercial complex, the leader of the women's gardening group, the principal of the Ilanga Preschool, and the manager of the Lochiel depot for the Carolina Dry Cleaners. She also cooked and cleaned, along with her 25-year-old daughter, for a family of eight and sometimes nine or ten.

When I arrived to stay for good, Mrs. Ndzukulu greeted me with her 15-year-old grandson, Sandile. They came outside when I arrived in Lochiel on the evening of April 8, 1998. My supervisor, Mrs. Busi Ndlovu, had picked me up at the Peace Corps oath of service ceremony in Middelburg, a two-and-a-half-hour drive from Lochiel. She was the principal of the Lochiel Primary School and would be my "boss" for the next two years. She wasted no time in letting me know her style was personal and friendly, if somewhat less focused than I had expected. I was about to burst with anticipation. I had been in the country for three months and I was ready to start. I had even visited my community to whet my appetite, and I couldn't wait to get there, put my things away, and get settled. This was the first day of my Peace Corps experience. Yet we drove all over the province in her maroon BMW doing errands, picking up school supplies, getting a dress from the dry cleaners, forgetting the uniforms for the drum majorettes and going back to get them. I was jittery. She finally decided that she did not want to drive anymore because it was dark. We went to her son's house in Nhlazatje, in the north valley, and he agreed reluctantly to drive me 30 minutes up into the mountains to Lochiel.

The road was covered in fog, and it was hard to see more than 20 feet in the dark. After nearly hitting them, we picked up a hitchhiker and her infant daughter. She said she was going to TV, a place neither of us had ever heard of. After a while she asked to be dropped off in the woods and said she was going to her mother's place for the night and would go on to TV in the morning. She left and walked into the woods with her baby.

I told Mrs. Ndlovu's son that I had never picked up a hitchhiker before. He said he didn't normally pick them up either, but she was with a baby....

"No, it's fine. I mean, it doesn't make me uncomfortable at all."

"But you are right," he said. "I know they can be really dangerous."

I wasn't saying that they were dangerous.

In fact, I thought what we did was pretty cool. But my white skin made him defensive about this apparently normal practice, no matter how nice I was. It was difficult to explain without feeling condescending: "No, really, I think it's nice that you people help each other out."

Because we were strangers in South Africa, the situation demanded that our roles be defined by race. "Whites" did not pick up hitchhikers, and I was white, so I must automatically disapprove. I made him uneasy just by my presence, and there was nothing I could do.

We drove through the fog in uncomfortable silence until we reached Lochiel. I thought it was a little strange to step out of a BMW when I was serving in the Peace Corps, but as far as I could tell, no one else thought it strange at all.

Gogo and Sandile greeted me, and we immediately walked inside to eat dinner in the big house that was formerly the lobby and dining hall for the hotel. We walked under the "Reception" sign that still hangs outside the door. We went into the once grand entry hall that now was lit by a single dim bulb and an eerie green light that streamed through the plastic roofing covering a skylight. Vinyl sheets with pictures of tiles covered the floor and met irregularly, curling up slightly at the edges. The walls were a sort of beige, darker at the bottom and lighter at the top after years with the same paint job. A wood-burning stove with a pipe chimney occupied one corner, and a large table the other end. Other than that, the room was empty. The Methodist Church holds services there, and it serves as the preschool dining hall.

We walked through swinging double doors to the left and into a small room with a glittery pink vinyl floor. The kitchen was huge and bright white compared with the dimly lit entry hall. It had white tile floors, and wainscoting topped by yellow walls. It contained two enormous, commercial-size coal burning stoves that went unused because anthracite was so expensive, two steel double-well sinks with large steel food-preparation areas on either side, two tables where people could eat or cook or do homework, and seven chairs. There was also an electric stove and oven that the family used for cooking, and a fancy wood-burning stove with a chimney and a temperature gauge that they used for warmth when the weather was cold. They kept most of their food in the refrigerator, but there was also a pantry, and several large tin boxes where they kept their maize meal—the staple food of southern Africa—safe from rats and mice and insects.

In an extravagant dining room, set in the lobby of the hotel, we sat down to eat. The family knew me a little by now because of the week I spent with them during the last stages of my training.

At that time, during my very first meal, I had been surprised to see such a nice table, a tablecloth, place mats, all kinds of silverware, and plates of food for everyone with chicken, rice, and mashed pumpkin. I was used to eating off a plate on my lap in the Khozas' crowded living room. Back behind the table were six orange-velvet, overstuffed chairs with dark wood frames and arms. Connected to resemble three love seats, they surrounded a small coffee table. At the open end of the U-shaped arrangement was the television.

That first week in Lochiel, I chuckled to myself about the Peace Corps and Africa Lite. But at the same time I was somewhat relieved. I had sat in other houses in South Africa—in Nkowakowa, in Kromdraai, in Nhlazatje—watching the *Super Dave Osborne* show and fretting about going to live up at Lochiel. I was nervous that there was no electricity and that people carried their water from the river. How was I going to handle it? In most Peace Corps countries, some 300 miles separate volunteers from the comforts of home, and those volunteers never have the chance to think about them. Here in South Africa the distance was all of nine miles. We sat down to eat at the beautiful table with Gogo, Sandile, Boni, the 25-year-old daughter, and Boni's oldest daughter, Twana, who was nine.

Eager to put everyone at ease, I began talking. The others, I noticed, were fumbling with their spoons and forks. I picked up the meat with my hands, as they did at the Khozas' house, and they all stopped and stared at me. Then they burst into laughter. I thought, of course, that they were laughing at me. It turns out that they were laughing at the instructions Gogo had given them, to eat like white people so that I would feel at home.

Two weeks later, the truck that the Peace Corps had rented to bring luggage to the ten or so volunteers in our region arrived about 9:30 p.m. Sandile came to help me unpack. We brought my belongings to the little house at the back of the garden. I was staying in one of the two-room suites with a bathroom. A small sink stood in a corner of each room, with a small mirror and a tiny pressboard shelf. The bathroom had a toilet and a bathtub. The water came from a deep well, and I found that I could drink it right out of the tap. But it was very cold. I would heat it in a kettle to shave and bathe.

Each room boasted an electrical outlet, and in the front room was a light, so I would be able to read at night without a candle. Each room also contained a built-in bed made from concrete blocks, wood slats, and a foam mattress. Although I had a fireplace, I still unpacked my space heater, and I would use both extensively. It was April, and winter was just beginning to settle in at Lochiel.

Even with Sandile helping, we needed two trips to carry all my bags. He sat with me as I unpacked my things. I had a portable CD player that fascinated Sandile. We plugged it into the wall and plugged the mini-speakers into the side of the player. He couldn't stop listening to the Allman Brothers. "No," he would say, "I think this one is OK. Let us stay with this CD."

I unpacked all kinds of new things that he had never seen before, and more books than he had ever seen in one place. I was putting some of my clothes on the shelf (which was an old desk from the school) when I heard Sandile scream, "*Hawu!*" I turned and saw him holding a piece of white-and-pink plastic with short blue, white, and green bristles poking out at alternating angles. He was feeling the handle—it was rubberized—and turning it around and around to examine the complex piece of technology. "*Litufbrush lengaga!*" he said. "That's some toothbrush!"

I finished unpacking, and Sandile reluctantly tore himself from the treasure trove of my simple possessions and went back to the big house. Alone in my room, I realized that I would live in that space for two years. With no idea if I would be able to survive in a wholly new culture or what I might accomplish or what the schools would be like or even if I would truly help a single person, I lay down in my sleeping bag, on a thin foam mattress barely covering the odd-size, irregular bed slats that stuck up at different heights and angles, and spent a long, restless night.

SHADOW AND SETTLING IN

CHAPTER SIX

EARLY EVERY MORNING IN LOCHIEL, SOMETIMES IN THE DARK,
a huge white flatbed truck begins picking people up at the border post,
12 miles to the east, and works its way back toward the Lochiel garage.
Another, smaller truck picks up a group of people from the large courtyard just behind the garage. The people are bundled in blankets and
scarves, and hats are pulled down tight over their ears. Most of the men
have complete coverall work suits. Some are one-piece jumpers that zip
all the way up the front, and others are jackets with matching pants.
The suits come in royal blue or yellow or bright orange so the people
can be seen by managers and motorists and identified as workers. Some
of the women wear coverall-style jackets, but dresses of various colors,
and then blankets and hats and scarves. The people are packed so tightly
that the trucks look like giant laundry baskets with sleeves poking out
and socks about to fall through the cracks. Thick wood poles stick up
on the sides of the truck's flat bed and give the people something to hold
on to while they are rolling down the highway. The people are also

carrying scythes and chain saws and knives and axes, but they somehow find a way to hold on.

Mr. Magagula, who drives one of the trucks, lives behind Gogo's big house, just below the lip of the hill on the way to the stream. He is a good friend of Gogo's and visits us often. Babe (pronounced bah-bay, and meaning "father" or "Mr.") Magagula has a belly that is famous. When people in Lochiel describe potbellies in general, or fat men, they compare them to Babe Magagula. When they tell me not to eat too much, they say, "Musa, you will look like Babe Magagula," and they make a motion to indicate a pregnant woman. His stomach pokes his navy blue T-shirt out through the sides of his orange coverall jacket. The zippers on his jacket are two feet apart, testing the one-size-fits-all theory.

Babe Ncongwane drives the other truck. I would eventually learn that he is an excellent chess player. No one else in Lochiel had ever seen the game. I got a board and a book, wanting to teach people how to play. Babe Ncongwane had learned years ago when he worked in the mines in Johannesburg. We played about even, sometimes in front of large crowds who thought it was wonderful that Babe Ncongwane was so good at the white man's *marabaraba*—a game that everyone else plays with stones or bottle caps on a board drawn in the dirt.

Babe Magagula and Babe Ncongwane have to drive through a dense fog that arrives every morning and lingers until ten or eleven. It makes driving terribly dangerous, especially with the children walking to school and the cows wandering all over the place. Some people with business in Swaziland speed down the road in their BMWs and Mercedes, weaving around trucks carrying virtually all of Swaziland's trade. Ncongwane and Magagula drive slowly, but I could never tell if they were safety conscious, or if 30 miles an hour was all their trucks could muster.

Their passengers work in the forest for Mondi Paper. Every morning, just as they pass the last home in Lochiel, they drive by a sign that says "Ermelo Tak Paaie." Ermelo is a town of white people 60 miles down the road, and *tak paaie* is Afrikaans for "branch roads." The sign indicates that the trucks are entering a stretch of road administered by the Ermelo District. This is the old homeland border.

Mondi, one of the world's largest paper companies, bought thousands of acres of land in South Africa proper and planted them with pine and eucalyptus trees. They then built a sawmill in Warburton, near the homeland border. During apartheid, the government subsidized "border industries" to provide incentives for companies that constructed factories or other businesses near the homeland borders. As the theory went, the companies would use "migrant labor" from the homelands. These workers would work in South Africa's economy, but go home each night to the homeland. This partly solved economic problems that the homeland policy presented and the sawmill remains the only industry near Lochiel.

They were exploited, but at least those workers had something to do. I arrived during the fall break, so the schools were closed for several weeks. That left me as a stranger with time on my hands and no clue about how to spend it.

Being alone was a scary prospect. I had been living with the other volunteers, and I had no idea what life would be like by myself. In America, I had never sat in a restaurant and eaten a meal alone or seen a movie by myself. I had lived with roommates since the day I left home at 18. And here I was in a little room in Africa without knowing where the nearest phone was, what I would eat, what my schedule would be like, whether or not I should drink the water, or where I would go if I had a medical emergency or even a routine sickness.

I fumbled through those first days. I made calendars and schedules and programs. I wrote in my journal and read for hours every day. I tried to predict how many books I could read in two years, and the date when my journal's pages would be full. Anything to give the seemingly endless stretch of time some meaning. At night I made an audiotape for Kate, my girlfriend, who was still in college. I left dinner with the family every night, went back to my room, and talked to her through that tape recorder. I looked forward to that conversation every day.

Still, during the days I learned a little more about the place and the people who would become my friends. Lochiel, at first glance, is a pretty simple place to get to know.

In the morning, standing behind the bottom half of my Dutch door, I could look across the garden, past the fat and gnarly "nut tree," the towering cactus branches, the purple jacaranda, and several other shrubs to the arbor that covered the walkway leading from the entry hall. In those winter months, when the vines on the arbor were bare, I could see through to the courtyard between the gas station and the hotel. The barbed-wire and small stick fence around the garden provided one boundary, and the long building that housed the general store and other small shops provided the other.

The courtyard was the center of the community. It was paved with concrete and splotchy blacktop, and potholes dominated the surface. Cars could not cross the courtyard without scratching the running boards or the muffler. On foot, in the summer, I was constantly dodging puddles that might be a foot deep. In the middle of this concrete yard stood a tree and a fountain that hadn't pumped water in 20 years. Magagula and Ncongwane would park their Mondi trucks in the dirt lot behind the courtyard, opposite the back of the gas station, which faces the highway.

Across the courtyard was the general store. It provided necessities, but was so expensive that everyone I knew tried to avoid buying things there. Being 70 kilometers from the nearest town with a grocery store, the owners could charge a tremendous mark-up. They sold bread, spices, dried soup mix, flour, matches, cigarettes (by the pack or, more often, one at a time). They had a rack of clothes in the back, several different pots and pans, plastic plates and bowls, lots of soft drinks, and frozen meats. The hotel/gas station complex was the only area in the community with electricity, so the refrigerated and frozen meats were valuable commodities, especially when people started to run out of chickens.

Doris, the cashier, took most of the blame for the high prices. She, like most older women, wore simple dresses made from patterned blue cloth and a headwrap. There was nothing particularly African about Doris's clothes, except maybe for the shoes.

None of Lochiel's citizens really needed shoes, but everyone felt obliged to wear them. Doris's sandals were woven out of thick brown straps of leather and had rubber soles. They weren't homemade; they were just cheap. Because she stood with her heels on what should have been the backs of the shoes, the leather was flat against the bottoms and black. The sides were falling apart and her small toe stuck out of a hole in the weaving. The shoes were unable to hold her feet.

Doris opened every morning at 7:30, just as the forestry workers left for work. She began by cleaning the floors of the store, on her hands and knees, and would not let anyone in until she was finished and the floors had dried.

Her store occupied the rearmost section of the large building across from the hotel. When I arrived, the next section of the building sported a huge metal door that secured a garage Mr. Ndzukulu used on the rare days that he was in town. Next to that garage was the post office.

Gogo, as I said, was the postmaster. There were no post office boxes, but because Gogo knew everyone, it didn't matter.

"Do I have mail?" people would ask.

"No, sorry."

"I am expecting something from my son in Witbank."

"OK," Gogo would say. "When it comes, I'll send a child."

That was how it worked. My address for the first year of my Peace Corps service was "Jason Carter/ P.O. Lochiel" and then the zip code. We had reliable mail service every day because we were on the main route to Swaziland, and all of their international mail came through South Africa.

Next to the post office, on the end of the building facing the road, was a small door where the shoe repairman sat, surrounded by old leather shoes. Like a junkyard, his four-foot-square shop was completely full of wrecks that could be used for spare parts. When he was sitting on his stool, with his brown leather apron so old and used that it shone, he almost blended in with his enormous pile of old shoes. You could see only his face and his hands at work on a pair that might be 50 years old.

Above his tiny shop was a sign that read "Carolina Dry Cleaners." It advertised the dry-cleaning depot that Gogo ran from the post office. People dropped off their most important items, and once a week Gogo's cousin, who lived in the township outside Carolina, came to pick up and drop off the dry cleaning in his little white covered pickup truck.

Above the sign for the dry cleaners was a painted sign saying "Dressmaker." It pointed to a small blue door at the top of an outside staircase that ran up the narrow front side of the building. But there was no dressmaker.

The gas station was the busiest part of Lochiel, as could be expected. When I arrived, a Caltex sign with a big star stood near the road, and across the top of the white gas station building were big red letters saying "Lochiel Estate Motors." The owner lived elsewhere, but you could always go in and find Chris, the manager. He wore a balaclava with eye and mouth holes, but he rolled it up on his head instead of pulling it down. Because of his job, he was a rich man and had at least two sets of worker's coveralls, one gray and one blue. He spoke good English and every day he let me read his copy of the *Sowetan* newspaper or the *Sunday Times*. I sat on a bench out front, under the canopy that sheltered the four pumps, and read the paper.

Three women sold fruit and cheese curls to whomever passed through. The apples, oranges, and bananas cost 50 South African cents. Peanuts were 20 cents a scoop, and the "snacks" or cheese curls cost 50 cents a bag. The exchange rate was about six to one, so I found the prices ridiculously cheap. The women sat there all day nursing their babies and talking about the weather or about how expensive bananas were getting.

Their main customers were people traveling by koombi from Nhlazatje in the north valley to Dundonald in the south.

Lochiel is a stop along the highway and little else. The economy is based almost entirely on the gas station and the taxi drivers who live in Lochiel and travel from Swaziland to Ermelo or Carolina, or to and from Nhlazatje. Like most places in rural South Africa, many families have relatives in Johannesburg or Ermelo or Nelspruit who send money home. And people over the age of 60 receive government pensions. A few entrepreneurs have small shops or wheelbarrows and are able to provide services, and two truckloads of people work at the sawmill. Outside of that, there is no economy at all. The land is too overcrowded to farm, and the livestock, while widespread, are scrawny and sick and have no commercial value.

The only people who really made money were the owners of the bottle store, where alcohol was sold. When the trucks unloaded their laundry in the afternoon, Lochiel square would be hopping. Men and a few women crowded the bottle store and the porch outside, drinking until they were fall-down drunk. They would stumble around and yell and break bottles.

Others would simply sit in small groups and share a quart bottle of Castle or Black Label beer. I cannot estimate what percentage of Lochiel's gross income is spent on liquor, but I know it is significant.

The worst part was watching the children walk by. Many of the men who worked would get staggering drunk every day, out in the courtyard for all the world to see. Parents would often send their children to buy beer. In the mornings Gogo's preschoolers would walk around the garden and the hotel picking up bottles and cans.

The hotel was the center of this alcohol abuse, and even though Gogo hated it, there was nothing she could do. Her husband was first and foremost a landlord, and the owner of the bottle store paid too much rent to be thrown out.

In addition to me, Mr. Ndzukulu and Gogo had five other permanent tenants. One of them was Albierto Pihlapahla, a young Mozambican who worked in the Mondi forest and lived by himself hundreds of miles from home. His first language was Shangaan, the dominant language of southern Mozambique, but he also spoke fluent Portuguese. Albert was infatuated with America and with learning English. Clearly, he had a gift for languages, as he had been in Lochiel not much longer than I and, without the intensive training I had, he could speak comprehensible, if somewhat accented, Zulu.

Albert was so interested in English that he would harass me. "Musa, come here. Please teach me English. Give me some work to do in English. Do you have a book? When can I learn?"

"Albert, I'll come by soon," I would say. I was extremely busy setting up my activities. Still, I wanted to maximize my impact, and one day I told him I would organize a class to teach English to several people who wanted to learn.

The next day he said, "Musa, come here. When do we start? Look, I can read this payroll sheet from the forests. When do we start? Can you just teach me alone?" And the next day. And the next.

I started avoiding him. If I saw him across the courtyard, I would turn and go around the other way. He would come and knock on my door. Everyone else was afraid to even come near my room, with the strange, unfamiliar white man inside. But Albert would knock and beg: "Please teach me English, Musa."

"Not right now, Albert."

I did give him some books, and I made a worksheet for him, telling him to list all the English words he heard, but it was never enough. He always seemed to catch me when I was on my way somewhere, or busy with someone else. "Look, Albert, I'm sorry, but I have to do this now. I will come back later." I would say the first part in English out of frustration, and then the second part in Zulu because I felt bad. Albert's constant requests were frustrating, but Albert was one of the most pleasant harassers in the bunch.

Past Albert's one-room home by the kitchen, with its bed set on the floor under his soccer posters, up the ramp to the porch behind the kitchen door, other tenants were lurking.

Grandma Jo and her husband were alcoholics. They received a pension from the government every month and drank until it was gone. Grandma Jo was a Tswana from the other side of Jo-burg; at least, that's what she said. Her husband wore a hard hat and yellow knee-high rubber boots every day. The two of them had probably worked on farms, moving from one to the next, until they ended up in Lochiel. By the time I got there, all they did was drink and ask me for money.

"Musa, *asseblief....*" Jo would say to me in Afrikaans. For more than two years, she always addressed me in Afrikaans.

"Hey, Jo! *Angazi iAfrikaans, Angisikhulumi isibhuno. Ngibuya eMelika, siyakhuluma singisi*—I don't understand Afrikaans," I would say in Zulu. "I am American, and we speak English." Apparently she didn't believe me.

Other people would tell her, "Look, he doesn't understand what you are saying." Eventually she would speak in Zulu and ask me for a "shoom" (one rand) or "five bob" (50 cents). Sometimes she would just ask me to buy her a beer or a *sikhubu,* the container from which people drink the traditional sorghum beer sold at the bottle store.

I never once gave her any money or bought her a beer. But every time she saw me, she would speak in Afrikaans and ask me for money. Sometimes her husband would get up from his upturned milk pail stool, grab her by the arm, and say, "He doesn't speak Afrikaans. Speak Zulu."

One day I walked out the kitchen door and was caught off guard. Both Jo and Albert were standing there in my path—Jo yelling at me in Afrikaans and pointing at her swollen foot, and Albert, as smiley and excited as ever, ready to learn English. Another boy from the high school was standing there with Albert, and Jo started grabbing my arm. I decided the time had come for Albert's English lesson.

I grabbed Albert and the boy and told Jo that I had promised them that I would teach them English. I'll be back, I said. *"Ngiyabuya."*

"Well, Albert," I said, looking around his tiny room. A pot was set on a small gas burner on the floor where he cooked. The soccer posters and the four or five shirts hung on a window handle. Albert's only belongings. "What do you want to do in English?" I asked.

"I want to write a letter."

"To whom?"

"To a girl that I like," Albert said.

I chuckled and so did the other boy, who was apparently a close enough friend that Albert was unembarrassed. Albert told me what he wanted to say, with some input from his friend. Albert wrote down the words.

> *Dear Nombulelo,*
> *Hello. I hope this letter find you well. I think you are beautiful and I would love to see you sometime soon.*
> *Maybe you would like to come and visit me at my place on Saturday at 4:30. Or I, of course, could come visit you.*
> *Please tell me what you think.*
> *Yours truly,*
> *Albert*

We all decided it was a fine letter, and I left, feeling guilty that I hadn't done more with him before. Some days later Albert caught me in the courtyard and thanked me profusely because Nombulelo had indeed come to visit.

Gogo's fourth tenant was a mysterious man named Mthembu. He stayed in a tiny room, about three feet by seven, outside the back door. Maybe it once was a furnace room, or maybe a garden boy's quarters before the homelands. I would peer in and find nothing in there except for darkness, maybe a pile of rags, and sometimes Mthembu. He never spoke to me or to anyone else. If we forgot about him at dinner, sometimes he would emerge from the darkness of his tiny room and knock on the kitchen door. He was stooped over, maybe five and a half feet tall, and dressed only in a tattered, greasy, once blue coverall that hung on him like a loose sack with holes at his elbows and knees. He might actually be a hundred years old. He worked in the yard during the day, chopping wood, raking leaves, cutting the grass, and each night Gogo included him in the meal.

"What's his last name?" I asked Gogo.

"Mthembu."

"Well, then what's his first name?"

"Mthembu."

"Gogo, come on. How old is he? Where is he from? Boni told me that when she first came, he was already here and that he has looked exactly the same for 20 years. What do you know about him?"

"Nothing. He was here when we got here in 1975. He's Mthembu wakaMthembu. He just stays here."

"Well, where is he from? How old is he? Haven't you asked him?"

"He doesn't know. He's from somewhere else. He is more than a hundred years old. He came here when they built the road. When we moved in, he was staying here. We always try to help him. We tried to give him some clothes, Mkulu bought him a new coverall, but he only wears that old dirty one."

Mthembu was probably mentally ill. He had no family, and in other cultures he might have been forgotten. But every night we counted out an extra plate and passed his food into the darkness outside the kitchen door. I saw Mthembu during the day every once in a while, chopping wood with an impossibly heavy ax or cutting the grass with a long, bent machete.

The last of Gogo's tenants, who became one of my best friends, lived in the small house near mine. It was half the size of my place and had no bathroom, but it was connected to the big house on the garden side and had electricity—nowhere else in town did—so it was a choice piece of real estate. Mtunzi didn't have any more money than anyone else, really. He just lived there because he acted as though he deserved it. He held himself in a different way than almost everyone else in the town.

Tall and confident, Mtunzi had a tall, flattop haircut. He had a broad smile and spoke perfect English. Often he would introduce himself with the English translation of his name, "Hi, I'm Shadow. Like the superhero."

Mtunzi quickly became the person I asked for advice and, in many ways, my ambassador to the community. People who were afraid to come talk to me would talk to Mtunzi. They would inquire why I was there, or if I would help them with something. He would in turn come and ask me.

A year older than I was, he also worked in the forests. Mtunzi had graduated from high school in Lochiel, but he did not have the money to continue his education. He worked for a while in Ermelo loading trucks, but decided it would be better to live in Lochiel with his family. He desperately wanted to learn more and get a better job. The first thing he asked me to do was help him with his English. I told him the best way to improve was to read books, and I gave him *The Life and Times of Michael K* by J. M. Coetzee. I thought Mtunzi would like that Coetzee wrote about South Africa.

In two days he came back. "Musa, I really liked this book. Can I have another? I especially liked the part about him growing pumpkins. But this guy is a little crazy, Musa. Do you have another book? Maybe one that is a little longer?"

"Try this one," I said. "It is 500 pages long." And I gave him *Native Son* by Richard Wright.

Two days later I saw him again. He had huge bags under his eyes. "Mtunzi, man, you look terrible. Are you sick?"

"Musa, I am too tired. Yesterday, I slept one hour. I stayed up until 4 a.m., Musa, reading that book. And then I worked all day, Musa. It is too good, that book. And then this morning I woke up with my face on the pages. I was almost late for work. That guy, Musa, is so smart. He is writing about apartheid in America! But, Musa," he flashed a wide white smile, "I can't take another book for some time. I have to rest. Thembi is so angry with me, yesses!" Thembi was his girlfriend.

Mtunzi and I spoke every day. He would come home from the forests and I would return from wherever I had been, and we would talk. His younger brother, who was still in high school, would bring his friends over to Mtunzi's place and play music on the radio. We would make a fire in a metal barrel and stand around outside, listening to music and talking.

Other neighbors would come and go. Shongwe was the mechanic who fixed cars in the repair shop behind the post office. Like Madonna, Shongwe had only one name. He was a huge man, by far the tallest in town. Born in Swaziland, he had dreadlocks and always wore a full-length brown jacket that almost touched the ground.

Shongwe's hands were huge and so tremendously callused that his palms were gray. Both my grandfathers had farms, and if, as the songs say, you should judge a man by the palms of his hands, Shongwe was a hero. He was also one of the only skilled workers in town and played a crucial role in Lochiel's economy.

Another visitor, Piet, was Shongwe's right-hand man. He not only worked on cars, but also taught Afrikaans at the adult education center at the high school. He was trustworthy, and when the community needed something done, they often called on Piet.

Vusi wore a shirt from Fox Chapel High School. I recognized Fox Chapel, which is just outside Pittsburgh, because one of my best friends went there. Many American church groups and other organizations send clothes to Africa, and often they are prized possessions. I would always laugh when I saw little boys at school wearing Florida State sweat pants or ΣAE pledge shirts. Vusi was cool and good-looking, and all the ladies loved him. He was a "too cool for school" type, but he secretly pulled me aside and asked if I would help him with English.

Bongani was a mechanic who looked exactly like Jimi Hendrix. His Afro was 12 inches tall, and he wore a headband tied around it. He also had somehow acquired a brown sheepskin coat. He had never seen Hendrix before, and I eventually dug up a picture and showed it to everyone. We laughed and after we listened to some of Hendrix's music, Bongani put the picture on the wall of the repair shop.

The guys were great. They drank every day and bummed money, but they were young and energetic and worked hard, too. They taught me a number of Swazi and Zulu songs about being in jail and missing their girlfriends or about their cows running away. I got out my Johnny Cash CDs and taught them a few American songs that covered the same ground.

They were my friends, but Mtunzi was the only one who treated me like an equal. Others were intimidated by my skin and the fact that I was from America.

We would all be talking, and someone would touch the hair on my arm. "Why do white people have such hairy arms, Musa?"

"I don't know. But I think they are not so much hairier. The hair is just straighter, so it looks longer. On my head, my hair is straighter. If you take Bongani's hair and pull it straight, it is much, much longer than it looks. Even on my legs, the hair is straighter. That's why it looks so different."

Later I went to my room to sleep, and Mtunzi knocked on my door. They had one other question that no one was willing to ask, so they sent Mtunzi. "Musa."

"Yeah?"

"On white girls, you know, the hair down there? Does it just grow straight down their legs?"

And if I had ridiculous questions I could go to Mtunzi and ask. He would be my guide. Often, though, the most important advice he gave, he had to give without me asking.

"Musa, you know, everyone is suspicious of you. You never go to see the old people. Why don't you see them?"

"Who? I didn't even know it was important, Mtunzi. Are there some old people who do things with the schools?"

"Hawu, Musa! They do nothing. But you must go see them anyway." And he told me exactly whom I needed to see. I went to see them. They did indeed do nothing; even so, I was glad to introduce myself, and many people in town appreciated the visits.

Without someone like Mtunzi, unembarrassed to ask silly questions or tell me when I was wrong, I would have been miserable and ineffective. When I hung out with Mtunzi, I realized how much it meant that he wasn't afraid or intimidated. I had not anticipated how paralyzing the problem would be until South Africans began to treat me as a white man first and foremost. Mtunzi—Shadow—was my first real line of communication.

BY THE LAST DAYS OF FALL BREAK, MY HORIZONS HAD EXPANDED. I HAD spent my time exploring the area around Lochiel. I had walked down into the forest behind the soccer field, all the way to the swampy marsh in the little valley between Lochiel and Dundonald. The pine trees were the same kind that my family grows on our farm in Georgia. Eucalyptus trees, imported from Australia, also grew in rows, and some areas had a ground cover of ferns. I had climbed well past the houses on the ridge and found a large field on a point protruding from the mountains. The grass was beginning to turn brown, but the view was breathtaking. The mountains dropped off all around me and allowed me to see for miles in almost every direction.

On one end of the valley was Kromdraai, the mine dump shining white on the green mountains. At the other end was Nhlazatje. This homeland settlement, and the smaller community or neighborhood within it, eLukwatini, had electricity, nicer homes, and a township-like atmosphere. After the homeland was created, the homeland government invested money in a few communities to attract professional people to the far-flung, rural homelands. The government built a small shopping complex in eLukwatini and wired the neighborhood for electricity. They also built a magistrate's court and government office building, a police station, a hospital, and a very nice two-story high school. That school, Bantwabetfu, was the only two-story school I saw outside of white towns. The electricity and development brought to the community the region's elite, which included almost all of the people with professional jobs. Today, eLukwatini is a town of teachers, health care professionals who work at the hospital, and others with government jobs. A few people run small businesses and stores. eLukwatini is the closest thing to a commercial center in the area, but, as I mentioned, it has no bank, no proper grocery store, no clothing stores, and, perhaps most important, no culture of patronizing local business. Throughout apartheid, the government discouraged development in black parts of the country and gave incentives to white business owners. White towns were often the only places to get things that one might need. Today, everyone still travels 70 to 100 kilometers to shop in town.

In eLukwatini, at the "Complex," is the only real restaurant in town—called Southern Fried Chicken. People always eat at home, and they think that going out to eat is a bit ridiculous. There are, however, enough single teachers and professionals who work all day and grab lunch to keep the place in business. It also has a bakery and sells snack foods. The owner is one of the wealthiest men in town.

The local government administration is still in eLukwatini, and the official name of the entire area, including Nhlazatje, Tjakastad, and everything between Lochiel and the border post, is called Greater eLukwatini. Since the end of apartheid, several other ministries have opened offices in the area. The Department of Education opened a large teachers' center, and the Department of Natural Resources and Tourism opened an environmental education and training facility. The Department of

Education Circuit Office is also located in eLukwatini, and over the next two years I would spend many hours there working with the staff and the circuit manager.

The valley surrounding Nhlazatje and eLukwatini is spectacular. Lochiel's mountains make up one wall, and the mountains of the Songimvelo Nature Reserve and the escarpment between the Highveld Grasslands and the Lowveld region make up the other. Everywhere you look, the green rolling hills and the scattered acacia trees of the valley collide in the distance with the rich green mountains. Huge tan domes and other rock formations rise out of the grassy plain.

The region's tourism industry is thriving. Aventura Resorts, a very successful business created by the apartheid government, developed a spa and resort at Badplaas, just 20 miles from Nhlazatje. ("Badplaas" in Afrikaans translates as "bath farm," referring to the region's hot springs.) White people flock from the small towns in the region to visit its water slides, miniature golf course, and hot-spring-fed pools and saunas. But the striking natural beauty of the land is what makes the resort truly wonderful. The light green rolling hills in the valley and the steep, dark green mountain walls allow uninterrupted vistas of grassy plains dotted with trees and blond boulders.

A road runs from the spa at Badplaas up to the crossroads at Lochiel. From there, a family during the apartheid era could travel to Swaziland to continue a beautiful vacation in the more mountainous deep green of Swaziland's own spas and casinos, or they could cruise past several family farms in the high elevation of the Highveld Plateau, where the fields are flatter with fewer trees and the grass and wildflowers move in waves to the horizon. Eventually the family traveling past these farms would also pass through Ermelo and reach the industrial East Rand and Johannesburg.

And they could have made this trip without seeing a single black person. To be sure, they might have passed small huts on a farm, and they might have stopped for gas in Lochiel. The scattered mud-and-stick homes of Lochiel and Beeskop are visible from the road, but, then again, the family members would have known that they were visiting a foreign country anyway.

Down in the valley, only the most perceptive white tourist coming up to the mountain crossroads would have noticed a small dirt road extending off a turn near Badplaas, and then another dirt road just before ascending into the mountains. The two tiny dirt roads snaking over the rolling hills could easily be mistaken for farm roads.

But in reality, on these roads just past the crest of the first hill and the 200-foot towers of yellow-and-brown rock that shoot up out of the grass like skyscrapers, the entire sprawling community of Nhlazatje and eLukwatini opens up—a mass of tin roofs and dirt yards full of laundry and cows and barefoot children, grids of dirt streets, and small handpainted signs scribbled with the name of a store. About 150,000 people live their lives in a place that is totally invisible to the rest of the country.

The people who built the road made sure it avoided Nhlazatje, the largest community in the region. The two dirt roads were paved only in 1993, and the Aventura Spa at Badplaas allowed black people into their pools in 1994.

Four years later, I was excited to explore these roads where I lived, and where I would soon begin my work.

SCHOOL

ONCE SCHOOL STARTED, MY SCHEDULE FILLED UP. I HAD A JOB
that spanned three Third World schools. Lochiel Primary School
was located on one side of Lochiel's amphitheater hills. Masakhane
Combined School was eight kilometers down the road. Mlondozi
Primary, the oldest and biggest of the three, was five more kilometers past Masakhane. I rotated between the schools, spending a
few days at each one. I walked to the one in Lochiel, but the morning travel to the other schools was slightly more complicated. I was,
in a way, lucky.

Ninety percent of the teachers at these schools live not in the com
munities around the schools, but in the larger and more developed town
of eLukwatini. Because it was given electricity by the homeland government before the rest of the huge Nhlazatje area, it immediately
became the high-rent district. The houses are nice, almost like the upper-
class township houses, and the people are well educated and wealthier
than the inhabitants of Lochiel.

eLukwatini was a community of teachers. Those who worked up in the mountain schools commuted every day. Each paid a certain amount of money every month to hire a koombi that drove around eLukwatini and picked them up. The taxis drove past the garage at Lochiel every morning. If I got out there by 7:30 or so, I could catch a ride.

The schools themselves were riddled with problems. Most of the parents of the children couldn't read or write. Many children walked for miles to school. Riding in the teachers' koombi on the way to school, I saw children lining the road on both sides, sometimes walking in groups of 20 or 30, spilling on to the blacktop as trucks and cars sped by.

All of the schools were poor enough to qualify for government-subsidized lunches; every child received a peanut butter sandwich and a cup of powdered milk each day during break. The school hired three or four women to spread peanut butter, mix the milk, and dole it out to the kids. The students lined up, standing silently until they received their two pieces of bread and cup of milk. For some this meal was the most substantial of the day.

The area's schools were overcrowded. Sometimes 90 children sat in a single third-grade classroom. No child had his or her own desk, and many even shared chairs. As winter approached, I would often pause outside a classroom and be unable to hear the teacher because of all the students coughing. Eighty tired, underfed children can create quite a racket.

The instruction was given in English. The textbooks, each one shared by several children, were at least eight years old. The lessons, left over from the apartheid curriculum, often made no sense at all to the students. I observed one class in which the English teacher asked the children—as the textbook suggested—to write a short paragraph about their trip to the beach. I looked around the room and shook my head. The windows were missing panes, and the wind, whipping through the mountains, ruffled papers and battered already wind-burned faces. The children's school uniforms were threadbare around the collars and cuffs.

Apartheid's residue coated these schools from top to bottom, and yet the sight of these children in uniforms recalled a hopeful memory. Other children dressed in these same uniforms had marched through the streets of Soweto to resurrect the antiapartheid struggle. As I walked in the schoolyard, sometimes turning my back to the wind to keep the dust from stinging my eyes, I was excited to work here.

My initial excitement was not shared by the teachers. I had come to South Africa to battle hardships in schools. I regarded the challenge with a sense of optimism and relished the idea of making progress. For the teachers, however, these schools were not a once-in-a-lifetime opportunity to spend a couple of years righting the wrongs of apartheid. They worked in these schools to put food on the table, and doing their job was difficult because the schools and communities were poor. Almost every single teacher would rather have been working in a better school in a wealthier community. And how could I blame them?

The challenge of educating children in this environment was extraordinary. The teachers had been trained at teachers' colleges in Nelspruit or Johannesburg, and adapting those techniques to Lochiel's classrooms was difficult. The children received very little academic support outside of school. The teachers' English was often the only English that the children ever heard. Resources were extremely limited, because the schools collected school fees from the parents. Most of the schools set the fees at 20 or 30 rand (less than $5) per student per year, and they still had trouble collecting this amount from impoverished parents. Mr. Boschoff's school at the mine near Kromdraai charged 120 rand *per month,* and even he was strapped for cash. At Lochiel's schools, with one-fiftieth the budget per student, textbooks, paper, pencils, and even chalk were in short supply.

On top of the problems they already faced, the teachers had to implement a brand-new curriculum with a new methodology that was almost exactly the opposite of what they had been taught. Many of the teachers were overwhelmed and frustrated.

The legacy of apartheid went far beyond the physical poverty of the community. In my first demonstration lesson, I began by asking the students what they wanted to be when they grew up. The teacher and I listed all of their potential occupations on the blackboard. There was a limited number: nurse, doctor, taxi driver, truck driver, security guard, mine worker, teacher, principal, gardener, maid, mechanic, store owner, police officer, soldier, and forest worker.

I repeated the lesson at every school in every class of fifth graders. Each class produced exactly the same list. One boy said he wanted to work for the phone company because that was what his father did. Another girl said she wanted to work at the border post because her mother did that. No one else had parents with other jobs.

When I got to the last school, on the third day, we had done the lesson five times. It was a simple demonstration, and the teachers understood how it brought different subjects together. After the children listed the occupations, we asked them to write five sentences about what the person they chose does at work, and then two sentences about what the students needed to do in order to become a police officer or a mine worker or whatever. Then some of the students had to read their sentences aloud. The teachers understood the activity, the lesson-planning procedure, and the reasons behind the different parts of the lesson. I showed them my written plan, and some of them went on to use that model for writing their own. It was a successful demonstration.

But I couldn't get over the lists of jobs. The teachers never commented on the list, and I am sure they would have been able to predict the list perfectly. These were the only jobs that this community ever had. I mentioned my concern to Eddie Msithini, one of the English teachers. "These are the careers that they know," he said. "They believe that there are only some options, because it is true. There *are* only certain options for them. None of these kids believe that they can be anything more. They don't know about other jobs because they have never seen them. They have never seen them with their parents, or their grandparents. Not even in the community. They tell you what they know, and they tell you what they think is correct to say in school."

Eddie was a great teacher. He loved his Siswati language and culture and taught his subjects—Siswati, English, and history—with passion. I found out, though, that he was not a teacher by choice.

Eddie was in his late 20s, and his family lived outside Nelspruit, where he grew up. When he was young, he wanted to be a land surveyor. He once saw a white man surveying in the location and asked the man some questions. Eddie liked the idea, enjoyed the trigonometry involved, and wanted to wear shorts. Yet all of the teachers in his school, his parents, and everyone else told him he should become a teacher. They would love to see him in a suit and tie because he was so intelligent. Most of the people in his community who had become someone of importance were teachers. What's more, no one in his community knew how to become anything else. Even though apartheid's job reservation policies were nominally at an end, land surveying was not an option for Eddie. He tried to get a scholarship to the University of Port Elizabeth, even going there for a semester. He enjoyed it, but his money ran out and there was no interest in funding a black boy who wanted to be a land surveyor. Eddie returned to Nelspruit and entered the two-year teaching college as one of many who would rather be somewhere else.

Venturing into the unknown world outside of their communal knowledge required a new way of thinking. This was difficult for the students to grasp, and often the teachers were not equipped to guide them. Many teachers, like Eddie, had been molded by apartheid and denied the life of their dreams. This pain and powerlessness engendered among the teachers a range of attitudes that shocked me again and again, from the first time I noticed them until the day I left South Africa.

Some teachers did not speak to me for months because I am white. This was not out of defiance, but because they considered themselves inferior and were afraid to talk to me. In the first meetings I had at Lochiel Primary with the first- and second-grade teachers regarding OBE, only one teacher spoke. The others would sit silently. If I asked a question, they would whisper "I don't know," with their heads hung and their eyes focused on the ground.

At another school, one teacher would stop in mid-sentence if I entered the room. He was a well-respected leader, the assistant principal of the school. Once, in the midst of explaining something to a colleague, he stopped when he saw me and asked me to do it for him.

"I don't know exactly what you were talking about," I said.

"I'm just speaking about math."

"That's great, you go on. I was just coming in to get some paper...."

"No, I can't explain it," he said. "Please help us. We do all of these things wrong. Why are you keeping things from us?"

The teachers uniformly underestimated their own ideas, their skills as educators, and the resources in the community. Simultaneously, they greatly overestimated the ability of the South African government, the United States, and even me to change things in Lochiel or Beeskop. Over and over teachers told me that in order to teach science, they needed a lab or that black teachers could never teach English perfectly or that the government needed to come in and build them a new classroom or hire new teachers or that the kids could not learn if their parents were not educated. Many simply did not think it was possible to provide worthwhile education without the resources that the white schools had. The overwhelming consensus was that attention from outside the community would be needed before they could teach effectively.

This feeling was understandable. After all, these teachers had spent their lives in the top-down, strictly controlled system of Bantu Education and in the government-centered system of apartheid. They had constantly been told how and where to live, learn, and teach. This upbringing poisoned their beliefs in their own potential.

One of the teachers offered to show me his wedding pictures. But they were in a black plastic film canister, undeveloped.

"Why don't you develop them?" I asked.

"Hawu! It is too expensive for us blacks. I could never afford it."

"How much does it cost?"

"Oh, Musa, I don't know, but those stores where they wash the film are not for us."

"So what are you going to do?"

"Someday, if I get rich, I may go and get them washed."

He had been married for six years. He had never even asked how much developing film cost. And he was expected to teach the future entrepreneurs of South Africa.

Teachers asked me, the white man, about everything under the sun. "Jason, what do you think about this car? Should I buy it?"

"Um, sure, it looks fine."

"But do you think it will run well? Is it all right mechanically?"

"I have no idea. Why are you asking me? Mr. Nkambule knows more about cars than I do."

"Yes, Musa, but you are white, and white people's cars, they don't break down like our cars do. Even Nkambule, his car breaks down sometimes."

"Do you really think that is because the people are white?"

"Yes. White people made the cars, Musa. These cars, they are not really for us blacks. But we must learn to use them anyway."

In my two years spent in the staff rooms of schools, I met plenty of teachers who talked to me like this until the day I left.

In her BMW, Mrs. Ndlovu (my supervisor) and I had a conversation that she brought up almost every day afterward. Mrs. Ndlovu is also the principal at Lochiel Primary. We were on our way to Ermelo on a school day to pick up the latest batch of drum majorette uniforms being made by a seamstress in town. At Lochiel Primary, the drum majorettes was the only extracurricular program that functioned at all. They met and practiced, under the supervision of two teachers, twice a week. The squad went to eLukwatini in 1998 and won the district meet. From then on, resources at Lochiel (including me) were devoted heavily to the one part of their school that was succeeding. There was therefore no use in questioning whether Mrs. Ndlovu and I should be spending our school time going to Ermelo to pick up the new uniforms.

As she drove, Mrs. Ndlovu asked me questions about school management. She was studying for a test and wanted to know the "Four Steps to Effective Human Resource Development." The South African government pays teachers and promotes them according to their education credentials. All of the teachers study constantly for certificates in Management and OBE, or Physical Science II, or even in Drum Majorettes. A résumé consisted only of the certificates earned and the courses passed, even if the lessons learned in correspondence courses (passed at 50 percent) rarely made it into the classroom.

"I don't know what that book says," I told her, "but I know there are certain things you could do to help develop your teachers."

"Yes, but I need to know for this test. Can you look in the book and explain it to me?"

"Ma'am, you speak English perfectly, and I think that you won't remember it for the test if I just read and then tell you about it."

"*Marra*, Musa...Look, you know these things. Just help me with the concepts."

Five more times I started to discuss ways that I thought she might be able to help develop the teaching capacity of her school, and five more times she interrupted me, asking if what I said fell under step one or two or what, and explaining that her sheet from the school where she was doing her correspondence work said she needed to know specifically the "Four Steps to Effective Human Resource Development."

I gave up. Frustrated, she changed the subject. Soon we were talking about other things and having a good time. We always got along wonderfully, and I respected Mrs. Ndlovu. She fell victim to the same apartheid-induced blind spots as others, but she was one of the rare people who could see past them.

When we got into town, I sat in the car while she went into the fabric store. She came out with a clear plastic bag containing a single uniform, a sleeveless white dress with gold trim. "LPS," for Lochiel Primary School, was written in gold across the front. She stood outside the car and held the uniform so that I could see it through the window. "Musa, is this OK?" she asked.

"Yeah, it looks nice," I said truthfully.

"Yes," she replied. "But look at this stitching. Do you think it will fall apart?"

"Ma'am, I have no idea. I have never sewn anything in my life."

"OK," she said and went back inside the fabric store. She returned after a few minutes and I got out of the car to help her carry the other 30 or so uniforms. We loaded up the car, and she put it into gear. As she did this, the rubber knob on the top of the stick shift broke off. "Hawu! Musa, what happened?"

"Ma'am, I don't know."

"Can we get it fixed? Is it broken forever?"

I examined the BMW symbol on the side of the rubber knob and at the diagram showing where each gear was located. I had no idea if it was broken forever. I did not know anything about stitching or about the way a drum majorette uniform is supposed to look. This woman was intelligent and experienced, and yet she was asking me about everything. I grabbed the broken piece of the stick shift and said, *"Bheka! Ang'azi! Tsina belungu, asikwazi konke!*—Look! I don't know. White people don't know everything!"

She paused for a moment, shocked. And then she laughed. She took the knob and stuck it back on the stick shift backward, and it worked just fine. She laughed some more. "You know, Musa, you are right. We really do think that white people know everything. You have taught me something today…hee, hee, hee."

She reminded me of this conversation every time she saw me. And even today I never look at a stick shift without thinking of that morning.

I met other superb teachers with wonderful ideas, open minds, and great expectations. Mrs. Mashinini, a teacher at Masakhane School, was one of the few teachers who sent her child to the school where she taught instead of a school with more resources in eLukwatini. In contrast to the broken-down dinginess of others, Mrs. Mashinini's classroom was decorated with homemade mobiles, pictures, murals of the alphabet, number posters, and exceptional work done by the third-grade students in her class. At night the wind would blow through the cracked windows and the emptied panes, and rain might leak through the ceiling, but every morning Mrs. Mashinini would pick things up off the floor, straighten them out, and hang them back up. She took great pride in her teaching and demanded excellence from her students. She would have been a great teacher with or without apartheid, in white schools in South Africa or any school in Atlanta, Georgia.

Another teacher at that same school became my guide for the first months of my job. Zwelithini Enoch Mthethwa went by the name of Chiluga, meaning "sweat." He was famous in Lochiel as an intelligent leader and an iconoclast.

I respected Chiluga immediately because he lived in the community. Virtually all of the instructors had gone away to a teachers' college, and the impact of leaving the community for a while is impossible to overestimate. They mingle with others who have different lifestyles, join a more diverse and cosmopolitan community, and acquire tastes for things that people who stay in Lochiel never experience.

Many teachers took jobs at the rural mountain schools only because they could find no other job. Almost all of them traveled to some faraway place to stay with their family during school breaks, or at "month's end," when they got their paychecks. Chiluga had grown up near Masakhane School and now lived minutes away from where he taught. His wife taught at Mlondozi. They could have lived in eLukwatini, but chose to live at home, in the mountains, with no water and no electricity.

Chiluga was fun and creative. He would come by my place to ask questions or just to talk about the news. Typical of his questions was: "Why is it, Jason, that they do not call Bosnia's fighting tribal warfare?"

In the beginning, he was the only teacher I worked with outside of school. Almost every day at least one teacher would tell me that he or she was sorry, but he or she had to go. "You see, Musa, I would love to do this after-school project, but I am using a common transport and they are waiting for me."

Like Mtunzi, Chiluga devoured books, and he especially enjoyed South African history. He read *The Mind of South Africa* and then stood in the Lochiel square giving history lessons to whoever would listen. He taught me constantly about his culture and his language. Like Tsimanga and Zakhele, he was adamant that I learn pure Siswati. We would sit, sometimes with Shongwe at the mechanic shop and sometimes in the staff room at school, and he would teach me words and explain the technical aspects of certain Swazi customs. I was fascinated and enjoyed his company.

On my first cycle through the schools, I put up a suggestion box in each of the staff rooms and attached a note saying that people should fill the box with anonymous notes about problems in their schools, or positive ideas for improving on the things the school did well. After a few weeks I went back to check. At the first school I found not a single note in the box. Another symptom, I thought, of the apartheid-induced inferiority complex. No one thinks they have anything worth saying.

I wrote another note above the box: "This school must be perfect! No one put a single suggestion in this box, so there must be no changes to make. Perhaps I should go to another school that needs me more?" I thought this would surely get people to put suggestions in the box.

I decided to change my schedule and went, unannounced, to Masakhane the next day. I saw Chiluga as I walked into the principal's office. He said hello, but he did not want to talk and hurried away. After a few minutes with the principal explaining a schedule change, I went to the staff room to check the box. The staff room is actually a small metal shack about ten feet square. As I walked through the metal door, Chiluga put his red marking pen into his pocket and stood up. "Hello, Jason. I must go to class now. I will see you after."

As he left, I looked at the suggestion box. Inside were 20 pieces of paper, all written in the same handwriting in red pen:

"The United States embassy should fund the building of a science lab."

"We should raise money from the rich people who drive by in cars and endanger our children as they walk down the road."

"We should learn how to make teaching aids from local materials."

"We should have after-school programs."

"We should have a basketball team."

They went on and on. I could not believe how many there were. My personal favorite, and the first one I tried to implement, said, "We should stop using class time for meetings with no agenda."

I was heartened by Chiluga's creativity and his ability to see beyond the limitations that had traditionally been applied to his community. He had fresh ideas, and in a society that, through Bantu Education, had sustained a full-scale attack on its creative thinking, this was all too rare.

Even with friends like Chiluga and Eddie, and exceptional teachers like Mrs. Mashinini, it took me a long time to understand the teachers' motivations and their expectations.

The Peace Corps tells its volunteers that they should use their first months to "settle in." Our program in South Africa was designed specifically to allow for this time and to capitalize on the learning of the culture and knowledge of the community that the volunteers developed. Our policy stated that we had certain goals: to empower teachers to use the new curriculum and methodology, to empower the people at the management levels to use new administrative and management techniques that would improve the learning environment, and to empower communities and teachers to create linkages that would benefit both. But the policy also stated that volunteers had the freedom to figure out the best way to meet those goals in their community. As the theory goes, after months of living and working with teachers and other community leaders, a volunteer knows his or her community better than almost anyone in Pretoria, and certainly better than anyone in Washington. He or she can then make decisions and craft a plan of action.

As I became better friends with more teachers, I began to go to eLukwatini more often. The teacher community in eLukwatini is close-knit, and they socialize together. I became close friends with Eddie and Nhlanhla Ndlovu (Mrs. Ndlovu's son) who both teach at Lochiel Primary. We liked to go to a place in eLukwatini called Club 2000, or Two Gs.

Two Gs was a concrete-block building with unpainted concrete floors, split into three different levels connected by short three-step stairways. A lounge with three couches and a table took up the top area. One level down was a room with another couch, a few plastic chairs, and the bar. The bartenders worked behind a metal cage with a small square opening through which they collected money and passed the quart bottles of beer. Just to the right of the prison-like bar, stairs went down to the last level, which had a pool table and a few more plastic chairs. The windows looked out at the rolling hills and steep mountain walls of the valley.

On good days, the breeze blew through, the beer was cold, and the company was great: school principals, building contractors, medical lab workers, and teachers. All spoke English and were politically astute and active; they all had something to say. Once again, like the times with Zakes, I was learning around the pool table, just hanging out with the guys.

At Two Gs, with Chiluga in Lochiel, and eventually with teachers in the staff room, I talked about the differences between the United States and South Africa. Being American was the coolest thing anyone could be. Everyone who followed the news wanted to know why we cared about Bill Clinton and Monica Lewinsky. "The amazing thing," some said, "is that the Americans think that we care. It's hypocritical."

Misusing words like "hypocritical" was pretty common among educated blacks in Greater eLukwatini. The teachers knew the words and clichés, but sometimes a teacher would use a word or phrase out of context. A person who was outraged by something might say, "I could not believe it! That Thabo Mbeki would do such a thing! It is out of this world." Mrs. Ngwenya, who lost her right arm in a car accident and wore a prosthetic from her bicep down, often said that she had to do something "single-handed." The English language in South Africa is spoken by most as a second, third, or fourth language. No one in Two Gs or in Lochiel grew up in an English-speaking home. Their slips of tongue often made me think about my language in a new way.

Teachers, like everyone else in South Africa, constantly asked me about America. Their questions were more informed than the average question in Lochiel or at the preschool, and I soon found that I could not always answer the way I wanted. "I read that people in America don't vote. Why?" A good question. I would have to say, "Because we take our democracy for granted in America."

"Are their tribes in America?"

"Well, not really anymore."

"So there were tribes?"

"Yes."

"What happened?"

"The white people took over their land."

"So where are they now?"

"They live mostly on what we call reservations."

"Oh, like the homelands?"

"Well…" I would stumble. "Not really. I think the difference is, uh, that there aren't nearly as many Native Americans as there are black South Africans."

"Why?" Some days I would be too embarrassed to answer, but on others I would be forced to admit that it was because our forefathers killed many of them.

Most people wanted to know how we did things in the greatest country on Earth. "Is there apartheid in America?"

"No," I said quickly. "There is no apartheid."

"So, then black people and white people just live together?"

"Well, not exactly."

"Do black people live in locations?"

"No," I answered. "They live right in the center of town." I marveled at my answer and wondered if that makes some sort of difference.

"Do black Americans speak many, many languages?"

"No," I said, "not like South Africa. Most speak only English."

"Hawu! It must be so easy for black people and white people to communicate!"

THE MORE PEOPLE ASKED ME ABOUT AMERICA, THE MORE I REALIZED the power of the idea of America. Being American gave me a special prominence. People would ask questions about everything. Are there cows? Are there black people? How big is it? Do you use koombis? What are the cars like? The teachers would listen intently to me, even if I was talking about bathroom passes or some other trivial element of American society. Almost immediately, I found that when I talked about America, people listened.

So I had different conversations about my culture and theirs. My progress in my job was painfully slow compared to the speed with which I progressed in cultural spheres. This learning was interesting and exciting, but it was also a prerequisite for being effective at my job.

As my relationships grew, I tried to implement parts of a plan. Keeping in mind both the good teachers and those who did not believe they would ever succeed, I conducted workshops with the teachers at all three schools. The Department of Education, I explained, spends 90 percent of its budget on salaries, preventing them from physically improving their crumbling schools or from investing in textbooks or other teaching aids. This means that the teachers are the only real resources available, and they need to be utilized to their fullest extent. In the workshop, which a few friends and I had designed during training, the teachers talked about using their colleagues as resources to help with problems, to create interesting and entertaining lessons, to come up with new ideas about teaching, and to solve whatever problems a school was having with the community.

Accustomed to a system that encouraged strict adherence to instructions, many of the teachers struggled with creativity. But they also were reluctant to ask questions or solicit advice. The result was a stifling work environment with very little reason to grow or change as a teacher. Many of the teachers had never observed another teacher in a real classroom.

At the workshops, we listed factors that inhibited cooperation. At each of the three schools, almost every barrier was attitudinal. "People will think I am stupid if I ask a question." "People are selfish with their knowledge because they want to get ahead." The only actual barrier that teachers listed was a lack of time to sit and compare notes.

We discussed strategies for cooperation and ways to change old attitudes, and I had the three principals make some changes in the requirements and timing of certain committee meetings. Under the old system, the teachers had been organized into subject committees, and at each workshop I conducted, the teachers decided to resurrect that idea. I arranged with the principals to require these meetings, and then made schedules so the meetings could occur during school time while all the teachers in a given subject had free periods. I met several times with each committee.

Often I found that the teachers of a given subject did not even know what students were taught in previous or subsequent grades. In one meeting of math teachers, a fourth-grade teacher mentioned that students were having problems with a particular function of fractions.

"What is that?" asked the third-grade teacher.

After the first teacher explained it, the third-grade teacher said, "Oh, well, in the third-grade textbooks we call that by another name."

When the fourth-grade teacher reintroduced the concept in his classes, the students quickly realized that they had done it before and grasped it more readily.

I spent a lot of my time asking teachers about the attitudes and practices spawned by the old "inspector-based" system, and how to change them. But, because so many of the thought processes were so deeply ingrained, this work was excruciating, and the progress was slow. To have something concrete to do, I also began teaching computer literacy. This instruction was fairly straightforward and required less knowledge of the teachers' underlying culture or motivations.

Two of my schools, Masakhane and Mlondozi, had computers. At Masakhane, they had a brand new Pentium computer with Windows 95 and all the business software installed. The principal, Mr. I. J. Nkabindze, was a jovial man with a beard who fancied double-breasted suits and V-neck patterned sweaters. He drove a tiny white pickup truck with a covered back, and he was known far and wide for his voice and prowess as a choir director. Like many well-to-do men in rural South Africa, his tie rested somewhat horizontally on his shirt front, and his jacket was either unbuttoned or stretched tight across his stomach. He was a good principal and was well respected by the others in the region.

He told me "a man from an NGO" had set up the computer with the school's name in the registry and then left it in the staff room for the school to use. No teacher had ever known how to turn it on. So I taught Mr. Nkabindze whenever I could, and some days I helped groups of teachers learn the basics of computer literacy. Everyone wanted to learn "computer," and besides speaking the language, this teaching was by far the most popular thing I did. I used my laptop along with Masakhane's desktop, providing two computers that a small class of teachers could use for practice.

We took the cover off the computer and looked inside; we learned how to use a mouse, how to type, how to save files, and where those files could be found. It was utterly foreign to every one of the teachers. Some of them had seen computers before, but none had any idea how one worked.

Mlondozi's principal, Mrs. Norma Ngwenya, purchased an old IBM PC with a five-and-a-half-inch floppy drive. I asked around in Ermelo and Nelspruit for software, but could not find anyone who had any access at all to the old-style floppy disks. I never really understood the term "obsolete" until I realized how little we could do with the computer. It was not an informed purchase, and the person who sold it to the principal was a crook who should be ashamed. Mrs. Ngwenya, who has the prosthetic arm, is one of the toughest people I met in South Africa. After her accident, she had to relearn how to write, drive, eat, brush her hair, wash, and perform every other function of her daily life with only her left arm. She was by far the youngest of all the principals I met, but more than made up for that in the way she demanded respect and discipline. I hope, for his sake, she never finds the man who sold her the obsolete computer.

The computer was not completely useless, however, and I worked with a teacher Mrs. Ngwenya assigned to learn how to use it. I taught him how to use the outdated software that had already been installed, and I taught him and some other teachers with my own computer.

As I developed relationships with the teachers, I was able to begin breaking down some of the barriers that apartheid had constructed. I was the first white person to ride in Mrs. Mashinini's and Mrs. Ndlovu's cars, to enter Chiluga's and Eddie's and Nhlanhla's and Mr. Manana's homes. Teachers became friends and began to confide in me. I began to confide in them. My respect for the people and their willingness to move beyond apartheid's leftover barriers grew. Every time I saw a person breaking through, I was impressed.

After our conversation about careers, Eddie and I walked into his class. I was going to perform the demonstration lesson about jobs for the sixth time, after having received the exact same list of possible careers from every single fifth grader in the region. Then a little girl raised her hand and said, in a quiet voice, *"Ngifuna kushiyela indisa. Ngifuna kuhamba ephezulu, emoyeni."* She wanted to become a pilot, she said, and fly airplanes through the sky.

Everyone laughed, as she knew they would. I told her she was great. I looked at Eddie and he smiled. Those were the moments when my job was wonderful. A ray of hope had shone through the cracked school windows of that fifth-grade classroom.

TOWN
CHAPTER EIGHT

I SHOULD MENTION THAT I WAS ALWAYS WELL DRESSED FOR WORK.

The teachers at my schools were obsessed with their appearance. I was not, and that created problems at first. I had envisioned a Peace Corps volunteer as down and dirty, barefoot, in shorts and a T-shirt, digging trenches or fish ponds. But at schools in Lochiel I was expected to wear a tie. Some of my most vivid memories of those two years were made standing in my room fretting over my clothes. If my pants weren't pressed, or if my shoes weren't polished, it was virtually guaranteed that one or two teachers would make a comment. That is, if I even made it to school. Gogo would often stop me. "Hawu! Musa! Today you do not look like a teacher!" She would head to my room, collect the dirty clothes, and spend the entire day washing and ironing. This I tried to prevent at all cost.

The southern winter of 1998 was bitterly cold in Lochiel. The workers leaving in the trucks, amid clouds of breath, wore extra blankets and trudged through thick frost on their way to be picked up each morning. I would wake up, teeth chattering, in the middle of the night and not remember where I was. Life made no sense: I was freezing in Africa in June. Yet I saw in a magazine that Lesotho has a ski resort. The Swazi and the Zulu have a word, *sitwatwa*, that means "snow" or "frost." No one in Lochiel thought the bitter cold was unusual.

I woke up one morning and put on a nice shirt and tie, some wrinkle-free pants, and my sports coat. Freezing, I added my North Face jacket. After I ate breakfast, though, Gogo wouldn't let me out of the house. "No, Musa. *Ungafaki two amacoats.* No. *Hamba kuwathenga amajersey aytwo. Hamba edolopeni.*" She did not want me to wear two coats because she thought that only poor people dressed like that, and it would not be suitable for a teacher like me. She told me to go to town and buy some jerseys (sweaters).

The term "town," in South Africa, applies only to a place where white people live. No matter how small a community may be, if it contains a group of white people, it is a town. Black people live in *emakhaya*, or country homes, or they live *e-lokhashini*, in the locations (they seldom use the word "township").

The apartheid government limited commercial development in the locations because they did not accept that the black people were permanent residents of South Africa until the 1980s. In the homelands, it was difficult to find investors ready to put up money for a bank branch or a grocery store. As a result, blacks spread across entire regions had to travel to white towns, spend their money in white-owned stores, and then had to return to their wasteland communities. Many white stores in tiny towns were able to stay in business only because they served the black people in the surrounding areas. I soon became one of those people who traveled long distances to keep them in business.

On my first trip to town, when Gogo sent me to buy sweaters to wear to school, I walked up to the Lochiel taxi rank at the top of the hill, a half mile from the garage, and got in a taxi. They said it was going to *Imlomo,* the Zulu/Siswati word for "mouth," and the name that many black people have given to Ermelo. There were only three other people in the fifteen-passenger koombi, so I had to wait.

I sat there for 45 minutes before it filled up. I grew to love sitting in koombis because most of the time people would leave me alone so I could read. And read incessantly. Besides books on South Africa, I had subscriptions to the *Economist*, *Sports Illustrated*, *Foreign Affairs*, and *Newsweek*. (The *Newsweek* subscription was courtesy of the Peace Corps.) I learned more about the structure of international capital markets in koombis than in any classroom, and during my time in the Peace Corps I was more up-to-date on world issues than I had ever been in my life.

These taxis are an enduring legacy of apartheid. Only blacks ride in them. White people have cars and would never think of riding in taxis like these. Blacks have no choice; they have to use them to get to town to buy food or clothes. Koombis are dangerous. Accidents happen every day, and the people who ride in koombis are without seat belts and are so tightly packed that the accidents are almost always fatal. Yet taxis remain the only option.

Padding and vinyl hang like stalactites from holes in the roofs of most koombis. The flooring is ripped out when drivers replace the original three rows of seats with four. Overloaded on every trip, the miles take a brutal toll on the machinery. The shocks are always shot. The speedometer is always stuck at zero because the odometer is disconnected so it doesn't register all those brutal miles. The speed is regulated only by the amount of shaking. If the windows are shaking too loudly for the driver to hear his music, he slows down.

Still, these rickety old taxis are always full. Grandchildren travel to and from grandmothers' houses. Maybe a father has sent for his family because he had finally made enough money to support them in the location near the town where he works. Most people travel into town with very little, but the taxis going home are always packed with groceries or people loaded with sweaters to sell in Lochiel, or with a crate of baby chicks to be raised and sold as chickens in a few months' time.

My trip to Ermelo to buy sweaters was typical. A few babies and tod-dlers with their mothers, a man going back to work after a few days at home, some younger men going to look for work or to pick up a rela-tive, someone having a problem with his identity documents, or with her pension so that she has to go to town to clear it up, and several older women going to do their shopping.

Ermelo is approximately 100 kilometers from Lochiel, or 63 miles. Carolina is approximately 75 kilometers, but it is not even half the size of Ermelo, so most people go to Ermelo to buy things. It is a mining town, originally built because the area rests on top of vast coal reserves. During apartheid Ermelo grew into a commercial and administrative center. There are several large banks, offices of a few national ministries, and numerous supermarkets, furniture stores, clothing stores, and the like. It is not very different from a small town in Georgia, except that almost all the people speak Afrikaans as their first language.

Pulling into Ermelo, the taxi drove past a fancy brown-and-white Old-German style restaurant on the edge of town and then into a small res-idential area. The lawns were manicured and the fences all had gates and mailboxes with signs announcing the owners' pride in their family names. The houses, mostly brick, were quaint, often with small porches and landscaped bushes and shrubs on either side of the front doors.

The taxi pulled into the rank behind a large beige-and-aqua build-ing called the Sanlam Sentrum, the main shopping center in down-town Ermelo.

In the back of the Sanlam Sentrum, where the taxi let us off, every-one was black. The storefronts were cluttered with signs for discounted meat, vegetables, meat pies, Dark and Lovely cosmetics, hair relaxer, perms, braids, phone calls paid by the minute, Zulu gospel, kwaito music, and other products targeted at black consumers.

In front, the population and products change. White parents rushed their kids around and in and out of cars in the huge parking lot. There were a few chain restaurants, electronics stores, and clothing stores. There were many black people as well, most walking, but some getting in and out of cars.

Inside the Sanlam Sentrum was an OK, part of a supermarket chain similar to those in America. Next to the OK was a cell phone store, a few shoe stores, a sporting goods store selling rugby balls and cricket sets, a jewelry store, a bakery, and several others selling whatever a small town may need. A mall, plain and simple, and very American.

Past the parking lot was a grid of quaint divided boulevards lined with trees and little family-run stores. For my sweaters I went into a place called Ermelo Outfitters, said hello in English to the white man inside, and bought two V-neck sweaters. I felt strange putting them on my Visa card. I used the word "jerseys" instead of "sweaters," but the man behind the counter still had a little trouble understanding my English. I apologized for not speaking Afrikaans. He laughed and smiled, said it was no problem, and apologized for not speaking perfect English. "It's been a long time," he said. "We don't get much practice here in Ermelo."

I had not seen much of the town before, and I walked around for a while, went to the ATM machine at the bank where the Peace Corps kept our accounts, withdrew some money, and bought myself a pepper steak pie at King Pie. I got a blanket for less than three dollars at a place called Pep, which catered to black people and was very inexpensive. I knew that Gogo had a daughter who lived in the location and worked at Beare's Furniture. But I didn't know where Beare's was, and after walking around the streets of Ermelo, I started to feel uncomfortable anyway.

As I walked around, I said hello to people, just as I did in Lochiel. *"Sanibonani!" "Sawubona, kunjani?" "Yebo Mama! Ninjani nine?" "Heita."* On the dirt footpaths of Lochiel, I had encountered few problems. At first people were taken aback and would stop and ask me questions. But because it was a tiny community, the people eventually came around. I could count on almost everyone to respond when I greeted them. "Yebo, Musa!"

In Ermelo, it was different. Everyone looked at me like I was crazy. No black person looked me in the eye the entire time I was there. I would say hello, and they would shuffle on by or look up in disbelief. The only ones that approached me were the taxi drivers once I got back to the taxi rank. Maybe they knew it was their home turf, so they weren't intimidated, but on the streets white and black people ignored the other's existence. I would have felt strange just showing up at Beare's and telling Gogo's daughter I was living at her mother's house.

Perplexed, I continued walking, exploring Ermelo and seeing what the town had to offer. I saw a sign for a travel agent and decided to stop in. I said hello to a young Indian woman sitting at a desk on the right, and to a middle-aged white woman in the back. Brochures hung on the wall advertising Mozambique's beaches, Victoria Falls, Cape Town, Durban, Port Elizabeth, the Garden Route, and skiing in Lesotho.

"I need to get to Cape Town for a few days. Do you have any suggestions?"

"Please sit down," the Indian woman said. When I did, she asked, "Where do you want to leave from, and how would you like to travel? It is much easier to leave from Jo-burg."

She turned to her computer and began typing on the keys and quoting me prices. The woman in the back interjected every once in a while to tell me how uncomfortable the bus was. "You really should take a plane." She also knew several places to stay that were "just delightful."

They recommended I also go to Durban if I ever had the chance, and the woman in the back really loved her trip to Mozambique last winter. "But you have to be willing to rough it, you know. It is not like America." She laughed at her joke.

As we were talking, a black man came in. He opened the door just enough to slip in, took off his hat, and lowered his head. He was dressed in a nice sweater and clean pants. I noticed him only because both women stopped talking and stared at him.

"What do you want?" the white woman said sharply.

"I would like to know how much it costs to go to Port Elizabeth." He asked so quietly that I could barely hear.

"What, by bus? I don't know," she said, and waved her arm.

He turned and left. Both women slumped back in their chairs as though they were exhausted.

"Whew!" said the Indian woman. "I always get so scared when they come in here. I think they are going to steal something."

"Oh, my God!" said the white woman. "Could you see it on my face? How scared I was?" They both chuckled for a moment, clearly relieved.

They asked me how often I made it to Ermelo. "Every few weeks."

"Oh, you must come more often. You should check out the nightlife in Ermelo." The Indian woman chuckled at her, so the white woman added, "It's not much, but the Riverside can be fun. They have live music. It's in Afrikaans, but it is really nice for young people like you. Where do you live?"

"Near the Swaziland border on Highway 17."

"Oh, I love it out there. I drive past it when I holiday in Swaziland. It is charming. Where do you live?"

"I live in the old hotel out there."

"There's no hotel there." Everywhere in the world people think they know their place better than any foreigner.

"Yes, there is. It's behind the petrol station in Lochiel."

They were both alarmed and began to talk interchangeably, saying the same things.

"My God! Isn't it owned by blacks? What on Earth are you doing there?"

"I'm working with teachers in the schools there to help them with the new curriculum."

"Aren't you scared?"

"No, the people are really nice and I have been there a while so they know me. It's really great."

"Are you going back there right now?"

"Yeah, and actually, I need to go catch a taxi."

"A black taxi?"

I should have said that most of them were actually red or green or white, but I just said, "Yes."

"My God." They were still interrupting each other to show their concern. "Honestly, you must be careful. You know, they'll kill you and take your money just like that." Snap. "Please be careful.... My God, you just walk over to the black taxis? Behind the shopping center?"

"Yes, ma'am, and I actually do need to go. Thank y'all so much. I'll be sure to go by the Riverside next time I'm in town."

I walked down the street and across the parking lot to the taxi rank. In so doing, I realized I was crossing a border that few others could cross. As I sat in the taxi, I reflected that I must be one of the freest people in South Africa. Both in front and in back of the Sanlam Sentrum, people were paralyzed by their fear of each other. Black people couldn't approach a travel agent, and white people couldn't take a taxi.

Fear is the key emotion between white and black in South Africa. It defines their relationships at all times, throughout the country. Black people in Ermelo wouldn't look me in the eye because they were afraid. White people thought I was crazy, and they thought the same thing about the other white volunteers in my group.

Anna Domenico, for example, is white, from Boulder, Colorado. She speaks Zulu, English, and maybe a little Italian, but she doesn't like to speak unless she really has something to say. She was a good friend of mine during training. She loved Bra Sphiwe, my father in Kromdraai, and taught him a bunch of new songs for his guitar. If you had asked me to describe my idea of a Peace Corps volunteer before I left the U.S., I would have imagined Anna.

The Peace Corps had placed her on a farm near Piet Retief. That town was more conservative than Ermelo, and farmers in general were not known for their cosmopolitan views on racial justice. Anna's supervisor, the principal of one of the schools built on farmers' land, had asked permission from the owner of the farmland for a volunteer to come and live in a tiny community of mud houses on his farm. He agreed.

When Anna arrived, she had a nice place to stay. It had no electricity and no water, but she met fun and friendly people. Eventually she went to see the farmer and his wife. They had a beautiful home with a computer, Internet access, plenty of food, extra guest rooms, and satellite TV.

"We think you should stay with us," the farmer said.

"No, really, thank you so much," Anna replied. "But I like the place where I am staying. The Peace Corps requires that you live with the people you work with, and that you live as close to their lifestyle as possible." The last thing she needed, as a white American, was to be set further apart from her community and teachers than she already was.

The farmer would not have it. Anna eventually had to leave the community until the Peace Corps leadership came from Pretoria to explain their policy to the white community. The farmer remained obdurate. Yes, he had agreed to allow a volunteer to live there, but he had no idea it would be a woman, and he certainly had not known she would be white. "If they think they can live with her, in the same house, what are they going to think about me and my wife?"

It was an interesting question. Not everyone, it seemed, was ready for the answer.

IN CONVERSATIONS WITH WHITE PEOPLE, I FOUND THAT MOST WERE not necessarily against the idea of Americans coming to South Africa to live and work in the black community. But such a lifestyle choice was outside the realm of their imagination. They themselves would have never even considered it an option.

One nice sunny day I was sitting in front of the garage in the grass next to the road. My friend Piet and Piet's brother were sitting with me, and we were talking and laughing. A car sped by on the highway, stopped, turned around, and pulled up next to us. The driver said something in Afrikaans. "Hello," I said, "how are you?"

"Good," he said, talking across a boy sleeping in the passenger seat. "Is everything all right?"

"Yes," I said. "Everything's fine."

"Do you need a lift somewhere?"

"No, I live here."

"You must be joking," he laughed. "There's nowhere to live here."

"I live back there in a room at that hotel. I've been there for quite a while."

"You live here alone?"

Confused, I looked at Piet, then at my sister Boni and Babe Chris. A woman was walking across the street with firewood piled on her head. Some of the kids from Gogo's preschool were running around. "No, sir, not alone. I live with all these people."

He shook his head, muttered something in Afrikaans, and having stopped to check on me, sped away, his tires screeching.

TAXIS WERE NOT MY ONLY MEANS OF GETTING AROUND. HITCHHIKING is an exercise in patience and trust, and as I grew comfortable in the community, it became my primary mode of transportation. On corners in Lochiel, at certain spots in Nhlazatje, on the outskirts of any small town in South Africa, or even at crossroads in the middle of nowhere, people stand and wait for a ride. A car drops off a person who is going to Hoedspruit instead of Lydenburg, and it picks up a person waiting to go to Lydenburg, who had been dropped off earlier by a car going to Hoedspruit.

Black people would rarely ride with an empty seat in their car, for the drivers charged passengers the same as a taxi. People without a car could go anywhere for a cheap price without having to ride in a crowded koombi. All of the bad things I had heard about hitchhiking from my mother were outweighed by my need for transportation and the ease with which I could find a ride.

Eighty percent of the time, I was picked up by black people, and most of them were strangers. Every time, they were surprised to see a white man hitchhiking on the side of the road, and many were nervous until well after we started talking.

I never once had a problem. Coming back from Nhlazatje in the late afternoon, I got rides in small cars that puttered up the hills to Lochiel, or in a nice Mercedes that zoomed around those little cars. I rode in the back of countless pickup trucks, with or without camper tops. Sometimes, friends in nice cars would pass and see me in the back of a pickup truck struggling to make it up the mountain, and they would point at me and laugh. Other times, though, they would flag down the truck and let me ride with them. I even piled into the cabs of pickups with two or three others, trying to get enough seat without too much gear shift. Often, the arrangement was so tight, or awkward that the muscles in my legs would burn from balancing myself the whole ride.

Once, coming back from the circuit office in eLukwatini in my best school clothes, I rode in the back of a covered pickup truck with three live chickens. They were flying around, defecating and pecking at the floor and my shoes and my bag. This was not the ride I was hoping for, but it was late and I had been waiting a long time. When I got out of the truck after 30 minutes with the chickens, I looked like I had been splatter painted from the waist down, and my nerves were frayed from dodging the spray. Gogo looked like she wanted to both kill me and laugh hysterically. She opted for the latter, bending at the waist and laughing so hard that she had to put a hand on the table to keep from falling over. Boni giggled every time she saw me for three days. There was no "Hello, Musa, How are you?" It was just "Ha ha ha, Hee hee, Musa and his chickens...ha ha ha."

On other rides, I spoke with businesspeople who wanted to participate in career days at school or with Department of Education officials who had heard of the Peace Corps, but wanted some clarification on certain points. "Do your salaries come from the DOE budget?"

"No sir, the United States government pays our expenses."

"Hmm, what a great program...."

I rode in an RV that the hospital in eLukwatini had converted into a traveling health clinic and AIDS education mobile. I had to sit on the bed in the back, but the people remembered me and helped me when I started my AIDS education work near the end of my Peace Corps service.

Hitchhiking is one of the most liberating experiences I can imagine. Jack Kerouac writes about traveling the downtrodden avenues of America and seeing that "everyone seemed to be in on it." Hitching in South Africa, I felt the same way. When other hikers saw me at a crossroad, we shared a wink that crossed borders and defied language.

I could go anywhere I wanted: Johannesburg, Pretoria, or Ermelo to see my friends and buy some food; Nelspruit to go to the mall and see a movie; Harare in Zimbabwe, Gaborone in Botswana, Maseru in Lesotho. I could turn around and be in Swaziland in 15 minutes. I could just run down to Badplaas to go swimming and eat at a restaurant. If I wanted to see another Peace Corps volunteer, I could go to some less glamorous places: Tjakastad, eKulindeni, Nhlazatje, eLukwatini, Mpuluzi, Silobela. I spoke the language and I knew my way around. I have been stuck near Breyton, in the middle of nowhere, as the sun was going down without a car in sight, and I jumped in the cab of a coal truck and ended up with a free ride. I once fell asleep and woke up in downtown Johannesburg, well past where I wanted to be dropped off; I struck up a conversation with a man on the street who found me a taxi to the station and was only 15 minutes late for a meeting in Pretoria.

All this freedom was dangerous. Going back and forth to town in koombis or in pickup trucks was eye-opening. I began to understand the layout of the area and the racial politics behind its geographic divisions. As I traveled, I began to see the borders of South Africa more clearly, and I realized I could live on both sides.

NEW ROUTINES
CHAPTER NINE

IN LOCHIEL I STARTED TO FEEL LIKE I WAS ON A ROLL. I HAD
been to both Ermelo and Nelspruit. My world was expanding. Chiluga
had taken me to some of the tiny shops around my schools, and I knew
a little about the communities near Lochiel and away from the road. I
had been to eLukwatini and knew my way around.

At home, I was feeling much more comfortable. In the beginning I
had felt that I was imposing, eating someone else's food. But after pur-
chasing groceries a few times, I felt better. I had also helped put the food
away, so I knew exactly where it was. This was no easy task.

Gogo put dried soup mix and flour in the kitchen cabinets. Milk and
meat went in the refrigerator. Canned food went in the dresser in the living room; corn flakes and ramen noodles (and nothing else) belonged in
the large chest in the dining room. Under that chest, on the floor, went
the eggs. Peanut butter? Behind the couch in the gallon tub with the lid.
The bread had its own breadbox on the kitchen counter. Then there was
the food for the preschool, which could be found in the pantry. Gogo

liked to keep the preschool food separate so she could account perfectly for expenditures, and, she said, because she suspected that the teacher or the cook would snack on any food they could find. I knew the teacher, Joyce, and was slightly startled to hear that she might be a food thief.

Gogo also kept several bottles of cooking oil in the cabinet next to the stove. Both she and Boni used ounces of oil just to fry an egg because their pans were thin, and the pan bottoms were creased and dented. I immediately realized that I could not absorb that much oil into my diet, and I bought Gogo a nice new nonstick pan.

All the food and cookware contributions I made gave me some confidence in the kitchen. I was finally able to have lunch without buying it at one of the tiny shops and was able to cook my own breakfast. This comfort, however, could be easily shaken.

I came home one day after school and decided to make myself a grilled cheese sandwich. I bought a loaf of bread from Doris's store. I got out the cheese that I had purchased in town the day before. I put the pan I had given the family on the stove. I knew where the knives were. I started slicing the bread and smiled. Unsliced bread is the most underrated thing in the world, I told myself. I was in a good mood.

I grilled the sandwich until it was golden brown and perfect. Twana walked in with Lindiwe, a girl who was staying with us for a few weeks. I knew these girls well and said hello. Putting the grilled cheese on a plate, I washed the cutting board, the pan, and the knife. I was feeling great and thinking that I was really getting settled in to this life in Lochiel. And then I noticed that Twana and Lindiwe were sitting on the steps by the door watching me and Twana was crying.

"*Unani?*" I asked. "What's wrong?"

She said nothing; after a moment, Lindiwe said, "*Ulambile*—She's hungry."

I asked Twana if she was hungry and she nodded. I asked her if she wanted half of my sandwich and she nodded, clearly ashamed and refusing to look up. I tore it and gave her half. I felt awful and confused.

From this vantage, one could see virtually every house in Lochiel as the town was in the spring of 2000, a few days before I returned to the United States.

ABOVE: I often bought lunch, like this roasted maize, at one of the taxi ranks in Nhlazatje, where *kombis* waited to transport people to destinations as far away as Johannesburg. The phone shack where I collected my e-mail is in the background. **OPPOSITE:** Gogo oversees afternoon tea in the kitchen. The children, clockwise from the right, are Andiswa, Nombhuso, Twana, and Thembilihle, whom we called "Rabbit."

OPPOSITE: A student peers through his third-grade classroom window at Lochiel Primary School.

RIGHT: At the Oshoek border post I talked with an entrepreneur who buys chickens and then transports them in his wheelbarrow to sell in his neighborhood.

BELOW: Children walk along the road to school, under power lines servicing First-World South Africa.

ABOVE: Children leave the schoolyard for home and follow a footpath that snakes through the grasses and crosses the creek midway through.

OPPOSITE, ABOVE: As teachers and students look on, schoolgirls perform a traditional dance with whistles at my going-away party in Gogo's backyard.

OPPOSITE, BELOW: Ms. Shongwe involves her students in a lesson at Lochiel Primary School. In my job as a Peace Corps volunteer, I worked with teachers to help them implement a new curriculum designed to establish a more creative environment for the first post-apartheid generation of South African students.

My grandfather took this photo of me with Nelson Mandela outside the President's House in Johannesburg. The morning that I spent with the two of them was one of the most inspirational of my life.

Without meaning to, I had tortured these poor, hungry girls by making a grilled cheese sandwich right in front of their faces.

Then I noticed that Twana had two white pegs in her earlobes. I remembered that I had seen several older people with large holes in their ears, and thought it must signify some rite of passage. Immediately, I wondered if the pegs had something to do with her tears and maybe even her hunger. Perhaps fasting was part of the ritual?

I couldn't keep track of all the rules and nuances of the culture. I had been told by several teachers at the school that it was especially important to avoid offense when it came to sharing food. Anytime I turned down food, people thought it was rude. Had I put Twana in a position where she could not refuse?

I left the kitchen confused and hungry.

But before long these discomforting experiences happened less frequently. I would go days without facing an issue that I had never encountered. Looking back, I am sure that Twana was crying for other reasons. Maybe her mother had yelled at her, or she had been in some kind of trouble. Lindiwe was probably just making an excuse.

As I settled into a routine, I uncovered more small revelations. Some were still shocking. One day I was sitting with Chiluga discussing the value of early childhood education while the preschoolers ran around us in the garden. Chiluga had always been very interested in the preschool, and I would soon find out why. "Musa," he asked, "do you know Sesi Joyce?"

"The preschool teacher? Yes, she is great." In fact, I had discovered Sandile and his friends sneaking peanut butter sandwiches, and I soon found out that the phrase "It was the preschool teachers" was an excuse that covered not only Sandile's snacking, but Gogo's and Boni's as well. It became a family joke.

"Joyce is very beautiful, don't you think?" Chiluga continued.

"Yes," I said, telling the truth.

"Well, I think I am going to marry her."

Chiluga's wife was a teacher at Mlondozi, and I knew her well. "What does your wife say?" I asked, thinking he was joking.

"She insisted, Musa, because you see, I am having an affair," he said, smiling. "Just like your president."

He liked to show how much he knew about the world. "So he's having an affair, but doesn't your wife care if you marry another woman?" I said.

"No, she thinks it is the right thing to do. She is going to give us a new bed for a present to show that she says it is good."

"Chiluga," I said, floored. "What does your mother say? And Gogo? What does she say?" His mother and Gogo were sisters.

"Hawu, Musa, Gogo is my small mother; I already told her. And what would she say? Mr. Ndzukulu has three wives."

All of this was coming too fast. I knew that multiple marriages were legal, but not that they were so widespread, and I certainly did not know that my best friend at school, and the family I lived with, participated in the tradition.

"You look surprised, Musa," Chiluga said in English. "Do you think it is wrong?"

"I—I don't know. I guess not."

"You know, Jason," said Chiluga, who always claimed to be an atheist, "the Bible says adultery is wrong, but this is not adultery. It's polygamy. Abraham had many wives."

"Wait a minute," I said. "Mr. Ndzukulu has how many wives?"

"Three. Gogo, the one in Mayflower, and another at his house in Pretoria."

I did not believe him. Mr. Ndzukulu was the high official in the Methodist Church who had so intimidated the Peace Corps with his religious fervor that they had lectured me about it several times before I left to go live at his house. I had not seen very much of him and was unsure how I felt about him, but this was a shock. Why hadn't I known?

Later, I asked Boni where Mkhulu stayed in Mayflower.

"At his house," she answered.

"With who?"

"His wife," she smiled. I had discovered a secret. I never spoke to Gogo about it. I am sure they thought that white people disapproved, and so they did not want to tell me. Later, in the kitchen, I heard Gogo talking to Joyce about being married. I asked Gogo later that night about Chiluga and Joyce, and she shook her head and said, "*Akusi*-easy, Musa—It's not easy."

I also found out that Mtunzi had a son, and his new girlfriend was pregnant. Boni is not actually Gogo's daughter, and Sandile has an entire family, with parents, brothers, and sisters in Middelburg. The familial relationships could be very confusing.

Other revelations made my life less complicated and were quickly absorbed into my routine. There were certain items that everyone in Lochiel had, but that I could not find. People had not purchased them in town, and no place in Lochiel sold any of them: grass mats that roll up; school shoes for the children; sandals like Doris's at the store; metal boxes to store maize meal; even the workers' uniforms and pants. They had to come from somewhere, but I couldn't find any place in Ermelo or Nelspruit that sold them. I especially wanted a mat. I figured that if I was going to live here for two years, I might as well get in shape. If I had a roll-up grass mat, I could do sit-ups and push-ups. I also thought I might need a hat, or some work clothes, and I wondered if such basic items came from some major source I had not found.

In fact, they did. One Monday morning, a month after I had arrived, I walked out of my room and could not believe my eyes. A thousand people were milling in the square and in the parking lot where the Mondi trucks parked. Some people had small tents sheltering their merchandise, and some just had blankets covered with goods. They were selling hats, shoes, dresses, work clothes, pants, boots, two-foot-long bars of green dish and body soap, pots, frying pans, sets of drinking glasses, silverware, roll-up grass sleeping mats, mats for wiping feet, oranges, apples, pears, bananas, cow tongues/intestines/feet/flanks/ribs/heads/other parts I had never seen, corresponding sheep and goat parts, cheese curls in 40-pound bags, cassette tapes, sunglasses, metal storage boxes, metal chimneys for wood-burning stoves, mattresses, blankets, brooms, and every other item I had ever seen in Lochiel. Two people had also put out blankets covered with roots and leaves, carefully divided piles of dirt, spices, specific animal parts in jars, and small bottles of various liquids with pieces of paper or cardboard stoppers jammed in the tops to keep the jars from spilling, all to be used in traditional medicine treatments. I wanted to ask for "eye of newt," but I did not know the word.

Every month on the second Monday, a truck comes to Lochiel to distribute the government pensions. All South African citizens over the age of 60 are eligible, and to avoid making people go to town to cash checks, the government sends a truck full of cash and a computer. People line up, then each person goes to the truck and shows his or her identity document. They are given cash and checked off the list in the computer. When I lived in Lochiel, the pension was R440 per month (about $75).

The pension truck is followed by people who sell things in a kind of traveling pension-day carnival. Pension day is the only day when people in Lochiel have any money, and it serves everyone's interests to have the goods come to them. The older people who cannot walk very far would rather come out once a month to do all their shopping, and the sellers know that no one saves any money, so it will all get spent immediately.

I bought a grass mat and a Kaizer Chiefs stocking hat. The Chiefs are a Soweto soccer team that, along with the Orlando Pirates and the Mamelodi Sundowns, dominates the Castle Premiership Soccer League—plus conversations in every taxi rank and pool hall in black South Africa. I supported the Chiefs because Gogo told me I should. Everyone loved my hat, and now I knew what I could find every month on the second Monday.

MY LIFE SETTLED INTO A ROUTINE. WHEN I WOKE UP IN THE MORNING, I heated water in a kettle, bathed from a bucket, and put on clothes for school. I gathered my schoolbooks and my magazines to read, and I walked through the garden to the big house. Some mornings the reception door was still locked, so I walked around to the back. I passed through the square and saw Doris unlocking the doors and cleaning the floors in her store across the way. I passed the bottle store, finally locked from the night before, and Albert's room, which he had left hours ago to work in the forests. Sometimes I had to bang on the kitchen door to get Gogo or Boni to let me in, but they were always awake and most days they had been for hours.

In the kitchen I found Gogo making tea. Some mornings she was dressed up to go to town or to a meeting in Nhlazatje. Almost every week she had to go to Ermelo to do government paperwork or deal with the bank for the preschool. Every other Wednesday she had her Methodist women's group, and she dressed in her red coat and red dress with a white collar and white hat. But most mornings she wore a head scarf and her old pink flowered muumuu with the holes in it, and she had not yet put in her teeth.

"Yebo, Musa!"

"Yebo, Gogo. *Kunjani?*—How are you?"

"*Sengiphilile*, Musa—I've lived," she says.

We rarely spoke in English, unless I did not understand something important that she wanted to tell me. Her patience with my sometimes stumbling Siswati/Zulu was infinite. She would go on in Zulu. "Where are you going today? Masakhane?"

"Mlondozi, Gogo."

"How is that school, Musa? Is it better than ours at Lochiel? I am very angry with Ma'am. She doesn't work." Gogo was the chairperson of the School Governing Body and was constantly trying to improve her school. At Mlondozi and Masakhane, the principals ran the SGB, but Gogo often walked over to Lochiel Primary uninvited and unannounced to drop in on the principal. Her kitchen was the true seat of power.

Twana would walk in wearing her school uniform—a black dress and white shirt—and black shoes. Sometime she would stand in the doorway listening to us talk about her school and watching me cook my breakfast. Gogo would eventually yell at her: "What are you waiting for? Go to school!"

Twana would look pained, as though Gogo had unjustly accused her of a crime she did not commit, even when it was obvious that she had been dawdling. "I'm going," she would say in a quiet voice.

By that time Nombuso would be waking up and rubbing her eyes and scratching the still-unidentified-after-ten-months sores on her stomach and maybe crying a little. Some mornings in the winter she would already be placed in a red basin in the corner behind the stove, naked and bathing. She and Andiswa went to the preschool with the other children, who, if they arrived early, sat in the kitchen and waited for Joyce, their teacher, to come. Every morning a few children sat on the step just inside the door, wearing stocking caps and little sweaters that were purchased on a pension day many years ago and were often being worn by their fourth or fifth child.

I ate eggs and bread for breakfast almost every day and walked back out through the square to the road. I said good morning to Babe Chris and the others at the garage. If I was going to Lochiel Primary, I would cross the road, walk down a path through the tall dried grass, and jump the creek to get to school. If going to Masakhane or Mlondozi, I would wait at the road for a ride. The teachers coming from Nhlazatje would pick me up if I was waiting. Every once in a while a white person would stop to give me a ride and then try to figure me out during the 12-minute trip to my school. I am sure that some Afrikaners told their wives after their trip to Swaziland: "Honey, I gave a ride to this okie who worked out in the black schools near the border. Odd guy. He said he was American but that he actually lived out there in the *bundus*. Can you believe it?"

Every morning at school, the children lined up for assembly. They would sing and listen to announcements. Then I hunkered down in the trenches and got to work.

After school, I began to travel more. As I became comfortable with the area, it shrank in size. Trips that had once taken a full day began to be only a half day, as I was less afraid to stay in another town until five in the afternoon before trying to get back home. I went to eLukwatini and Nhlazatje more and more to see my teachers or my friend Bill, a fellow volunteer, and to e-mail. I bought Internet access in Nelspruit for 19 rand a month (less than $4) and found a phone to use with my laptop, a public phone in a tiny clapboard shack in Nhlazatje. A meter recorded the length of the call, and the attendant meter-watchers charged people accordingly. After I convinced them that I was not going to put any strange charges on their phone, they let me use it regularly, and I e-mailed almost twice a week.

Of course, every time I took my computer out of the bag, I had to explain what it was to everyone who was making a phone call that day.

"OK, this is a computer. It uses the phone to talk to a big computer in Nelspruit. That computer is connected to other computers and is sort of like a post office. My computer checks my 'box' and gets all my messages for me...." The process is pretty complex, and I did not have all the necessary words in my Siswati lexicon, but I stumbled through and, I hope, broadened a few horizons. By the end of my service, I did not have to explain because the meter-watching women in the phone shack did it for me. "Hawu! You don't know computers? I'll explain it to you...."

I enjoyed my routines in places like the phone shack and Two Gs, where I could teach people about American ways and could learn more about their language and the culture. At first I had the same conversations over and over. I became fluent first in conversations about computers, soccer, pool, and cars. I learned words and phrases constantly, but I remembered these snippets only if they fit into the conversations that I repeated every day. I added little bits each time until the conversations I could have were fairly substantial.

By far the most common of these went like this: I would say, "Hello, how are you?" And every person I spoke to would invariably ask, *"Ha! Ufundepi LesiZulu?"* or *"Uwazelani le siZulu?*—Where did you learn Zulu?" I had a routine that I used to respond. It grew gradually, and I added to my repertoire as time went on, but I recited basically the same phrases over and over, as though I were in a play and these were my lines. "You must be very smart," they would say. "Your mind catches and holds things very well."

"Why would you think that? Don't you speak English?" I would answer.

"Yebo, and Afrikaans."

"So, how many language do you speak? Four or five! I speak two, English and Zulu, and you say I am smart? No, you are the one who is smart!"

They would laugh and say I was "clev-ah," a word for smart but a little crafty, like I might try to pull a fast one.

I remember clearly the day I stopped consciously thinking about using Zulu. I had just taken a long walk to the top of the ridge at Lochiel and was enjoying being outdoors. The sun was setting behind the line of trees that made up the old homeland border. Lochiel's mountainside, dotted with the houses of my community, was lit with pink and gold. I saw a young woman I knew from the square, a friend of Piet and Shongwe and Vusi.

"Hello. How are you?"

"Fine, Musa. How are you?"

"Good. Where are you coming from?" I asked her.

"I am coming from the garage. I got some gas here"—she held up a jug—"for the generator so we can watch TV."

"Oh," I said. "Are you going to watch soccer tonight?"

"Yes, I love the Chiefs!"

"Me too, I'm sure they are going to win. I'll see you tomorrow."

"OK, Musa, bye-bye."

And we both walked on. It was an inconsequential, everyday conversation. But after a few steps I realized something: The last sentence she said was in English, but I could not remember which language we spoke before that. Even now, looking back on the conversation, I think we intermingled both languages.

MY EFFORTS IN TEACHING COMPUTER CONTINUED. SOME DAYS I TAUGHT lessons to Sandile and his friends, or the few teachers who lived in Lochiel. Sandile, Chris, Dumisane, and Doctor were my most loyal students. After they learned the basics of computer literacy, we made all kinds of documents. Eventually, I would just lend the laptop to Sandile so he could play games or teach others how to use it. He and his friends knew more about computers than any other high school students in the history of Lochiel.

Many afternoons, however, I spent alone in my room. School was draining, so I welcomed this downtime. I had no television, only two radio stations and books and magazines. Sometimes I read so much that my eyes stung. Papers and magazines piled up around me. Books covered every flat surface in the room. When people would come to visit me, without fail they would make comments about the number of books—and the fact that I needed someone to help clean my house.

Every evening I emerged from my privacy to sit in the kitchen while Gogo or Boni cooked dinner. We usually ate a large helping of pap, a thick porridge made from maize meal and water that had the taste and the stiff consistency of old grits—which is to say, very little taste and a paste-like texture. Still, I grew to like it. Because the family was relatively well-off, most of the time we would eat meat with our pap. Plus there was my Peace Corps salary. Some nights I bought the meat, but after Gogo had collected the rent at the beginning of the month, she often would buy enough meat to last for days. Gogo would boil it in a pot with a little water and then mix half a packet of dried soup into the juices to make a kind of gravy. On nights when there was no meat, we would eat pap and greens mixed with nuts, a dish they call *phidvo*. On other nights in the spring and summer when we had milk from Gogo's cows, we would eat milk or amasi with phuto, a dry, crumbly version of the regular stiff pap.

Many families in Lochiel ate only pap. Its purpose, like any staple food, is to fill up the stomach. On some nights at Gogo's house, we would have a football-size helping and a small slice of meat or a chicken leg. But we would never go hungry.

Gogo's favorite dish was sardines canned in hot sauce. She liked this meal because it took only 15 minutes to prepare. She'd pour the maize meal into the boiling water to make the pap, heat up the sardines, add some tomatoes and onions, and dish it out for six or seven people. We ate it so often that near the end of my service, Twana, the nine-year-old, rebelled. In defiance of all the South African cultural protocols I had learned, she told Gogo it was gross and that she didn't want to eat it anymore. I secretly thanked her.

People in Lochiel used every bit of what they had, and nothing illustrates this better than the way we ate chicken. Boni would buy a live chicken for twelve rand or less (two American dollars), wring its neck, boil it for a minute to loosen up the feathers, pluck it, cut it up, throwing away only the lungs and few other tiny internal organs, and then boil the opened chicken in a pot. The family ate the feet, head, heart, intestines, liver, several other organs, the breast, back, wings, neck, thighs, and legs. They generally gave me a thigh or the breast, but on occasion I ate other parts as well.

The first time I saw how efficiently they devoured a chicken, I could not believe it. They ate every single particle of meat, breaking up the pieces to get to the meat in the hard-to-reach places, such as between the chicken's tiny ribs. They ate the tendons, ligaments, and cartilage off the ends of the bones. And then they ate the bones themselves, crunching them up in their mouths, sucking the marrow, and putting the little bits of bone enamel back on their plates.

The first time I ate chicken, I had a leg. At the end of the meal, everyone else had only a small pile of wet white dust on their plates. I looked down at mine and saw a dumbbell with two enormous-looking tufts of skin and meat on each end. Eventually, I learned to eat more efficiently, though I could never eat the bones. I would give them to the kids when I finished.

In training, Zakhele had taught me a Swazi saying: *"Kudla ematambo wa incondo*—To eat the bones of the mind."* At the time I did not understand it fully, but after seeing chicken bones picked clean and crunched up by my family in Lochiel, I had no doubt what it meant—to make a thorough search of your thoughts, to think deeply.

Whatever we were eating, we always put out an extra plate for Mthembu, who lived out in the darkness.

After dinner, Boni and I would watch the news or another TV show or talk about the day. She never missed an episode of *Days of Our Lives*. It came on in the late afternoon, and after she helped out at the preschool, cleaned the house, did laundry, or helped at the fish and chips store, she would watch her soap. After dinner, we watched *Generations*, a South African soap opera about competing ad agencies and life in Johannesburg. *Generations* was by far the most popular television show in Greater eLukwatini.

Boni and I would sit in the living room, and she would laugh and tell stories about Nombuso's antics. Sometimes Nombuso or Twana or Andiswa would come in crying because one of the others had hit her. Then the other would run in behind saying, "But she poked me with a stick" or "She took my paper and crumpled it up" or " She broke all the pencils." Boni would scold them, just like any mother with kids, and they would go away to play again. Sometimes the girls would show me a picture that they had drawn, or Twana would show me the "good job" she got on her homework.

Gogo would usually sit with us and laugh, but some nights she would talk business. What was the plan for Lochiel Primary? What exactly was I trying to do? she wanted to know. How could I help her at the preschool. "Musa, what does this form mean? Do I have to go to town?"

More often than not, the answer was yes. Gogo had no car, no phone, and a very small operating budget. And she was constrained by the paperwork and bureaucrats in Ermelo. I saw the social workers in charge of preschool funding only once during the two years I spent at Lochiel. The rest of the time Gogo would have to go to town to see them. Often she would have to go two days in a row, because she would be told that the person who handled a particular section of the form, or a specific area of the regulations, was out of the office or busy. Or getting an answer to her question might require a return to Lochiel to get a form or piece of information that she had left at home.

I did not enter or even peek into Gogo's room until well into my second year at Lochiel. When I did, it looked eerily familiar. A rack of clothes stood in one corner. Stacks of papers—some teetering two feet high—countless folders, and three-ring binders covered every flat surface in her bedroom. The bed was piled high with papers and folders, reports and receipts. She lived alone in her room, struggling with the burden of liberating her community, one government form at a time. She stayed up, lucky to have an electric light late at night, with a calculator and a pencil trying to get the paperwork done.

EVERY DAY SHE WOULD SIT IN THE KITCHEN WHILE THE FOOD WAS cooking and talk about being sick of all the travel or about the pain in her foot or her back. But every morning she would get up, arrange the necessary paperwork for her project, and if she had to, go back to town. I can't say what kept Gogo going. She never explained to me or even gave a hint about why she did what she did. But she never hesitated, never expressed any thought that she might quit her work in her community. It was as though there were no other way for her to be. The most she ever said when she looked around the schoolyard, reminisced about the now overgrown garden project, or considered the enormous burden placed on rural preschool administrators, was "Akusi-right, Musa—It's just not right."

She never talked much about her feelings. At least, not to me. She sometimes preached on Sundays at church in the old reception area. And she led the singing and praying with such emotion that I would worry that her body couldn't take it. These moments were perhaps the most personal I ever saw of Gogo.

We would sometimes sit in the kitchen and she would tell stories about being a child, or a young woman. She spoke frankly, without exaggeration. Her stories were unadorned and to the point.

Gogo grew up in Carolina. The school she attended as a girl is still standing, she told me, on the edge of the township. She used to walk to school. "But, Musa, even now you can go to Carolina and see the places where the houses used to be. They were so close to school. Then, one day, the white people came and told everyone to move to the other side of the river because we were so close to town. They said we made too much noise." She paused. "So we moved. And we walked a very long way to school."

She also worked for a time sewing sweaters in a factory in Johannesburg. "You know what, Musa?" she asked me one day when talking about the worst part of living at the height of apartheid in Alexandra, a township outside Johannesburg. "There were men who traveled in the location, criminals, and if they did not like you, Musa, if they did not like you for one second, they would take your bucket from the latrine and they would turn it over into your living room or your kitchen." That was the sort of story left out of the books I read about South Africa.

Indeed, she would look at the books I carried and say, "Musa, you know, I don't need to read those books. I was there. What is your book saying now?"

I told her that the material I was currently reading was about the riots in Alexandra in the 1960s.

"Hawu, Musa. I was there," she said. "I still remember." She recalled riding on a bus coming home from her job in the sweater factory and seeing smoke rising from the township. Police were patrolling all around, and they would not let the bus enter the area. She sat in the bus with no food and no water for five hours. "Musa," she said. "I had worked all day, and I was so hungry and tired! I got really angry."

She almost never told stories about her time in Pretoria. Perhaps she simply found it uninteresting. She worked as a "domestic" for an elderly English-speaking couple, cooking and cleaning. She lived in their maid's quarters, but some weekends she had off and went to Alexandra to visit her friends.

The proudest she ever sounded was when she told me that in Lochiel she once cooked dinner for the entire Kangwane cabinet. "Right there at that table, Musa. Whoo! It was so nice. All of them were here, even the president. And they ate a nice meal, let me tell you."

"Is that your favorite memory?" I asked her.

"Hawu! Musa. No. Once, I rode in an airplane."

"To where?" I asked, shocked.

"From Nelspruit to Durban," she said. "Because a woman came from the UN to give me an award for my garden. In the sky it was just like sitting here. You can get up and walk around. Do you want to see the magazine with my picture in it?"

She went to get the picture, and sure enough, she was highlighted in a newsletter from an international environmental organization that had given her an award for her garden project in Lochiel. But then she became occupied with the preschool and stopped working on the garden. There was much to be done in Lochiel and it was perhaps impossible for a community-minded person like Gogo to forgo the next challenge.

BONI EVENTUALLY WARMED UP TO ME AS WELL. AS WE SAT IN FRONT of the fire in the old reception area one night, she said, "You know, Musa, I want to do something with myself. Always, I do things for other people. I went to Pretoria to help my brother-in-law prepare for his party, and then last week I went to Ermelo to help his wife with some things at their house there. And only because they promised me that they would buy some sweaters for the girls." Twana, Andiswa, and Nombuso were all her daughters. "Do you see any sweaters? No. What can I do? Everyone is suffering. We are all poor, but why haven't they bought me those sweaters?"

Tears welled up in her eyes. "I want to go to school. To do marketing. I have a friend who wants to start a travel agency, to tour people around South Africa. Then I will be able to buy sweaters for the kids myself."

She had no money for school and had no way to get any. "But the life that people live here in Lochiel is nothing," she said. "Look at the young women: They wake up, maybe ask someone for money to drink, cook twice, and maybe get some man to give you some money to get extensions in your hair. Then they say *siphilile* [We've lived]."

She wanted her children to go to good schools, not like the ones here in Lochiel. "The one I don't want to see fail is Nombuso," she said. "I look at her, I watch her, and I know that her mind is too clever. She is so funny and so happy that it would be terrible to see her go to school here. But where would I go? I can't leave Gogo here alone...."

Sitting in the kitchen, I watched Gogo and Boni raise the little girls. Andiswa, like many five-year-olds, often cried. At the first stern word from anyone in the family, she would raise her arm to cover her eyes and run to the other room to bury her face in the couch or in the bed she shared with her sisters. She drew pictures of horses and played with dolls. She walked barefoot around the house with a legless doll tucked into a blanket tied around her back, just as all the women in town carried their own babies.

Twana, the oldest at nine, had many chores and often took care of Nombuso. While Andiswa was walking with her dolls, Twana would struggle to keep Nombuso, the real baby, from slipping off her skinny nine-year-old hips. Twana also had homework every night, and Gogo made her sit at the dining room table until it was finished and Gogo had inspected it. The girls played together with the neighbors in the yard, and they found rats and snakes and spiders and collected birds' nests. They complained to me almost every day that they were bored.

I watched Nombuso sprout teeth, learn to walk and speak, and eat by herself. In the beginning, Gogo mashed pap in her bare hands and mixed it with a little gravy to make a suitable version of baby food. One night Nombuso watched me eat, confused by my fork. She reached out her hand, clutching for it. Gogo simply said, "Hey, Nombuso, you don't need that thing. Musa, he eats with a white man's fork. You eat with the one that God gave you."

SATURDAYS

CHAPTER TEN

SATURDAY, *UMGCIBELO,* IS THE DAY OF BURIAL. DEATH BECAME A PART of my life to a greater extent than I had ever experienced. In my two years in Lochiel, I went to more than 30 funerals. The first one occurred only three weeks after I arrived. I went to Masakhane School one morning, where the principal asked me to exchange the dates on my calendar with Mlondozi School because at Masakhane they were busy with the arrangements for the funerals of several children. I asked what had happened and he said we could go and see. As we got in his car, he told me he also wanted to drop off a letter at the chief's place to notify him about the deaths.

Just to the east of Masakhane, the road rises slightly to cross a low saddle in the hills. As we drove toward Swaziland, the principal pointed to a footpath 20 yards off the road to the right. "There, where those boys are walking right now," he said.

We stopped. A truck coming from Swaziland had blown a tire. From the skid marks, it seemed to have veered into the right lane, then swerved back to the left and off the road. It struck three little girls as they were walking home from kindergarten. This terrible tragedy, I would learn, was not so unusual when every day thousands of children walked along the side of the road to school.

As I stood there with the principal, three days after the accident, the tire that had exploded was still lying on the side of the road. A fender rested in the tall brown grass, and a very clear trail of tire tracks cut through the grass and across the footpath.

The bodies had been retrieved three hours after the accident, and the truck was picked up two days later. The funeral for one of the children was that weekend. The funeral for the others was to be "another day" because their parents did not live in Lochiel; one lived in Natal and the other lived between Piet Retief and Volksrust. Those children had lived with relatives near Masakhane. We passed their houses on the way to the chief's place, and the principal pointed them out.

At the chief's offices, the secretary of the Tribal Authority, Godfrey Mayisela, and the principal discussed the accident. The principal spoke Siswati too rapidly for me to understand, but from his hand gestures I could tell he was describing the bodies. Apparently, one was almost severed at the waist. After we left, the principal insisted that I attend the funeral.

It was held on Saturday at the little girl's home. The house was off the main road, and when we drove up in one of the teacher's cars, we followed the tracks in the grass on the side of the road, which had been left by the cars that had preceded us.

The service was long. Representatives from the school, the Department of Education, and the local government each gave speeches in Zulu. I understood almost none of what they said. We then went from the house to the graveyard. A few men put a tiny white coffin into a grave. A minister said some prayers, and then all the men from the community formed a line to shovel dirt, two at a time, to fill the hole. Each person got about three shovelfuls, threw them in the hole, and then laid the shovel on the ground for the next one.

I was nervous, but I stood in line, took the shovel, and cast three shovelfuls of dirt into the hole. Afterward, I was shaking. I had never mourned a death that way, and I was terrified I would do something wrong.

I slinked to the back, weaving my way around other graves. All around me, people were standing on top of the grave mounds to get a better view over the heads in the crowd. They all seemed to be from out of town. Once the hole was filled in, the men from the community formed a new line and handed stones from one person to the next along the line until they were laid on top of the grave. Eventually, the grave was completely covered with rocks. Throughout this ritual the women sang in support of the men.

Afterward, we all went back to the family's house to eat. Once the meal was over, the girl's father came up and thanked me for coming. His eyes were tired, and he held his hat crumpled in his hand. I was the first white person they'd ever had in their house, he said.

Only a few of the people from the community had ever seen me before, and they didn't know what to make of me. Some thought I was the owner of the truck. Others, apparently more sophisticated, thought I was a representative of the company. The teachers who knew me straightened that out with a chuckle. There was no one from the trucking company at the funeral.

A FEW WEEKS LATER, ONE OF THE BORDER GUARDS I HAD KNOWN FROM the square at Lochiel died in a car accident in Johannesburg. Some of my friends from Lochiel and I went to his house near the border, and the community conducted the funeral in the same fashion. All the men lined up, shoveled dirt onto our friend's coffin, and passed the shovel to the next man. The women sang. The men lined up and passed rocks to cover the grave. We went back to the family's house, washed the dirt from our hands in a small bucket, and ate. On the way back to Lochiel after the funeral meal, I rode in Shongwe's light-blue pickup truck with Piet, Vusi, Bongani, and 12 other people. Being among them made me feel like a part of the community.

Two weeks later, I went to Piet Retief with several other volunteers. When I came back on Sunday, I found out that Shongwe's truck had turned over with 15 people aboard, injuring many of them. I saw friends with bandages, cuts, bruises, one broken hand, and a broken foot.

Vusi, who wore the Fox Chapel High School shirt and who was loved by all the girls, had died. Sandile went with other high school boys to recover the car from the ditch on Tuesday morning. They lifted it with chains and ropes and towed it back up to Shongwe's garage. Later that day, I went over there and sat with Shongwe, Bongani, Piet, and the rest of the guys, some of them wearing bandages and slings.

Vusi had been sitting in the passenger seat, and I saw the crushed-in space in the totaled truck, parked outside. Some of his friends sat on the bed of the truck, some leaning against it, in total silence. Others came to sit, and people left when they wanted, sometimes shaking hands with Shongwe or Bongani or me, but no one said a word.

From then on, I attended funerals about once a month, and learned more about the rituals each time. Many died of sicknesses and a lack of health care, in addition to car accidents. And many died of AIDS-related illnesses—South Africa has one of the highest rates in the world—but no one in the community talked about the disease.

Initially, I went to funerals simply because everyone went. But the first time I attended a funeral in Lochiel proper, I learned exactly what funerals mean to the community. I arrived late at the graveyard, back behind the soccer field in Lochiel. The funeral was being held for an old man, a friend's grandfather. I knew every face I saw, and they knew me. I shoveled and passed rocks. In Zulu, they say "*Ngasebenza*— I worked."

I caught up with Mtunzi as we crossed the square on the way back to the family's house. At the gate, he bent to wash his hands in a small red bucket full of dirty water. I hesitated, noting that every person in Lochiel had just "washed" their hands in the same bucket. There was no telling what was living in the brown water. "You must wash your hands, Musa," Mtunzi said as he shook the water from his own.

I ignored my reservations and dipped my hands. "Now," Mtunzi said. "We have conquered the death."

"Why do we wash our hands?"

"Because, Musa, we don't want to take the death back to our own homes. The community comes together to conquer the death. Then we all go to the family's home for a meal, because all of us are still here. Let's go eat."

A few months later, Herbert Zwane, a teacher at Lochiel I knew well, drank so much at the Lochiel bottle store that people said he needed help getting home. As darkness approached, someone put him out of a taxi at his house. He found that the car he had just purchased had been delivered, and he decided to take it for a spin. One of his sons and a few of his brother-in-law's children, all in primary school at Lochiel, went with him.

Mr. Zwane's son survived the accident. He later told the police that they were driving when a car swerved into their lane. His father dodged it. Then another car swerved into their lane, and his father dodged again. A third car entered their lane, and finally, an 18-wheel truck coming from Swaziland, but Mr. Zwane could not swerve in time. No one was wearing a seat belt, and two of the children died.

Mtunzi told me the story about the boy talking to the police. "Musa," he said, "do you think that those cars really came into his lane? No, they did not. He was so drunk, Musa. It is terrible." Mtunzi also told me that one of the children died because she crawled down on the floor of the car in fear; her neck was broken under the front seat when the car collided with the truck.

Mr. Zwane also survived, but he was still hospitalized when the other teachers and I went to the funeral of the little girl at her father's house in Mayflower. The father said that he was going to kill Herbert, but nothing ever came of it. Mr. Zwane had three major surgeries to repair a broken leg, a collapsed lung, and serious damage to several other internal organs. I saw him back at school almost four weeks after the accident. He walked with a cane, and his face was badly scarred. Days after I saw him, he died of an infection resulting from the surgeries.

School was suspended for three days while the teachers prepared for the funeral. Because he was a member of the teaching fraternity, his death had to be treated with extreme respect. I made programs on Masakhane's computer to be used at the Thursday memorial service in eLukwatini. An obituary, cataloging Mr. Zwane's academic achievements, degrees, and honors, was read, and two speeches were given in remembrance. We pasted a picture of him in his academic attire—cap and gown—to the front of the program and the announcement was made that he would be buried in this scholarly garb. On Friday, three teachers and I (the only ones with passports) hooked a small trailer to Nhlanhla's truck and drove to Swaziland to buy food for the funeral. We bought pounds of beets, carrots, mayonnaise, maize meal, meat, potatoes, and pumpkins. We delivered the food in the misting rain. After the car slid and slithered on the muddy track that led back to the Zwanes' house, Nhlanhla and I left, and the female teachers stayed the night to prepare the food. Huge iron pots lent by someone in the community were set outside the mud walls of the homestead, waiting to be filled with boiling meat and vegetables.

Because Mr. Zwane was a member of Gogo's church congregation, Gogo and others from the church held an all-night vigil at the home. The next morning I met her at 7:00, the time Ma'am told me was appropriate. The fog was so heavy, I walked past the house two times. I could not see ten feet and would have been lost had I not heard the singing. I listened and followed my ears through the mist to the Zwanes' wooden fence. A few other teachers stood in the muddy yard. Ma'am Ndlovu arrived and insisted I accompany her inside.

The interior mud walls were crumbling around the wooden doorframe, and the thin sheets of vinyl flooring printed with pictures of yellow tiles were streaked with mud from the visitors coming to pay their respects. Ma'am Ndlovu went in to sit with the family, the minister, and the body, and I stayed behind in the tiny front room. Gradually more and more people came to stand with me, including a friend who was an assistant minister. Gogo came out of the room with other women who had held the vigil, and she stood next to me. People came from outside, and the room began to get very crowded. I was almost completely locked in my place; there was no room to move. Twenty more people arrived, until we must have had 70 people in the tiny mud room. Adding to my claustrophobia, only a foot or so separated my head from the corrugated iron roof.

I started to sweat. Ma'am Ndlovu and the last of the visitors came out of the room with the body, leaving only the family and the minister inside. All of our bodies were pressed together even more tightly. I was nervous that the mud walls would crack and collapse. Through the door, I heard the minister's booming voice begin to pray, and a few women in the family room screamed and cried. In our room, packed with people, we began to sing. I had been to a number of funerals, and by now I knew some of the words.

We sang louder and louder, and the crowd began to sway. I was lifted off the ground at times. The room was soon pulsating. The voice of the assistant minister, whose name was Mandla   power—rose above ours and led the group. "We are all together and we will walk in heaven as one." The roof of the house began to vibrate. We were a mass of living flesh packed into a room, singing with all our might, filling the room with life. In the other room, the family struggled with the death.

We sang for some time, pressed up against each other and dancing. The door opened, and we crowded together even more. Some people spilled out into the yard, creating a pathway. The minister and four pall-bearers emerged, followed by the women in Mr. Zwane's family. They were ready to proceed with the funeral.

Outside, in a cold rain, the crowd had grown, and we followed the casket out into the yard. The minister said a prayer, one of the teachers made a brief comment about Mr. Zwane, and we left for the graveyard. We drove, 15 people to a car, to eLukwatini, where Mr. Zwane's body was buried in his academic attire near the Teachers' Center, between two other teachers. I shoveled dirt and passed rocks to complete the burial. We returned to the house, washed our hands, and ate a meal with the grieving family. I went home exhausted.

CHOOSING SIDES

CHAPTER ELEVEN

MOST PEACE CORPS VOLUNTEERS HAVE TO LEARN TO LIVE IN THE Third World, removed from the comforts of home. Rivers carry their food from farms upstream. People make six-day treks to town or for medical help. My great-grandmother, Lillian Carter, served in India in the 1970s. She wrote letters home about peanut butter and cheese. When she got care packages of food, she rejoiced. But South Africa is very different.

Separating me from First World comforts—a quarter-pounder with cheese, or a burrito, or a Subway six-inch turkey sub—was only a ride into town. I could flag down a car at the border post and get a ride all the way to Jo-burg and see *The Matrix* on a big screen with THX digital surround sound. Contrast defines the world in South Africa.

Even the weather is a study in extremes. In the winter the highveld is freezing cold, with no rain for five months. In the summer, it is blazing hot with monsoons. Many days, on the radio news, there would be warnings of drought and brush fires in the Western Cape, followed by a story about massive flooding near Kruger National Park that left schoolteachers picking books out of the trees.

The contrast between sun and shade is intense. If you walk from the shade into the sun, the rays attack with an almost physical pressure. I sometimes shivered inside the classrooms and then burned while I stood in the schoolyard trying to warm up. I could stand under a tree in the garden and feel individual rays of sun on my hand.

On the highway, white BMWs zoomed past women carrying firewood or water on their heads. Riding in a taxi along the 60 miles between Ermelo and Lochiel, I would pass 10 farms supporting 30 families. Then, past the border of the old homeland, thousands of families could be seen lining the road. Power lines and phone lines carrying information and electricity to Swaziland ran right over the top of Lochiel without stopping. Those lines belonged to a different South Africa.

In TV, a community between Lochiel and Masakhane School, a tall red-and-white metal tower rises from a peak hundreds of feet above the road. Two white transmitter disks point north and west. When the tower was built, the community was given a new name. The people who lived in TV thought that signals shot out from the towers to the televisions some of them had at home (usually powered by car batteries). But the tower did not provide service to any of the community's televisions. I once got a ride from the white man who maintained the tower. He said it was used to link a home base in Johannesburg to transmitters implanted by his company into cars to track them in case they were stolen. TV should have been called "car locator."

I remember riding from the border gate to Lochiel with a man in a Mercedes on his way to Johannesburg who told me about his country. "Oh, you're from America. Well, let me tell you, you must be careful around these blacks. Look at how these people live. It's the Stone Age." Pointing around, he went on, "I'll tell you what, if we took a bunch of our blacks and put them in the middle of the U.S.A., you guys would be pulling your hair out as well. We gave them books and they burned them. We gave them schools and they vandalized them. I saw on the news how some schools spend more money on repairs than on teaching supplies. Can you believe it?"

"Yes, sir. I work in these schools in this area."

"Here? God, you must be brave. Can you really teach them anything? Because I have found it impossible to get through to them."

Sometimes the racial divide bordered on the ludicrous. One day I was standing in Doris's store, playing a video game. The store had leased two games from a man in Ermelo, and barefoot kids in threadbare school uniforms would pack in to watch their friends play Ms. Pac-Man or Street Fighter. For 50 South African cents at least 10 people got to watch a game. Many kids went without lunch just so they could play. I was pretty good at Ms. Pac-Man, and I always drew a big crowd. The other kids were always trying to beat my score.

That day I had just finished playing and was going to my room when I realized I had forgotten to get the item I originally went to the store to buy. As I turned to go back in, someone ran up and grabbed my arm.

"Thank God! Thank God! Can you please help me?"

A short, middle-aged white woman, wearing corduroy jeans and a sweater, was clutching my arm so hard I thought she was going to tear my sleeve. "Ma'am, what's wrong?"

"My gosh," she gasped, out of breath. "I am so glad to have found you. Do you know these people? Do you have a car?"

"No, I don't have a car, but what's wrong?"

"My car is out of gas," she said.

"There is a gas station right there," I said, pointing. "Where is your car?"

"Do they have gas there?"

I walked with her over to the gas station. She told me she was an artist, moving from Johannesburg to Swaziland, and had all of her belongings packed into her car, across the road from the gas station. I made a point to speak to Babe Chris in English. "Do you have a gas can? This woman has run out of gas."

"Yes, Musa. I will go and get it."

I promised him ten rand, and Chris poured some gas in a jug. The woman and I walked to her car, a brown Toyota piled to the top with boxes and bags. As I was pouring gas into her tank, using a piece of cardboard for a funnel, Nhlanhla pulled up with Vincent, a teacher from the high school, on their way to play soccer with some of the other teachers. I did not see them until the woman tapped me nervously. "Someone's coming."

"Heita!" I said in greeting.

"*Ini leyinkinga la?*" Nhlanhla asked, and we spoke for a minute in Zulu.

"Oh, she just ran out of gas," I said.

"You need to turn the car around," he said, "so that the gas goes to the engine. If the road is going up, the gas will never get there."

"OK," I replied, without translating for the woman.

Vincent went to get in the driver's seat so Nhlanhla and I could push the car around. "What are you doing?" the woman screamed.

"Oh, I'm sorry," I said. "These are my friends, Vincent and Nhlanhla. We need to turn the car around so that the engine is downhill from the gas tank."

She was reluctant and tried to start the car herself several times before she agreed to let us do it. We pushed it around to the other side of the road, and Nhlanhla rolled it 20 feet down the hill; he popped the clutch and the car started. The woman thanked me directly, got in her car, and left.

"She didn't like me," Nhlanhla said, speaking English for the first time since he arrived.

"She just doesn't know you," I said, smiling, and he laughed.

Once, coming back from Mlondozi School in the teachers' koombi, the valley of Nhlazatje opened up before us as we rounded the mountain. At the bottom of the hill, the road turns to the left and a large grassy bank rises on the right side. At that bank we saw a truck, overturned, and the blue Venture that Sam Malaza used to carry the Sisukumile teachers to and from school. A huge pile of something pale tan was strewn on the ground. The grass has turned to ash, I thought. "What is that?" I asked. "Is it people?"

We approached slowly, nervous about the possible carnage. As we pulled up behind Sam's car, we saw the teachers from Sisukumile, all of whom I knew well, standing in the pile picking up pieces and inspecting them. "What is that?" I said again, alarmed.

"Izinkhukhu," one of the teachers said, smiling. "Chickens." The koombi stopped. Sam was standing near his Venture with the back open, piling in box after box of chicken. There must have been 10,000 chickens, divided and wrapped, ready for supermarket shelves, in packages that said "Braai Pack," "Mixed Portions," "Legs and Thighs," "Wings," and "Whole Chicken." The boxes had mostly been destroyed, but the plastic wrappings were intact.

I saw Vincent standing in a pile of Mixed Portion bags. "Hey, Musa!" he said. *"Bheka lezinkhukhu!*—Look at these chickens!" He switched to English: "It's unbelievable, don't you think?"

Vincent followed my eyes to the red truck cab and the driver sitting up, hunched over and bleeding. The trailer had apparently been disconnected because it was 20 yards or so behind the cab, which was jammed into the grassy bank. "Is he alive?" I asked in Zulu.

"Yes. He is very lucky. We saw the whole thing from the top. He was running so fast and he couldn't make this turn," Vincent said in Zulu, motioning with his hand. He switched to English: "We called the police and the hospital. The ambulance is coming. I think he is OK."

I agreed with Vincent's assessment. "He's lucky."

"Let's go get some chicken," Vincent said. "Sam is loading up his car."

By this time Sam's Venture was almost completely full. A silver BMW pulled up, and two white men got out, grabbed two cardboard boxes of chicken, put them in their trunk, and sped off. In the distance, the police and the ambulance were approaching from Nhlazatje. The other koombi of teachers from the schools near the border pulled up behind ours, and they stormed the pile, too, picking chickens and packages of parts. Only I hesitated. "Musa, what's wrong?" someone yelled.

"Ah, these chickens aren't ours." I said, unsure what to do.

"Musa, this is food. If we don't take it, it's going to spoil or be eaten by the dogs. Take some home to Gogo."

The ambulance arrived, and they treated the driver. The police also arrived. They said nothing about the teachers grabbing the chicken. "Heita, Musa!"

"Heita!" I replied to one of the cops I knew from eLukwatini, and I started to relax. I did want to pick up some chicken for Gogo. I picked up a braai pack, a bag with several big pieces of meat—no wings and no internal organs.

Then a family of white tourists pulled up and stopped. The father got out to see what was happening, telling the rest of his family to stay in the car. The father reached into the car, fumbled around, and pulled out a video camera.

Through the viewfinder he must have witnessed quite a scene. Thirty-five well-dressed black people running back and forth, filling their cars and koombis with chicken piled on the ground. The police standing by the wrecked truck chatted, and the paramedics worked on the driver on the ground.

I was paralyzed. Was he planning to show the video to his friends and talk about how barbaric these blacks were?

The man yelled over to the police, "They're stealing! Can't you see they're stealing? Can't you do something?"

He then yelled to everyone, "These are not your chickens! You're stealing!"

I laid down the braai pack.

The police began to shoo us back to our respective transports. Vincent, still holding a few chickens, explained that they could not leave because Sam had filled his truck to the top with chicken and had left. He would be right back to collect the teachers.

I climbed back into the koombi and sat down between bags of chicken, with my feet up on two boxes, and we drove off. "Musa, hawu! Why didn't you get any chicken?"

I could not answer. I had no real reason for not taking the chicken, and I could see the point of both sides. When the man had yelled, I had for some reason used his comments as my moral compass.

As we pulled away, the tourists continued to record the scene, and Sam's blue Venture appeared, relieved of its chicken burden, to pick up the teachers.

The news spread fast. On my way home a few hours later, pickups full of people holding chicken parts, screaming and honking their horns stretched in a line from the accident site to the crossroads where I was hitching. At home, Gogo and Boni were excited. "Musa, how much chicken did you get?"

"None," I said, ashamed.

"Gogo," I wanted to say. "I was intimidated by these white people with a video camera. I didn't want them to think I was a criminal."

Gogo was excited about the prospect of free chicken, and I was disappointed to have let her down.

A few weeks later, after getting used to chicken lunches at school, I had a chance to redeem myself. Sitting in my room one day with a book, I heard a commotion. I walked outside and found Chiluga trying to hide in the bushes. "Chiluga, what are you doing?"

"Hey, Jason, there is a white man here who wants me. I have to make sure he doesn't find me. He wants to take my car!"

"Why?" I asked.

"Because I was owing him and the court settled, but he still wants money. My attorneys are dealing with it."

That sounded like a reasonable excuse, so I said, "I'll tell him to go away if you want me to."

"Hey, thank you."

I left to go and talk to the man. As I walked across the garden, Piet and Shongwe looked at me, waiting to see what I would do. I passed more and more people; I was sure that all of them had seen Chiluga in the last few moments, because he had obviously walked past. But no one had said a word to the man.

I found him standing at the door to the bottle store. He was skinny and wore white jeans and a paper-thin, striped, short-sleeve shirt with buttons down the front. He was smoking a cigarette with one hand and holding the pack and his car keys in the other. The women in the store behind him smiled at me. They were in on the secret, too.

"Hello, my name is Jason Carter. I am from the United States. I stay here and work in the schools in the area. I heard that you were looking for Mr. Mthethwa."

"Yes," he answered.

"If you have a message for him, I can give it to him at school tomorrow."

"No," he said. "I need to speak to him personally."

"He told me yesterday that today he would be going to town...."

"But his car is still here," he interrupted. "I see it standing there by my bakkie."

"Well," I said, thinking quickly, "sometimes he drives another car, a red 323 hatchback with a Kaizer Chiefs sun protector in the back window. And often his brother or his cousin is driving that car."

"I'll just wait here at the bottle store," he said, pulling hard on his cigarette. "I know he'll be here sooner or later."

"OK," I said. "My name is Jason Carter again."

"I'm John Williams."

We said good-bye and I left. As I walked back around the corner through the garden and saw how many people were sitting in the square and in the garden, it occurred to me that there was no way Chiluga had spoken to them all. It was just accepted: If a white man comes looking for someone, you say you don't know where that person is.

As I approached Piet and Shongwe, a boy came up and said that the man was getting in his car. Soon Chiluga came out. "Now, Chiluga," I said, "be careful. I told him I would be seeing you tomorrow at school, so he may show up there."

"Oh, that's no problem," Chiluga said. "He was there today and yesterday. I just tell my brother-in-law to say I'm not there, and I stay in the staff room. He leaves immediately."

Two days later I was on my way to Nhlazatje, hitching at the crossroads, when a white pickup truck stopped. I climbed in and found John Williams, smoking a cigarette. He was going to Barberton, and I asked to be dropped off at the road to Nhlazatje.

"Have you seen that Mr. Mthethwa?" he asked. "He is a rogue! I'll tell you what: He must never work because I have been at his school every day for five days and he is never there!"

"Often," I said, disguising my smile, "they send teachers on errands and other assignments during the day. Why are you looking for him?" I was starting to think the matter must be serious to require his driving from Barberton every day. Had Chiluga done something really bad?

It turned out that the man, who worked for the Barberton Sheriff's Department, had sold a car to Chiluga, but Chiluga still owed him about a hundred dollars. The man had easily spent more than that in gas and driving costs going back and forth to Barberton. But the principle kept him going: If someone owes you money, they should have to pay. White people, he thought, too often are intimidated by blacks. People who disappear into those communities think they can do whatever they want. He was not going to let that happen to him.

Sitting in his car, I felt sorry for him. It is wrong to run from your debts, and the divide between the communities should not serve to undermine normal transactions. But I was ambivalent about the situation and again struck by South Africa's impervious borders.

THE LAW
CHAPTER TWELVE

ON BOTH SIDES OF SOUTH AFRICA'S BORDERS, CRIME DOMINATES conversations. Every night, television programs cover crime as the leading national or local issue. White people live in constant fear, and black people travel under perpetual suspicion, even though they are much more likely to be victims. Arguably, the worst violent crime in South Africa occurs in the Coloured communities surrounding Cape Town.

In Lochiel, as in much of black South Africa, the law lost much of its legitimacy during apartheid, when black leaders were sent to prison for standing up for their rights. Mandela, Biko, Sobukwe, Sisulu—all of them broke the law. The only regulatory sign I saw in Lochiel dated from the apartheid era and hung above the entrance to the hotel. Referencing a 1978 statute, it indicated that Mr. Ndzukulu was licensed to sell alchoholic beverages, but only to black people.

The police system under apartheid was organized not to fight crime, but to preserve the system. A Coloured taxi driver in Nelspruit once explained this to me in terms of the "rising crime" issue. I was with

another volunteer, speaking English, and when the driver learned that
we were from America, he began speaking in English as well. "How do
you like our country?"

"I think it's great," I answered.

"What do Americans think about South Africa?"

"Most of them," I answered honestly, "have only heard about crime
and AIDS and other problems. But I love it here and have never had a
problem at all."

"I'll tell you something about crime," he said. "We have always had
crime. I live in the Coloured location, and it is just the same now as it
was during those days. But now they come and *see* the crime. During
apartheid," he said with a crisp Afrikaans accent, "if I called the police
this time on Friday night and told them someone had broken into my
house, they would come on Sunday or Monday and take a report. If I
told them the guy next door was making pamphlets for the ANC, they
would come with a whole division with dogs and everything in 15 minutes. Now, they say crime is going up, and it is—in white parts of town.
Remember, there was a freaking curfew for 20 years saying that people
couldn't be on the streets in the white part of town at night. They
removed the curfew, people have a little more freedom, but they are still
poor. What did they expect?"

After apartheid, the authorities needed to regain the respect among
the black population that had been lost during the years when police
roamed the homelands and townships brutally enforcing racist laws.
Living in Lochiel, however, it seemed that police from outside the
community were changing very slowly, if at all.

When I came home one evening, Boni and Gogo were sitting at the
kitchen table looking distraught.

"What's going on?" I asked, setting my books down.

"Musa, it's bad," Gogo said, looking up from her clasped hands.
"Today, two white police came to get Albert. They said he should go

back to Mozambique. Musa, they took him and they hit him and hit him. They hit him up against the wall and he fell down."

I thought about the letter he wrote to his girlfriend. I recalled his soccer posters and his unrelenting desire to learn English. He had shown me a picture of his sister and niece in Xai-Xai, a town just north of Maputo. He had been obsessed with cowboys, and just days before, he had asked to borrow my cowboy boots.

After I let him, he polished them for a few hours and then wore them around the square for days, proud as can be. Now, apparently, he was sitting in jail ready to be deported, wearing the boots I had given him because I had felt guilty about not teaching him enough English.

I heard Nombuso start to cry in the living room. She had had a nightmare about the police coming for her.

"Did she see it?" I asked Gogo.

"Hawu! Musa, all of us were there watching. There were so many of us. Maybe 20."

Albert's door was locked when I went outside to look. Across the tiny corridor between the kitchen and the courtyard there was a splattering of blood where his face must have hit the concrete wall. With everyone watching (including two-year-old Nombuso), two white policemen had demonstrated the brutality of the past without shame.

Later, I was sitting in a taxi coming back from the border post with Piet's younger brother, Patrick, who was home from Johannesburg. We had not met before, and we talked for the entire ride. As we passed Litje Lembube, a secondary school closer to the border, he pointed at the trees that stood 30 feet high in a perfect row. He laughed. "I planted those trees," he said.

"When?"

"In school. Whoo! It was so hot. I was working and sweating so hard. I was so mad. The principal forced me to do it for punishment. They were very small trees, but there were so many, it took all day."

"Why did he force you to do it?"

"I was playing dice during school," he said, laughing again.

"Still," I said, "that is a pretty good punishment."

"Yes," he answered. "I never played dice in school again, and I can look at my school and see that I have done something. And the trees make me remember how hot and mad I was." He smiled, looking out the window, then became serious. "Jail is not like that."

Startled, I said, "Tell me about jail."

He had been arrested for "pointing a firearm"—one of those phrases that sneaks, entirely in English, into the Zulu telling of a story: *"Bangibopisa ngabo four ebsuku...Ba ngi tjaja na* pointing a firearm."

Another man had reported to the police that Patrick wanted to shoot him. They arrested Patrick in Tembisa, and he sat for four months in prison before having a hearing. When the witness did not show up, Patrick was told that the person never filed a complaint, and all the charges were dropped.

Sitting in a communal cell for four months had been difficult. "The food, Musa, was very bad. I could not even eat it." He said he lost several kilos, and his skinny frame did not have much to spare.

But, he said, it was a learning experience. He met people and heard about things he had never known. "It is all cock, Musa. If you have money, you never go to jail. I know that I could go to some police in Tembisa and buy a murder docket for 5,000 rand. They would give me the files and say, 'Here. Burn it.' And there are people who would pay me more than 5,000 rand to kill someone. I know some people who came in and out of that jail just in that way. Armed robbery is only 3,000. It's crazy. The police don't care." He paused. "And then they arrest *me* for four months." He held up four fingers and shook his head. "It's not right."

"No," I agreed. "It's not."

I asked him about people he had met. "Did you meet any murderers?"

He described one killing in detail, the type of crime that keeps white South Africa awake at night listening to every sound in their yard. Two teenagers broke into a white man's house, raped his wife and daughter, drank all their liquor, then killed him and his family and drove around all night in the family's car.

"How did you know they did this?"

"Hawu! I lived with them for some weeks. They told me all about it," Patrick said. "But you know what, Musa. I don't understand it.

"I know why you would want to break into the liquor cabinet and why you take the car out and drive it around. But rape? I don't understand it. In the township, you can get a girl for five rand. I just don't understand those boys."

VIOLENT CRIMES COMMITTED AGAINST WHITE PEOPLE WERE FAIRLY rare, but I came across several crimes of a more pedestrian variety.

Soon after my arrival in Lochiel, I went with a teacher to buy new tires for his car. We drove to the top of the ridge and pulled up in front of a house. Several children were playing barefoot in the dirt yard, one pushing a small car made from scraps of wire with crushed cans serving as the wheels. Behind the house the mountains dropped steeply into the valley, and one could see for miles. As we stayed in the car, the teacher told a little girl to go get her brother. She went through the door into the mud house, and a young man emerged. We all greeted each other. "I heard you had some tires...," said the teacher.

"Yes," the teenager said, and went to get them.

He soon returned with two tires, and the teacher got out to inspect them. Nubs of rubber stuck out from the tread, proving that they had never been used. "It would cost 600 rand for one of these in Ermelo," the seller said.

"How much do you want?" the teacher asked.

"Two hundred," said the boy.

"But," the teacher responded, "I would have to go buy two more in town if I want to put these on my car."

The boy looked down and shifted his feet nervously. "I think we can get one more," he said.

"OK," said the teacher. "I'll come back on Wednesday and buy them. Three for 300?"

The boy agreed, and we left. "Did you see those? Those are great tires," the teacher said. He dropped me off at home and set off to check out the full retail price for the single new tire.

That 300 rand would pay for the family's food and clothes. Perhaps it would replace a broken window pane. The teacher was a good teacher, one of the few who spent his own money on school supplies, in addition to supporting his wife, children, grandparents, parents, and a few siblings. He now had saved some money on tires. He was not a criminal, just someone willing to benefit from the thriving black market.

Another instance occurred right in my own family. One day Boni bounded into the kitchen, ecstatic. "Musa! I am going to start a business!"

"Oh?" I said. "What are you going to do?"

"I am going to go down to the border post and sell fried fish and chips and fat cakes."

"That is great!" I said. "There is no one down there selling those things, and there are so many truckers that they will buy a lot. Why did you decide to do it now?"

"Lindiwe's mother is going to give me her deep fryer, and Gogo is going to loan me money for potatoes and fish."

That struck an odd note. "She is giving you her fryer?"

"Yes. She got a new one."

"Is she making so much money that she bought a new one?"

"Hawu, Musa! All the money she makes goes to clothes and food. She does not live with any old person. They don't get a pension with the grandmothers."

"So where did she get the new one?"

"Her brother-in-law worked for a restaurant in Johannesburg. The white man closed the business and was going to sell all the things. He is moving overseas. So her brother-in-law got one of the fryers. It's big. With two places for cooking."

"He just stole it?"

"Yes, but, Musa," she said, smiling at my concern, "that white man didn't need it. He is moving to America. I told you, Musa: Now I can have a business of my own, and make money for the girls."

Boni deserved the chance to own a business and she would work hard. And where else could she have found the money to start an independent life for herself and her three girls? Still, her attitude required a certain disrespect for the law and was justified in her mind because they were only stealing from their oppressors.

Many people close to me benefited from crime. The taxi fares were cheaper because the taxi owners disguised the mileage on their vehicles by disconnecting the odometer. I don't know if any person in Lochiel paid income tax, or sales tax, or if any of the businesses declared their profits. Yet when my house was broken into and all of my things were stolen, I found out how the community members band together to protect their own.

I stepped out of a taxi at the crossing before Lochiel that day, and walked the familiar half mile to the garage. I said hello to Chris and the women selling fruit. One of the women told me that Gogo needed to see me immediately, but the woman was using words I had never heard and I could not decipher the reason for the urgency. Nonetheless, I went straight to the kitchen.

Gogo told me that someone had broken down my door and stolen everything.

"Everything?" I asked, incredulous.

"Almost," she said.

I ran around to look. "Somehow," I kept telling myself, "this will work itself out."

The wood around the door handle and lock had been splintered apart from the door. Inside, some of my clothes had been flung on the floor along with scattered papers. Several books had been stolen—my computer, all of my shoes, most of my shirts and jackets and pants and sweaters, all of the American cash that I kept in my small cabinet, my CDs and CD player. I looked around. Usually, there was a tangle of cords approaching the little old electrical outlet. All of the cords for the computer and CD player were gone. The person had also stolen the mouse pad, so he must have known, at least, that all these things went with the computer. And he had known to open my cabinet to get at the cash.

Gogo felt terrible. She apologized a hundred times and almost broke down crying. If the perpetrators had made it to Swaziland, my things would be gone for good.

I recruited people to help me. Shongwe, Piet, Bongani, Chiluga, Mtunzi, and Sandile all felt terrible and embarrassed. They apologized again and again.

This was Sunday evening. On Monday morning, I went to school— in the old jeans and running shoes I had worn the day before. My lack of proper attire caused almost as much trauma among my teachers as the fact that my home had been broken into. I guess the clothes really drove the point home. Mrs. Ndlovu and two other teachers accompanied me to the police station to file a report. This police station was manned by people I knew, black people from the community.

I filled out a report. I listed the things I could remember and indicated my estimate of their value. Because I had purchased virtually everything in the United States, the cost in rand was huge. I was embarrassed to reveal to my friends at the police station how valuable my things were. The officer taking the report did not say anything to me directly, but I saw his eyes grow wide when he read over the list.

After school, I went to Nhlazatje to call the Peace Corps and to talk to the circuit manager. That evening, I found Gogo in the kitchen. "We found it," she said.

"Where?"

"Ben was at Doctor's house and saw your alarm clock. He asked if it was yours, and Doctor wanted to fight. We must go and tell the police in the morning."

I spent a second sleepless night in my empty room. Doctor, who shared a name with one of my good friends from Kromdraai, was a friend of Sandile's. I had taught him how to use the computer and had even shown him what an American dollar looked like when he asked to see it. My thoughts fluctuated between "Will I get my things back? Can he get them to Jo-burg and sell them before we get to him?" and "Perhaps my things would be feeding his family." I might even have insurance to cover the entire cost. I agonized a little over what to do, but every single person I talked to the next morning at school told me to go to the police.

With some teachers from school, I went to the station and told the police that I had been given a tip: My things were at Doctor's house. A few hours later, as I stood with several teachers in the schoolyard, where we could see virtually every house in Lochiel, the police drove up to Doctor's. After a short pause they turned back around. We would later learn that Doctor had been prepared to fight them. The police went for backup and returned 30 minutes later with two trucks, more police, and two dogs. Barking and yelling and clanging followed, and we were told that Doctor swung an ax before being overcome by the police. They arrested Doctor and his cousin, and later that night they called me into the station to identify my things.

Every single article of clothing, all the money, the computer—everything was intact. The police were as proud as can be; I was happy to have my things back; Gogo and Mrs. Ndlovu were ecstatic.

"Yes," one of the teachers told me, "Doctor and his family have always been bad. They sit in their house all day and do nothing. But they have a TV that is this big!" He held his hands wide. "It is not right."

"You see," Shongwe said, "you don't take something from someone in the community. It is not right. And if you take some small thing, you take it to eat. But you don't take everything from a person. No, it's not right."

I was happy to have recovered my belongings, but I was perhaps more happy because I felt like I belonged to Lochiel. People from the community helped me find my things and supported me in every step of the process. They urged me to go to the community police, and the police recovered my belongings.

Days before I left South Africa, I went to court in Carolina. This was six months after Doctor was arrested, and both Gogo and I had been subpoenaed to testify about the incident. It was rare for a case to be referred to the regional court in Carolina instead of the magistrates court in eLukwatini, and when I asked the police officer who delivered the subpoena why, he said it was because the value of the stolen goods was so high. Apparently, if Doctor had taken every belonging from a poorer person, he would have been in less trouble.

On the day of the trial, Gogo and I left for Carolina before eight so we could make our nine o'clock court time. Once we got there, we paid the driver and walked up the ramp to the red brick courthouse.

Inside, we signed in with a black security guard who sat behind a desk. To our left were two small waiting rooms. This dual layout was presumably left over from segregated times. Gogo and I went into the first room, where two other people were sitting. The wooden bench we sat on hung from the wall and circled the small, shadowy room. There were no light fixtures and no windows, and the only light from the door created faint gray parallelograms on the floor. Another man came in, dressed in a ratty three-piece suit, frayed at the pant cuffs and the collar. As far as I could tell, I was the only white person in the courthouse.

We sat there for an hour, and nothing happened. I had not eaten and was getting hungry. I got up and walked around the lobby. The door to the courtroom was unlocked, and I went in. Ten rows of empty benches faced toward the front, which was laid out like an American courtroom: two long tables for the attorneys, the judge's seat above a seal of South Africa, and a witness box to the judge's left.

I went back to the lobby and asked the guard, in Zulu, when court would begin.

"Any minute," he responded.

"We're getting hungry," I told him. "Is there any way we can go buy some food and come back?"

"No," he said sadly. "If you leave, they will start without you. Sorry, but that is the way they do it."

The court date had already been delayed for six weeks because Gogo and I had been unable to attend the previous one. I sat back down.

"It's ten o'clock," Gogo said. "I'm hungry."

"Yeah, they're late. It's ridiculous," I told her.

The police from Lochiel arrived and begged Gogo not to leave to get some breakfast because we were important to their case. We sat until 11:00 without so much as a sign from the court that they would open that day.

At 11:45 a white woman came down the hall, said a few words to the bailiff at the sign-in desk, and left. I got up, walked out of the little dark waiting room, and asked what was going on. "They're about to begin," the guard told me.

I sat back down and told Gogo. We had been waiting for almost three hours. The older man had lain down on the bench and was sleeping. The other couple dozed as well.

Another uniformed bailiff opened the courtroom door and announced that court was in session. Gogo and I got up, roused the sleepers, and with the five or six other witnesses and observers from the other waiting room, entered the court and spread out on the benches.

The woman from the lobby stood in the front, conversing with a white man. Both wore robes and talked in Afrikaans. An announcement was then made in Afrikaans, and a man I had not noticed translated it into Zulu. We all stood up. The judge, a middle-aged white man, heavyset with dark brown hair, came in and sat down. The translator, a black man wearing a light-blue three-piece suit and glasses, leaned against the witness box, looking out of place next to the three white people in robes.

The proceedings began and were conducted completely in Afrikaans. Two black teenagers walked in, escorted by guards. They stood next to the white man, who was presumably acting as the defense attorney, with their heads down. The woman, whom I guessed was the prosecutor, spoke to the judge for a minute or two in Afrikaans. The judge asked her some questions and she answered them. The boys stood, staring at their hands while the attorneys discussed, I assume, their rights under the law and their future, in a foreign tongue.

After the discussions, the judge looked at the two teenagers and addressed them directly. The translator, who had been leaning heavily on his hand, perked up and said in Zulu, "Do you have a lawyer?"

"No," the boys answered, one after the other.

"No," the translator repeated to the judge.

The judge then spoke a few sentences in Afrikaans, and the translator told the boys in Zulu that they could hire a lawyer or, if they could not afford one, one would be assigned to them.

The judge and the prosecutor discussed a few more items in Afrikaans. Then the judge addressed the teenagers again and the translator translated. "Your bail is 20,000 rand. You are to come back to court on July 12."

Afrikaans is taught in South African schools, but the level of comprehension varies greatly from person to person. Clearly the court understood this and provided a translator. But, as far as I could tell, it was the court's decision that the translator need only translate certain parts of the process.

Gogo fidgeted next to me. "I'm still hungry," she said, half smiling.

"Me, too. Do you understand what they are saying?"

"Ay, I don't understand."

"Well, I think we must be next."

I was wrong. Four more defendants walked in and watched as the white people discussed them in Afrikaans. Only those same few sentences were translated into a language they understood. The court remained content to keep them in the dark about the rest of the proceeding.

After a few more bail hearings, the judge announced that the court would take a five-minute recess. This was translated into Zulu so we would understand.

The other people on the benches shuffled around. The police officer from Lochiel who was sitting just in front of me, turned around, knowing that Gogo and I would be angry. "Musa, we must be just after the break," he said apologetically.

Steamed, Gogo got up and walked back to the bench in the dark waiting room. The man in the tattered suit had lain back down to rest. A few of the witnesses whose hearing had been called were getting ready to leave. Others were standing in the room or leaning against the wall. A few complained that they hadn't had anything to eat. It was 12:15.

We waited 15 minutes and, ever the optimist, I made Gogo get up and walk back into the courtroom with me. "Musa," she said as we sat in court, "they are not going to start. They like to make us wait and make us feel hungry." "They" referred not just to the judges and lawyers in the regional court.

When Nelson Mandela went on trial, he wore a traditional Xhosa robe to make the point that he was a black African in a white man's court, and that their judgments and procedures were not those of his people or his society. Thirty-five years later, his point was still valid.

By one o'clock, Gogo was furious. "We have to eat," she told the guard. "This is not right. We have sat here from *nine in the morning*! You see?"

I had resigned myself to torpor. I sat in the dark waiting room between an old couple and the sleeping man in the suit and almost dozed off.

At a quarter to two, the prosecutor walked into the hall carrying a box of her leftovers from lunch and sipping on a straw stuck down in a can of Orange Fanta. Three hours earlier I might have said something. Now I was too tired from thinking about the unfairness of everything, and I just sat there watching.

"You see, Musa," Gogo whispered as the woman walked away down the hall. "You see? They eat and they make us wait for six hours...."

Just after two o'clock the bailiff called us all into court. We went in and sat down. Doctor and his cousin came in through the back door escorted by guards. The judge opened the court again. And then, as if to prove that this was a white man's court, he announced that they would proceed in English because the complainant was an American.

I was mortified. All day this court had shown disrespect to the black people in the waiting room. The police from Lochiel didn't like it or have any control over it. And now this court was singling me out as a person entitled to respect.

They called me as the first witness. I sat in the box next to the judge, and the prosecutor asked me, in my own language, to identify myself.

She then asked me a series of questions. I told her about the state of my room both when I left it and when I returned and found it had been broken into. I agreed that the list of things that were stolen was indeed the list I had written, and that all of the items had been recovered. She asked if I knew any of the defendants, and I said yes.

Doctor looked up at me. His face registered no emotion. I looked at the prosecutor and told her that I knew Doctor, and that he had been at my house several times.

The judge interrupted suddenly. "Wait a minute. You say that you let these boys into your house?"

"Yes," I replied. "On several occasions."

"Why?"

"Because they were learning how to use a computer."

The judge was slightly surprised. After I identified Doctor, the prosecutor had no more questions.

The defense attorney stood up, all smiles. "For the record, is it true that your grandfather is former President Jimmy Carter?"

"Yes," I said.

"Really?" said the judge, interrupting again.

"Yes."

"What exactly are you doing here?" the judge asked.

"I'm working with schools in the area around Lochiel."

He nodded his head.

The defense attorney asked his second and final question. "Is it safe to say that many other people knew where you lived and what you were doing? And that many people knew that you had a computer and other expensive items in your house?"

"Absolutely," I answered.

I was dismissed. The entire ordeal took less than ten minutes. None of my testimony was translated.

As I was stepping down, the prosecutor said something to the judge in Afrikaans. "No," the judge responded. "I think that because we started in English, we should continue in English."

The next witness was a police officer from Lochiel, who testified in Zulu. All of his testimony was translated into English. When the judge started asking him questions, another police officer leaned back to me and said, "This is where they try to confuse him."

When the policeman who had recovered my things was finished, Doctor's mother was called, but she was not present. The attorneys agreed that she was important to the case, so the judge called for a recess of a few weeks.

As we left, the prosecutor approached me to say thank you. I asked if Gogo had to come back. "No, that's fine," she answered.

Gogo and I had to laugh. There was no other option. We had traveled 50 miles with no car and waited for six and a half hours so I could speak for ten minutes, and the case had not even been decided. Doctor would sit for weeks before his trial was completed. I still do not know how it turned out.

We walked out of the courthouse and into the Chicken Lickin' across the street. I bought Gogo a small box of chicken, and we sat on the corner and ate, watching people walk in and out of the stores and down the trail to the location.

THE CODE

A WHITE PERSON WHO SPEAKS ZULU IS ONE THING. PEOPLE HAD heard about those in Natal and on some farms near Carolina. But a white guy who speaks Tsotsitaal, now that is something different altogether. Tsotsitaal is the street language of urban South Africa. A linguistic analysis of Tsotsitaal would be almost impossible. It is an amalgamation of Afrikaans, English, Sotho, Zulu, and countless other African languages that mingled in Johannesburg at the time of the great gold rush. Workers came from all over southern Africa and melded into an urban culture that needed a way to communicate. The result was a vibrant and almost complete vocabulary of street slang borrowed from whichever language had the coolest sound. Even the term "Tsotsitaal" is a mixture of the African slang word *tsotsi,* or criminal, and the Afrikaans word for "language" (*taal*). Kids in Lochiel speak Tsotsitaal among themselves, and it is the language of kwaito, South Africa's brand of hip-hop, the constant sound track of daily life in black South Africa. I heard the language in the staff rooms, playgrounds, and taxi ranks in Lochiel, and

more so in Nhlazatje. But in these rural areas the language is an imita-
tion of the way people speak in the townships of Jo-burg.

As far as I was concerned, a sketchy Tsotsitaal was all I needed to
be viewed in a new light. I spoke passable Zulu, and Tsotsitaal is Zulu-
or Sotho-based, drawing heavily from English and Afrikaans. Without some knowledge of all those languages, Tsotsitaal and kwaito both
need explanation. Tsotsitaal is, as they say, *pah-shah-sh*, a word meaning "cool," whose origins I cannot begin to glean, but whose sound
is indeed cool.

Because of my language facility, my friends and relatives liked to
show me off to their friends in town. In Lochiel I had become familiar,
but to people who lived in the townships and interacted with white
South Africans everyday, I was still very much a novelty. My Tsotsitaal
and Zulu, along with patience and brave friends who acted as my guides,
allowed me to cross the white-black border almost every time I went
to a location.

After his brother's lobola in Potchefstroom, Nhlanhla and I drove back
to Ermelo. We had left Lochiel at 4 a.m. and had been eating and drinking all day. I could barely keep my eyes open. We dropped off the family, and Nhlanhla asked if we could make a stop. "Sure," I said, though
I was struggling to stay awake.

Nhlanhla called his friend Eric on his cell phone to see which party he
was going to. Eric was in a park outside of town, but he and some friends
were getting ready to leave. He said he was thinking of going to a house
party somewhere in Ermelo, but he would wait for us in the park.

When we pulled up to the campground, there were only three cars.
On South African television, American rap and R&B videos play all night.
I couldn't help remembering this when I saw someone like Eric: He sat
by himself in his silver Honda Prelude, with black-tinted windows and
chrome bumpers, doors open, blaring TKZee or some other big-name
kwaito group. Sunglasses in the middle of the night.

We jumped out of Nhlanhla's car, and they talked. Eric looked at me nervously. "What are you doing, bringing a Boer?" he asked Nhlanhla, not realizing that I could understand his language.

Nhlanhla explained that I was his friend, and that I spoke Zulu, but Eric was skeptical. He said nothing to me and did not shake my hand when I held it out to say hello. He abruptly walked back to his car and got in. As we followed him to the party, Nhlanhla was uncomfortable and a little nervous that he had brought me. This was not a family outing. His friends were young, successful, and lived in Ermelo—a town not known for its flawless race relations. I was nervous, but more tired than anything.

The party, sponsored by a local radio station, was packed. The house was on a quiet street. Since apartheid's housing restrictions were eliminated, many upper- and middle-class blacks had moved into the white parts of town. Nhlanhla and I followed Eric's car down a few tree-lined streets, passing quaint houses with chain-link fences surrounding well-trimmed yards. At the end of one block were 20 cars, parked haphazardly in the street. I felt like I was in high school and someone's parents were out of town.

When we stopped and got out, Eric immediately came over and said hello to me. He had apparently had time in the car to feel guilty for being rude. The three of us walked around to the back of the house. The stone patio in front of the garage was full of people, the back door to the house was open, and bass-heavy kwaito was thundering out. It seemed that everyone was talking on a cell phone. Inside, the back room was full of people dancing. Charismatic and smart, Eric was hailed by everyone.

Almost immediately, it seemed, he accepted me as a friend. I could speak the lingo and that made me cool. He apologized again for being rude. I told him that I understood and that he should not worry. He actually worked with white people all day at a government job and had no problems in that regard. He had just been surprised. Once he realized I could speak pretty good Zulu and could greet in Tsotsitaal, he started introducing me around to everyone. "Hee-hee. This is the best white man in the world. His name is Musa. He's a Swazi, but he's from America."

Nhlanhla wanted to speak to one of his friends, so Eric and I went inside. Down the halls, in the kitchen, and in the side bedrooms there was almost no furniture. A few chairs and maybe one couch supported several drunk people in one room, but the rest of the rooms were empty except for the people. The house was packed with people dancing, talking, kissing in the corners. There were almost as many women as men—a drastic difference from Lochiel or Two Gs, where I would rarely see more than two or three women with thirty or forty men. A woman from the radio station talked to us in English for a few minutes, and I was happy to see such a strong, self-confident woman being treated as an equal. Off to one side, a small room had been blocked off with a table. Three people sat in front of stacks of cases, selling cans of beer and alchoholic cider. Eric and I bought a few cans and went back out to the patio.

When I walked into a room, everyone would stop and look. They would stop dancing and talking; some even stopped kissing in the corner. Outside, they would grow silent when I walked up. Eric would break the silence, and when I said hello in Zulu, everyone laughed and we continued our conversation with no reservations. Merely speaking the language melted the ice.

For example, Sihle, a hulking man with jet-black muscles stretching the sleeves of a small white T-shirt, refused to talk to me. He yelled at Eric, "I have to talk to these people all day, and now when I want to relax, you come with one here?"

He left and sat on a bench near the edge of the patio. I continued talking and laughing with several other people. Nhlanhla came back from wherever he'd gone and said he needed to go pick someone up. "Can you stay here with Eric?"

He looked at both of us. Less than an hour earlier we had not known each other. "Sure," Eric said. "There's no problem."

After a few minutes, Sihle called me over and asked how I was. I guess he had decided to give me a chance. He was amazed at my Zulu and that I was from America. He was well educated and worked as a prison guard. We talked for a while, and when I saw him on the street in the township a few months later, he yelled for me to come and meet his friends.

Eric became one of my best friends in South Africa. I went to his home on several occasions. Both he and his wife, a beautiful woman who speaks Sotho as her first language, had high-paying jobs, and he lived in a house in town. His six-year-old daughter went to a white school in Secunda, the town between Ermelo and Johannesburg where his wife worked, and the little girl spoke better English than Eric. They had a satellite dish and let me watch ESPN at night when I needed to see a big game.

The language was a code that, like a secret society, let me into the community. Knowing the code set people in black South Africa at ease. Without the language opening doors, I do not know how I would have coped. The code, like hitchhiking, was liberating; but, also like hitchhiking, it exposed the difficulty that others had with crossing racial lines.

Rian Malan, an Afrikaner journalist and a descendant of D. F. Malan, the first apartheid prime minister, wrote a memoir, *My Traitor's Heart,* in 1990. The book is a groundbreaking, beautiful articulation of the liberal Afrikaner. Many of us in the Peace Corps read it because it goes a long way toward explaining the pathologies of white South Africans. In almost every encounter Malan had with black people, the gulf between them was wider than it needed to be because he couldn't understand their language. The book is full of pain caused by "incomprehensible tongues." He and a companion picked up a crippled hitchhiker and then couldn't explain why they could not take the hitchhiker home. They ended up yelling: "We not take you home! Petrol finish! Understand?"

I arrived in Nelspruit after school one Friday night, ready to spend the night at a backpackers or youth hostel, after an especially hectic week. I decided to have a steak at a chain restaurant called the Lone Star Steakhouse. To my surprise, I saw two black men sitting at the bar in the expensive restaurant.

I read, drank a beer, and ate my steak. When the waiter came around, we talked in Zulu. Eventually the two sitting at the bar asked me in Zulu where I was from. We started to talk and they moved over, uninvited, to my table. That kind of personal intimacy was not uncommon in black South Africa. One was a teacher in the location, and the other said he was a businessman from Jo-burg. After a half hour the teacher had to leave. After a few more minutes of chitchat about his white girlfriend whom he was visiting in Nelspruit, the businessman turned serious.

Slightly heavyset, no older than me, he had been buying me drinks, I guessed, to prove that he was rich. He was wearing some kind of expensive sweat suit and had several rings and gold chains. He dressed like Zakes or any number of my teachers. He started speaking in English: "I have a proposition for you."

"OK," I said, having no idea what to expect.

"You are an American, and you speak Siswati and Zulu. You seem like a good guy. But you say you take taxis. How would you like to make a lot of money?"

"I think I'd like that a lot," I answered in Zulu.

"You seem like a good guy. You could sell cars for me. You see, I am a mechanic. I go to auctions, you know, and buy cars. Insurance companies, they sell their totaled cars for maybe 15,000 rand. I buy the totaled cars, fix them up, and then you could sell them. I think you could make 40,000 rand per month."

"That's a lot of money," I said. "How do you fix the cars?"

"I get the parts and fix them up all for about 15,000 rand. You could sell the cars for 150,000 or more depending on the cars."

"This sounds too good to be true. *Angiyithembi*," I said. "I don't believe it."

"There is no catch. After I fix up a car, I take it to the police so they can certify that it is not stolen, and then, after you demand the papers from the police, you can prove nothing is wrong with the car."

"Why don't you do this yourself?"

"Because I am black and this is South Africa," he laughed. "I could never get a loan or a zoning license for the property. And then the police would harass me constantly because I am getting rich and I am black. The banks want a nice white guy there to make sure their money is OK. And *labelungu* (white people) won't ever buy a car from a black guy. They are mistrustful. But you they would trust. And you could sell the cars for much less than the other dealers and still make a 200 percent profit."

"And what do I tell people when they ask me how I get my cars so cheap?" I asked, becoming interested, though still not believing what I was hearing.

"You tell them you have a great mechanic and he lets you check out the cars at any police station in South Africa and the police all say that everything is legal. They are rebuilt cars."

"So, how do you do it?"

"Oh, that you don't need to know. I do it with my guys. We get the parts, we rebuild the cars, and you get a perfectly legal product."

"Where do you get the parts?" I asked, smiling.

"Well," he said, "that's obvious."

I couldn't believe that I was sitting in a steak restaurant with this man proposing a venture into organized crime. I felt like I was in a movie. "How do you do it?" I asked.

"Can I trust you?"

"Hawu! Mfwetu," I said, *"Mhlambe Siyosebenzanana*—My brother, we may be business partners."

"We steal them," he said.

"I know that, but how do you get the police to say they are legal? Do you bribe them?"

"No, no. You could take these cars to any police station in South Africa, even to the head of police in Pretoria, and he will tell you that they are legal, rebuilt cars."

"Hey, *mfo, ayungitshela, pella. Niyenzanjani?*—Come on, man, just tell me how you do it," I said.

We were both getting a little drunk. Either he was making it up or he thought I had bought into his little scheme, because he explained the whole process. He and his colleagues buy a totaled car at an auction—for example, a 1998 silver Mercedes 300E with a tan leather interior. There are 14 points or so on that automobile that identify it. They strip all the identification and then find another 1998 silver Mercedes 300 E with a tan leather interior that is running well. They steal it and replace all of its identification numbers and plates with the plates from the totaled car, of which they are the legal owners. They then take the "rebuilt" car to the police, along with the ownership papers, for inspection. The 14 points clear, and they have a legally certified rebuilt car in perfect condition all ready to sell.

"Have you done this before?" I asked.

"Of course. I work for this guy from Nigeria who lives right in the nicest part of Jo-burg. His house is so big it has a huge wall and security around the clock. He only travels in limousines."

I decided he was lying. From the richest people to the poorest, everyone in South Africa blamed Nigerians for the organized crime, and everyone claimed that someone had a perfect way to steal cars. He had read about this in a magazine or had made it up completely. "What kind of car do you drive?" I asked him.

"A Ford Contour," he said, smiling. I must admit, I had not seen many American cars since I arrived in South Africa. A Ford Contour would be very expensive. "Do you want to see it?" he continued. "It's right outside."

We finished our beers. I had already paid my tab, and we went out to see his car, which was, sure enough, a blue Ford Contour. "Take this." He handed me a piece of paper with his number on it. I never called.

GOGO ALSO LIKED TO SHOW ME AROUND IN TOWN, SO I WAS ALWAYS invited to family events. Shortly after my trip to Potchefstroom, we went to a graduation ceremony. Mercy Lindeni Sibanyoni, Gogo's daughter who worked at Beare's Furniture in Ermelo, had a daughter a few months older than I was named Senzile. She was graduating from the teacher-training college in Soshanguve, the mammoth township outside Pretoria.

I had been to Pretoria several times, and though I was somewhat familiar with the white part of town, I did not know the townships at all. Mkhulu came to Lochiel with his truck, and Twana, Andiswa, Nombuso, Sandile, Gogo, and I climbed in. We borrowed mattresses from the preschool and put them in the bed of the truck for people to sleep on. Sandile and I got in the front with Mkhulu, while Gogo sat in the back with the girls. We left Lochiel on Friday at six in the evening. For some reason, many people in South Africa like to drive through the night. I was very tired and kept dozing off in the hot cab. Sandile laughed at me for bobbing my head, and Mkhulu accused me of not listening to the story he was telling. Late at night we passed through Witbank, and Mkhulu explained how its name had come about.

"Witbank," he said, in his best Afrikaans accent, pronouncing the *w* like a *v* and making the *a* short, "means 'White Bank,' and it used to be called Swartbank (pronounced *svahrt bahnk*). You see, Musa, *swart* means 'black' in Afrikaans, and the soil in the area was very dark in color. Then, when they discovered that this black dirt indicated that there were coal deposits in the ground, and that the town would be very rich, they changed the name from Swartbank to Witbank. You see, Musa, they believed that white was good."

When we stopped for gas, Gogo went to the front, and Sandile and I got in the back with the little girls. As we approached Pretoria, around midnight, Andiswa became very excited. She pointed and yelled at a gas station all lit up with a fast-food place next to a fenced-in area full of tractors. As we drew closer to the township, Andiswa banged on the window, yelling, "Look, Twana! Hawu! Did you see it?!" about the tiny establishments on the outskirts of town. At five years old, she had never seen any place so large.

The lights of Pretoria were a distant glow over the hills when we saw the first signs for Soshanguve, listing extensions and other alphabetized sections of the township. FF, PP, and E signs pointed off the highway, and we turned off for G. Sandile was asleep next to Nombuso. For an hour and a half I had sat on the tire guard and, having lost 30 pounds of cushion since I left Atlanta, I was bruised and ready to get out of the truck.

We turned off the highway onto a broken street. The township engulfed us on all sides, a hodgepodge of homes and small businesses packed side by side. Big numbers on signposts or fence posts identified each dwelling. Even late at night, people were walking in the street. Light poured from the windows and open garage doors of the homes that doubled as bars or small shops. Down one of the streets a huge ShopRite was closed for the night. It was the first supermarket I had seen in a township. We soon passed the teacher-training college from which Senzile was graduating, and across the street was a doctor's office. Clearly this township had an entire economy of its own.

The Sibanyonis, Gogo's daughter and her family, lived at 11248 G. To give an idea of how large Soshanguve is, I went to Pretoria a month later for Peace Corps business, and I decided to go back and spend the night at the house of these relatives. At the local taxi rank in Pretoria, I found 20 taxis heading to "Sosh." *"Ngiya amaG,"* I told the man who ran up to see where I was going. "I'm going to the Gs to visit my family."

"AmaG or AmaGG?" he asked. "The Gs or the GGs?"

Just the Gs, I said, and he sent me to the appropriate taxi.

I also knew a South African working for the Peace Corps who lived in YY. The systematic nature of Soshanguve's layout conjures up images of white men in rooms full of maps trying to lay out the township in order, so they could keep track of how many blacks there were. Only a bureaucrat could stomach addresses like G, and GG, and YY.

Up and down the dirt street, mismatched fences made from pieces of gates and other fences surrounded each lot. The Sibanyonis' residence was a four-room house with a small guest house in the back. A wrought iron fence rose 15 feet out of a concrete wall that divided their yard from their neighbor's. We pulled in and parked on the lawn.

Inside, the family was still awake. Through the back door was a crowded kitchen and the typical claustrophobia of black South African homes. Mr. Ndzukulu greeted everyone in Sotho as we waited, just outside the door, to enter the room. One by one we trickled in, turning sideways to pass between the people and furniture. A coal-burning stove took up one corner. Pressed against it was a countertop and sink. A table extended from the edge of the counter almost all the way across the room. On the right was a small table with two electric burners and pots and pans. People sat around the table or stood against the far wall, Boni among them. They had all heard of me, and I was introduced around.

I learned that the mother of the household worked at House of Coffees in Pretoria. A daughter, Masha, in her 20s, worked at a doctor's office in Soshanguve. A high school–age son also lived in the house. They rented out their guest house in the back. This night, I had no idea how the house would hold us. Other visitors were in the living room, and a few more were expected later. Some were staying next door, they told me.

Sandile and I went to the guest house with three other young men. Between the bed and the wall was enough room to fit two bodies. One person was already asleep in the bed. Sandile and a cousin took the floor, and I and another cousin climbed into the queen-size bed, trying not to disturb Mabutho, whom Sandile recognized as Senzile's boyfriend from Ermelo. Sleeping six in a bed was not uncommon, but three still made me uncomfortable.

Apparently I was not the only one. In the morning, I woke to a scream. Mabutho jumped up from the bed shrieking. He stood for a moment in his underwear and looked at me in terror before he woke fully.

"Heita," I said.

He laughed and said in English, "You must be Musa. You have scared me today!" Then in Zulu to everyone: "Men, this is the first time in my life I have gone to sleep alone and woken up in bed with a white person!" We all laughed.

The graduation, held at the college gym, was attended by thousands of people from all over South Africa. The new teachers wore caps and gowns, and speeches were given by faculty and guest speakers in English. In the audience I saw only five other white people.

After the ceremony, the 20 of us went back to the Sibanyonis for a celebration feast. People danced in the street and followed Senzile, marching in her cap and gown, through the mismatched gates of the house. After the meal Mabutho and I were sent on an errand and took a short tour in his car with Masha. "There's a nice jazz place there," she said, pointing to a brick building with musical notes bolted to the outside. "And there is a restaurant that sells chicken and has a place to buy *braai*." She pointed out her office, plus countless places to buy food or beer, play pool, or get your hair done. When we returned to the house, it was time to go. All of us bound for Lochiel piled back into the truck and drove away.

When I returned by myself a few months later, a stranger walked me down the same township street to make sure I would be safe. I had met him on the taxi, and he was concerned about my going alone. But when we arrived, three different neighbors remembered me by name and shouted from their yards, inviting me over for dinner or tea. Several friends I'd met came over to the Sibanyonis to sit with me in the living room, on two couches set so close we had barely enough room for our legs.

At Christmas, after I had been on a trip for the Peace Corps, I met Gogo and her family in Nyanyadu, the location outside of Middelburg. We were to spend the holiday there with Sandile's parents. I traveled alone in a township where I did not know my way around, and again, as would happen every time, someone insisted on helping me find my way. A complete stranger I met on the taxi accompanied me straight up to the door.

Sandile lived with Gogo, but his six-year-old brother and four-year-old sister stayed with his parents in Nyanyadu. Sandile's father worked for Eskom, South Africa's major electric company, and Sandile's mother worked at Checkers, a large supermarket chain. Their house had been improved from the original matchbox style to five rooms, and it had a nice yard. The street was paved and had sidewalks. The neighbors spoke Pedi, so I talked to them only in English. Several other people accused Sandile and me of being from Natal because we spoke a "pure" Zulu, instead of Ndebele, a related language prevalent in the area around Nyanyadu.

Christmas was wonderful. It was the middle of summer, not a cloud in the sky. We sat on the cool grass in the shade of the house, watching the children on the street. In the morning, Boni, Gogo, and Sandile's mother, Phindile, woke up the children. They all put on their best clothes. Sicelo, the six-year-old, wore a tie; the girls all wore fancy dresses with lace collars and dance shoes. There were no presents, though. Christmas is just a celebration of children.

I sat on the stoop, looking out over the hills of the township. Jazz poured out of the windows one house down. Sesi, the four-year old, spoke Pedi with her five-year-old neighbor and then yelled to me in Zulu. Sicelo rode his bike on the sidewalk. Families walked by in their Sunday best, going to and from church.

I was reading a *New Yorker* that my grandmother had sent me from home. One article discussed a famous hair stylist who commuted "by private helicopter from his impeccably appointed East Side apartment to a house on the best lane in the Hamptons." He knew, he said, from his youth in the south of France that he wanted to "be with the most interesting people." Another article, about Rwanda, intoned the usual litany about the hopelessness in Africa, its death and disease.

I watched Andiswa spinning around, trying to make her dress flare out. Nombuso mimicked her and fell down. Both of them had long since removed their shoes. This is the irony, I thought; this is the terrible, dark, disease-ridden continent of Africa people read about.

"Musa!" Gogo yelled. "Call the children." Dinner was almost ready.

In the distance, smoke from cooking fires rose above the tin roofs of the squatter camps. The houses were strapped together with maize meal bags and mattress springs. Children still played in the streets. Christmas dinner was almost ready, and I felt right at home in joyous black South Africa.

FOREIGNER

CHAPTER FOURTEEN

I HAD BEEN IN SOUTH AFRICA FOR A YEAR, AND I STAYED BUSY in Lochiel. Some of the now familiar obstacles at work frustrated me, but I was inspired to work around them. I truly believed that the tasks facing the teachers were the most important in South Africa's struggle to vanquish apartheid.

As the weather began to cool, the political campaigns leading to the June elections began. Mandela was stepping down, and the new constitution would be taking effect after the election. Copies of the constitution, in tiny white books and in all languages, were distributed throughout South Africa to inform people about their rights and the structure of their new, permanent, nonracist government. I picked up copies in English and Zulu. On any given day one might have found a politician who had been jailed on Robben Island for being a member of Steve Biko's black consciousness movement speaking before the Teachers Union, urging the strengthening of the "revolutionary alliance" between organized labor and the ANC. It was an exciting time.

In my struggle against the lingering oppression wrought by apartheid, almost daily I had new projects and ideas. Numerous teachers told me that they could not improve their teaching results because the students received no support at home. So, we conducted a survey to determine if this was indeed true. We asked each fifth grader to tell us who they lived with, how many other students were in their house, how many rooms were in their house, and whether or not they had someone at home who could help them with their homework. Only a handful of children had no one to help them. A vast majority listed brothers and sisters as the persons they turned to for academic support. This was less than ideal because these brothers or sisters were busy with their own work in secondary school—a school where less than 30 percent of the students passed the most basic of tests at the end of their schooling.

We engaged the secondary school to set up a big brother/big sister tutoring program to motivate both the younger and older students, especially those who showed potential for excellence. We discussed this idea with the primary school governing body and tried to find people in the community who would be willing to host study groups at their houses. All of this was new in Lochiel.

I worked with the principal of the secondary school, Mr. Tshabalala, a well-respected man in the community and a friend. We organized a committee of community leaders, young and old, to spearhead an effort to convert an empty room at the secondary school into a library. The committee met often and created a constitution for the group, a step that every organization must take before being able to solicit money from the government. Subcommittees met to make rules and look for opportunities for funding. I was insistent that the committee be run by people from the community, but I helped out as much as I could. Two committee members were selected, and I trained them in computer literacy and showed them how to use Microsoft Word. All of the committee's written material was produced by the members themselves.

The teachers in my regular Outcomes Based Education/Curriculum 2005 meetings told me that they did not understand the English in the materials given them. I could not blame them. The curriculum was frustratingly complex: divided into eight Learning Areas, with a set of Specific Outcomes under each one, for a total of 64 Specific Outcomes. Each had between five and twelve Assessment Criteria, making for a tremendous number. Each Assessment Criterion had a set of Performance Indicators that told the teacher what he or she was supposed to teach. Moreover, the teachers were told to document every Performance Indicator, Assessment Criterion, and Specific Outcome they addressed in every lesson, but they were given no guidance at all about what these lessons might look like. In addition to this, the language used in the materials explaining each Specific Outcome, Assessment Criterion, and Performance Indicator was very difficult to decipher. It all made little sense to me, and English is my first language.

I took the Specific Outcomes and rewrote them in simpler English. For example, one Specific Outcome in the Language, Literacy and Communication Learning Area said, "The learners will understand and apply language structures and conventions in context." My teachers were confused about what exactly that meant in a first-grade classroom. I looked at all of the Assessment Criteria and Performance Indicators, read some of the other descriptions, and rewrote it to say: "The learners will understand and use grammar." Breaking down the language barriers was difficult, but it was extremely effective in overcoming the intimidation that the teachers felt when approaching the new curriculum.

I met with the teachers both in groups and individually. I had weekly meetings with the principals of four schools—under the guise of Computer Literacy—and we spoke about school management and shared "Best Practices." I worked with teachers, including my good friends, on changing their teaching to allow more student participation and less rote learning and on helping other teachers with feedback and new ideas.

I helped the secondary school reframe its guidance policies so that all of the teachers would be involved and the students would receive more individual support. The teacher in charge of guidance, Mr. Thomo, and I took that plan to the Circuit Office.

Because there were so many qualified but unemployed teachers, the government of South Africa, correctly, did not want Peace Corps volunteers teaching classes. We only worked with the teachers and gave periodic demonstration lessons with the children. But whenever I interacted with the kids, I was amazed at both the attitude and intelligence of the students, and the difficulties of growing up in rural South Africa.

The most exciting interaction I had was during the creation of our Student AIDS Committees. AIDS is perhaps the single biggest problem in South Africa. Of all the teenage girls who have children in the hospital in eLukwatini, more than half are HIV-positive. Yet, the community where I lived was virtually silent about the disease.

Unprotected sex with multiple partners was the norm among the teachers with whom I was good friends. Extramarital affairs were more common than monogamy. Often, teachers from the primary schools would date girls from the high school. The government and the media had undertaken massive campaigns, creating posters about AIDS and setting up public discussions. But few people were willing to discuss it specifically, and no one wanted to talk about their own behavior.

A few teachers, however, were ready to begin tackling the problem of educating the students about AIDS. All of the students, boys and girls, had questions about the disease itself and how it was spread. Health care workers from the hospital in eLukwatini conducted workshops and supplied posters and pamphlets to explain the biological realities of the virus.

Most of the students would be discussing issues of sex for the first time in school, and we anticipated that there would be some discomfort. A few teachers and I decided that it would be best if we focused on the girls. We arranged for discussions, and the young women were excited to get a chance to talk without any boys in the room. The teachers who ran those discussions let the students know at the very beginning that, as young women in Africa, they were five times more likely to have AIDS than young men. The teachers asked the girls to come up with theories about why this may be true. The results were amazing.

At each high school, students were asked to list the factors that they believed led to the spread of the disease. There was one factor that every group of tenth and eleventh graders mentioned: prostitution. As one girl explained, "Many families are very poor. They do not have the money so they send the girls out to get their own food. They tell the girl that maybe she can get money for them. And they go to the border post and they go with the truck drivers. And the truck drivers say, 'If I am paying for this, I will never wear a condom.'"

Others talked about family pressure for girls to have babies—which, a student pointed out, leads to unprotected sex. Also, the students said that many wanted a man to take care of them, and most men would only have sex "flesh to flesh." If the man was older, or a teacher, he could have sex with many girls and they would find it almost impossible to say no. Each group of students also mentioned rape as a common means of disease transmission.

Another volunteer had similar conversations with young women in her community. The most telling comment about the power of women to control their bodies came not from a student, but from a female teacher. She said, "I know that someday my husband will cheat on me. He will have affairs. And when he comes home, I will not be able to stop him from having sex with me. I will not be able to make him wear any condom. So, there is no way for me to stop this AIDS. Why should I wear a condom if I am going to die anyway?"

Thabo Mbeki, the current President of South Africa, invoked international disdain by declaring that HIV may not cause AIDS and that "poverty" was the real cause. The other teachers and I who had worked so hard to begin remedying the problems caused by misinformation in our community were outraged by the first part of his statement. But after listening to the girls at the high schools around Lochiel, there is no denying Mbeki's right to claim that poverty is a factor.

IN LOCHIEL, I WAS ALWAYS ON. THERE WAS NEVER A MOMENT WHEN I could be away from my job. Everyone was watching me, which meant that I had to watch my every move and think before I spoke.

I really wanted to help, but there was only so much I could do. In Lochiel, in eLukwatini, at the taxi rank, outside school, I could not walk anywhere without drunken old men grabbing me by the arm to tell me how much they loved me, how happy they were that I was here, and how wonderful it was that I was trying to learn their language. Then they would pull me closer, and inches from my nose they would say, "Can I have just one rand?"

Even with my friends, Nhlanhla and Eddie and Chiluga, the conversations centered more on work and were intended to make sure they would participate in the school's subject committee plans or take seriously the fact that their behavior may give them AIDS. I grew tired of speaking a foreign language all day and trying to learn more in each conversation. Miss Lillian lived with another American when she was in the Peace Corps in India, and still she had problems with isolation and loneliness.

What's more, in South Africa, I was cursed with the option to run to strikingly familiar surroundings. Cars drove by, waiting to give me a ride. The television advertised cheeseburgers and grilled chicken sandwiches. Every morning when I woke up, I would stand in the tub pouring cupfuls of rapidly cooling water on my body, and I knew that in a matter of hours I could be in Nelspruit, sitting in a restaurant and having a hearty meal. The proximity made the temptation difficult to resist. And the knowledge that I could leave when I wanted deepened my isolation in Lochiel.

NELSPRUIT IS SITUATED IN THE TROPICAL, HOT AND HUMID LOWVELD. My house in Lochiel lay on the other side of the 4,000-foot escarpment that divides the Lowveld of Nelspruit from the Highveld of Lochiel and Ermelo. When the taxi or the truck twists down the mountains of the escarpment above Barberton, mangoes and citrus trees take over from the pine and eucalyptus of the higher and drier land of South Africa's central plateau, and the temperature increases dramatically.

Nelspruit is the citrus and fruit capital of Africa, and the surrounding countryside is lush and tropical. The city offers much more than Ermelo. With the fall of apartheid, the capital of Mpumalanga moved from Middelburg, near Pretoria, to Nelspruit, and the town now housed most of the provincial ministries and the provincial parliament. Nelspruit is also the gateway to Kruger National Park, the largest game park in the world, and lies on the Maputo Corridor, the primary tourist thoroughfare between South Africa and the spectacular beaches of Mozambique. Indeed, Mozambique opened a consulate in Nelspruit, and several luxury hotels were built. Restaurants in Nelspruit offered all kinds of food: Portuguese, Chinese, Italian, seafood, pizza, burgers, steak, and almost anything in between. Most important to me, Nelspruit had a "backpackers."

Backpackers are youth hostels with several bunks in each room where foreigners can stay for a very small fee. Most backpackers have a few common bathrooms with showers and a living room. Backpackers are havens for low-budget young travelers. Some are nicer than others, but in South Africa most have a pool and good company. In Nelspruit, a bed cost 30 rand a night after other volunteers and I cajoled the owner into giving us a Peace Corps discount. That owner was an interesting guy named Paul. In his late 20s, he had grown up in Pretoria and had attended one of the most prestigious Afrikaans boys schools. He was a blond, rugby-playing Afrikaner and had one of the best understandings of South Africa and its future that I ever encountered. I quickly grew to consider

Paul one of my close friends in South Africa, and his backpackers was a wonderful place to relax.

When a black person saw me on the street in Nespruit, he or she had no reason to think me different from any white South African. Though I came to town to escape being the sole white person, I went out of my way to define myself clearly to the black people in town. I spoke Siswati or Zulu constantly. I said hello to every person on the street, at the taxi rank, or in the restaurants. I was obsessed with ensuring that every black person I saw understood that I knew the code. Sometimes I took it to the point of absurdity, yelling to people across the street just to let them know that I was not like other white people. Their response was always one of wonder and excitement: "How do you know Siswati?"

I could leave for Nelspruit after school on Friday and be back to Lochiel on Saturday, after a hot shower or two, several restaurant meals, and a night of hanging out by the pool speaking English with Paul, a few travelers, and other volunteers who had made the trek to Nelspruit for companionship. We talked about our places and our problems with our jobs, about a new book we read on South Africa, and about the post-apartheid constraints gripping both white and black South Africans. Being with them was always a welcome break after living and working in a foreign environment.

The discussions I had with my fellow volunteers infinitely enhanced my understanding of South Africa. Female volunteers were constantly reminded of a cruel double standard regarding their sex, and of the possibility of harassment. Their communities, their families, and their teachers expected them to behave in a certain way. To keep the community's respect, the women in my group could not go to the pool halls or drink, regardless of the circumstances. Male teachers would not listen to a female volunteer with the same respect that they gave me. Teachers made repeated passes at them, so that the volunteers' schoolwork included the constant task of rejecting pushy men. Given all that I had heard about women from the male teachers in my community, I was not surprised.

The taxi rank and the travel that brought me such freedom was an exercise in harassment for women, especially for black women. Some men in black South Africa were at least slightly intimidated by a white woman's skin. Black women, on the other hand, enjoyed no such luxury, and the men were used to humiliating them in certain ways. For example, in the koombis a woman was required to sit in the middle seat next to the driver—who was always a male—and often the driver would have to reach between the woman's legs to change gears. Even if the gearshift was on the steering column, the harassment was the same. Outside taxis, women could not set out on their own to hitchhike.

Many female volunteers started wearing rings so they could tell people they were married. A few even had problems with good friends of mine from eLukwatini. Other times, Department of Education officials whom I respected very much would get drunk and knock on the door of two women who lived near me, trying to get them to come out with them.

Still, a large number of South African women held positions of power. The ANC demanded that one out of three parliamentarians from their party be female—four times the percentage in the United States Congress. Strong women like Gogo abounded, and provided great friends for the women in my group. The ability of the women volunteers to demand their dignity and respect also made it possible for many of them to participate in events that may have otherwise been male only.

When black South Africans met me, they saw a potential oppressor. I felt that I had to do everything possible to break that stereotype. When a male teacher worked with Serina or Nikki, two volunteers in my region, they saw a black woman that they could push around. Serina and Nikki did everything in their power to destroy that stereotype. They worked hard to give the young black girls in their communities role models and the men a new perspective on women.

At the circuit office in eLukwatini, for example, I assumed a posture of deference. I was overly polite to everyone. I volunteered for errands. But I got everything I needed. I would say, "Can I please use the phone when everyone is done? I am in no hurry. I can wait." The people in the office would scurry around, get off the phone, and give it to me immediately. Yet the two black women volunteers who used my circuit office, Nicole and Nikki, soon realized that if they did not demand the phone, they would wait all day.

On one occasion, when I walked in alone, one of the men who worked there said hello and then asked, "Do you find differences between women in America and women in South Africa?"

"Yes," I said. "Women in America demand a different kind of respect. Why do you ask?"

"Because," he said, "Nicole just left, and I have never seen a woman like that. She wants to be treated like a man."

C. D. Glin, a male African-American volunteer who became a good friend, pointed out that no one was excited when Nikki or Serina spoke Siswati, or when he spoke Pedi. They were noticed only when they were *unable* to speak the language.

Many people in black South Africa thought these volunteers were interesting, but the African Americans did not get any special treatment because of their skin color. Black South Africans who worked in stores followed them around to make sure they did not steal anything, and if a black volunteer tried to hitchhike, they would certainly never get a ride from a car driven by white people.

I had grown up with African Americans, gone to school with them and been good friends. I had walked out of my high school (which was about 50 percent white) with hundreds of other students to protest racist remarks by a teacher. I had taken undergraduate courses and participated in extensive discussions about race in America, in large and small groups. I had worked for Harvey Gantt, an African American who was running for Senate, as a political organizer in the "black belt" of rural North Carolina. But until I had to live as a minority in a community where I was forced to be conscious of my race every day, I had not scratched the surface of what racism meant. In America, like many people, I knew how to talk about racism. But I never really felt like I was living with it until I came to South Africa.

Coming to an utterly race-obsessed society where people in my small group of closest friends were harassed, where my job, my neighborhood, and my life made me constantly aware of my color, allowed me, for whatever reason, to finally look black Americans in the face and talk clearly and truthfully about race. And, I think, South Africa allowed my friends to talk to me in different ways as well. Perhaps we were able to discuss issues more openly because we could pretend to be talking about South African racism, as opposed to America's. Whatever the reason, I had never been as close to anyone of another race as I was to the three African-American women who lived as volunteers in the valley below Lochiel and a few other African Americans whom I shared times with while I was in the Peace Corps.

Pretoria was an ideal place to get together and test tolerances. A group of us, black and white, men and women, would go out on the town. If we went to white restaurants, we would get terrible service. We might go to a black club, and the people there would not know what to do when the whites spoke their language and the blacks did not.

Hatfield, Pretoria's nightlife center, borders the University of Pretoria, one of the finest colleges in South Africa and a well-known bastion of conservatism. Hatfield Square was often filled with college kids, and after months in dusty African villages, we would feel like sailors on shore leave. One night we walked into a club called Ed's Diner. The bar, located on a lively street, had an American fifties theme. We did not know that this theme extended to racist behavior as well. We went there because they have a dance floor in the back. Other than our group, there were no black people in the club. At one point, C. D., who had dreadlocks and played football at Howard, was dancing with Anna, my friend from Boulder, Colorado, who lived on the farm near Piet Retief. I was dancing with Marci, an African-American woman. Apparently Marcus, who is biracial and was dancing with another white volunteer, was just too dark for some of the boys at the bar.

I overheard: "Can you believe they're in here dancing with white girls? I'm going to kill that guy." They started bumping into us, spilling our drinks. We were all tottering a little after a night of drinking, and I started to get fired up. My freedom-fighter attitude was in full swing, and I wanted to tell these guys what I thought. Thankfully, someone in our group less belligerent than I decided we had better leave and began to usher us out.

As we left, a college student reached out and grabbed C. D.'s hair. C. D. pulled away and glared at him, but he refrained from saying anything and continued walking. The young man and two of his friends followed him out. "Hey, you! I can touch your hair if I want to! Are you telling me that I can't touch you, if I want to?"

"What do you mean?" asked C. D., maintaining his normal diplomatic demeanor.

"I'm from the Free State," the guy said, referring to the Orange Free State, a conservative province. "Do you know what that means?"

"What?" C. D. said. "That you're an asshole?"

I had had a few too many drinks, and I ran up behind them cursing and yelling, just in time to hear the man call C. D. "boy." I thought C. D.'s eyes were going to pop out of his head.

Kathleen, a white woman from our group, offered a few conciliatory words, and the group of Free Staters turned around and walked back into the bar. C. D., Marcus, and I were led back to the taxis yelling, but a fight was avoided. On some level our behavior was a provocation, and we should have expected this response. But that did not make our anger less justified. For the African Americans in my group, the possibility of this type of confrontation was always in the back of their minds. Their freedom in white South Africa was drastically curtailed, not because all whites were like the boys from Ed's, but because it was difficult to tell which ones were.

Several of the African Americans in my Peace Corps group had white South African friends with whom they stayed when they went to town, and all of us came to town to stay at backpackers and relax. Yet I had a much easier time being accepted by blacks than they did by whites.

IN NELSPRUIT, I WOULD TRY TO SHOW WHITE SOUTH AFRICANS WHAT a great place black South Africa could be. I asked Paul from the backpackers to come with us to kwaito concerts, and he would laugh and tell me it was dangerous. A few other volunteers and I finally got him to come to see M'Du, a famous and very talented kwaito star. We were the only white people in the entire club.

Many of Paul's best friends, including his business partner, Mpho, were black. He often tried to convince friends and family that the future of South Africa lay in relationships like the ones he had with these friends. I admired Paul for his desire to bring people together, and the more time I spent in white South Africa, the more I came to realize the difficulty that many white South Africans had.

Bill, the volunteer who lived in Nhlazatje, and I met one night at a Mexican restaurant in Nelspruit called Cantina Tequila. The first moments in town always seemed surreal. Minutes before, I had been let out of a car going to Kanyamazane, or Hazyview, speaking Siswati. Earlier in the day I had been at school trying to devise a plan to pay for candles so that parents would not feel that a child's late-night studying was a financial burden. Many of the children's caretakers questioned the value of education in the first place, and they did not see why their child, after finishing his chores, needed to waste a candle to stay up and read.

Now I was sitting in a Mexican restaurant at a tall table in the bar section watching a white waitress in a short black dress pouring upside-down margaritas into the mouths of several rugby-playing Afrikaners. Bill and I started telling jokes and stories with several of the white men in the bar. We were defending American football against their lame arguments that rugby was better.

Bill was drinking hard that night. He had just learned—he had to tell me four times before I believed him—that his former fiancée had run off with his congressman. He ordered one of those big blue drinks that comes in a fish bowl with umbrellas and ten straws. I refused to drink any, so getting to the bottom of the bowl was a challenge for Bill. When he neared the end, the other people in the bar took an interest and started cheering him on. He finally finished and everyone cheered. Someone came up behind him and turned the fish bowl full of ice onto his head.

Then Zakes walked in. He was visiting his family in a township outside Nelspruit, and Bill and I had called him and told him to meet us there. We had not seen each other since the end of training. Bill and I jumped up and hugged him. I was talking as fast as I could in my best Siswati to show him how well I could speak. Bill was babbling excitedly and asking him what he wanted to drink. Yet when we all sat down, we realized the rest of the room was silent.

We pretended not to notice and kept on talking in English, catching up and reminiscing about the good old days of training. Zakhele was now attending a technical college in Pretoria. He was dressed to the nines and had an even smaller cell phone. Gradually the conversations at the other tables picked up, and the atmosphere returned almost to normal.

Soon, one of the men with whom we had been drinking came back over to our table. "Hello, can you introduce me to your friend?"

"Sure. This is Zakhele. He was our Siswati instructor, and he is our great friend."

"Pleased to meet you, Zakhele. You've done quite a job teaching them Swazi."

We all talked, and soon he insisted on buying Zakes a drink. Others began coming over. "Hello, I'm Piet."

"I'm Michael, pleased to meet you."

"Hey, guys, my name's Janie. I'd like to buy you a drink as well. What are you having?"

The ice had been broken. These white people were falling all over themselves trying to shake Zakes's hand and to buy him a drink. One of the guys gave us his card and told us to call him if we were ever near Middelburg. "I've got a farm out there. We can sit and have a few drinks and talk about all this shit in our country here." Then Nicole, Nikki, and Serina, three other volunteers from the valley below Lochiel, walked in and convinced us to go to another bar. So Zakes, Bill, and I left with three black women.

I do not know what the people in the Cantina Tequila said when we left, but that experience stayed with me. It was as if they had been waiting their whole lives for a black man to walk in so they could jump up to welcome him. Because we were old friends, Zakes was able to overcome that initial shock of silence. I saw that South Africa, for all its borders, thirsts for connections.

I could walk into a township bar full of black people, and everyone would fall silent. But I knew the code. I could say, *"Sanibonani! Heitada. Nithini lapho? Bengicabanga kuthi niya groova la. Bengiyazi kuthi senithulile nje. Ini indaba?"* And everyone would laugh and we would get to talking. The language was my bridge to black South Africa. That night we were the white people's bridge to Zakes.

THINGS FALL APART

CHAPTER FIFTEEN

ANYONE WHO IS AN INTERLOPER IN ANOTHER CULTURE HAS TIMES of self-doubt. For all my efforts, I was never going to become a black South African. At times, I was too fond of white restaurants and bars and westernized comforts. What I was to learn, after my first year or so in the country, was how much black South Africans wanted these things, too.

This realization was triggered by a trip I took to the United States. I had been invited to appear with my grandfather at the Global Meeting of Generations, and the Peace Corps had encouraged me to go. My grandfather and I were to have a moderated conversation, on stage, to demonstrate the value of intergenerational dialogue. As one of my first public speaking engagements, it was an overwhelming experience.

I saw my grandfather just prior to the event. I was tan and had lost 20 pounds since I last saw him in Johannesburg.

"I almost didn't recognize you," he said. "You look like you're doing great."

"I am," I said. "South Africa is a crazy place, but I think I'm getting around pretty well."

"Well, what do you think we should talk about?" he asked.

We discussed what we might say onstage. I knew that he was going to speak about the widening global gap between the rich and poor, how stingy America is in giving foreign aid, and how Africa in general receives too little attention.

I would talk about being young, a member of my generation. I tried to explain why we often don't vote or seem to care about world issues. I told him we were alienated from the world's debate over "major issues" because we did not see how those issues affected us. We could not muster the energy to march for small changes in the tax laws or limits on international capital mobility. We needed some new rallying cries, something to latch onto as a cause.

Soon we were talking about the inspiration I received in South Africa. Participating in the post-apartheid struggle for equality and empowerment was exciting, and even to a former president, the thought of being in the midst of all the changes was intoxicating.

Charlayne Hunter-Gault, who would soon become CNN's Johannesburg bureau chief, moderated our discussion onstage. We re-created some of our previous discussion, told some jokes, and had a very good time. I was surprised by how relaxed I was.

Near the end, we took written questions from the audience. One person asked me—the 20-something kid sitting with the two accomplished figures—"Jason, what have you yourself done to affect change?"

It was a good question, and I was proud to have something of an answer. I had not done much, but I had worked for a year in a small South African homeland and changed a few minds, perhaps altered their teaching practices, and I had crossed hundreds of racial boundaries.

After the event I said good-bye to my grandparents.

"I'm impressed," my grandfather said. "The Peace Corps has been good to you."

"Thanks," I said. "I'm excited to go back."

"Well, we're proud of you."

"And a little jealous?" I asked.

"Maybe." He smiled, and I hugged them both good-bye.

For all the warmth of our farewell, though, that trip home was a mistake in one important respect. I did not know how uncomfortable I was in South Africa until I went to the United States. After this trip, I was still excited to return to Lochiel and see my friends, but I could see more clearly that I would only be a visitor.

Upon my return I learned that four of my best friends, all of whom had just been in Washington with me, had decided to come visit. Just before that, the Diversity Committee had put me in charge of "entertainment" for the Regional Diversity Conference that it was hosting in April. Volunteers representing all of the countries in the Southern Africa Sub-Region would be coming, and the Diversity Committee wanted to be able to direct the visiting volunteers to safe nightspots in Johannesburg. I was to scout out places to go and make recommendations.

Because my friends from home were also coming, I decided to check out Johannesburg right away. The city, as is widely publicized, has one of the highest violent crime rates in the world, and the Peace Corps had given us travel advisories warning against staying in certain neighborhoods. I knew of only one place, the Bass Line, a club in Melville famous for its African jazz. I called a friend of a friend whom I had met in Washington, and she referred me to a young South African woman. Zindzi was the resident nightlife expert in the office of an American media company, and she agreed to take me out one night in Jo-burg.

I asked around in Pretoria for the name of a backpackers and called them. All of the backpackers in Jo-burg pick up travelers for free if they are staying the night. When I told the man at the backpackers that I was traveling by koombi, he said they could pick me up only inside Park Station, and they recommended that I take a bus. I thought at first that he was just guilt- and fear-ridden, like the rest. Then I discovered that

Greyhound buses run frequently between Pretoria and Johannesburg and are not much more expensive than a koombi. So, I paid the extra dollar and opted for the air-conditioned, comfortable bus that dropped me off inside Park Station.

The main bus and train depot in South Africa's largest city is awhirl with activity. Just outside its walls is the hub of the minibus taxi industry. Blocks and blocks of central Johannesburg are devoted to transporting people to and from every township, homeland, or town in South Africa and beyond. From Bree Street or Wanderers Street you can find a taxi direct to Nhlzatje or to Swaziland, Ermelo, Nelspruit, Pretoria, and all of the surrounding townships, but you can also find one to Cape Town, Bloemfontein, Durban, Port Elizabeth, Maputo, Harare, and other destinations that would take 18 hours or more to reach.

At the taxi rank in Nhlzatshe ten different women sell fruit and snacks. Outside Park Station thousands of vendors sell everything from Coca-Cola, meat products, and pies to necklaces, marijuana, and religious paintings for your home. This frenzy of outdoor commerce and more or less informal travel attracts all elements of black South Africa, including the worst. Even Gogo and Boni dreaded walking around the area because they were scared of the *tsotsis,* or gangsters. Many of my friends in the Peace Corps and other travelers had had the straps on their backpacks cut off their backs and everything stolen.

So I was not necessarily upset to get off a bus inside the station and have the backpackers pick me up.

The only other major South African city that I knew was Pretoria. The capital of the Transvaal when gold was discovered 30 miles to the south, it has retained its more conservative Afrikaner leanings. Johannesburg, on the other hand, was founded as a boomtown, a destination for anyone who wanted to make a quick buck, and it remains the commercial center of the entire region. It is significantly less reserved than Pretoria.

Johannesburg is one of the most exciting and vibrant cities in the world. It is divided into many smaller neighborhoods, each with its own name and reputation. At one time, after apartheid's thorough "cleaning," the residential areas were all white. But many of the commercial areas still served the black population. Johannesburg was a black city by day and a white city by night. As apartheid began to lose its grip on South Africa, black people moved into certain areas of Johannesburg, many of which had long been vacated by whites. Today, entire neighborhoods in central Johannesburg are populated exclusively by blacks, and others are integrating. (Some of the fanciest, of course, remain predominantly white.)

In the minds of many South African crime watchers, the most frightening places are no longer in the townships of Soweto or Alexandra, but in the inner city of Johannesburg. Hillbrow, a central Johannesburg neighborhood once famous for its nightlife, was singled out in our Peace Corps instructions as an area to avoid at all costs. "The nightlife is dead and crime is rampant." But these neighborhoods could be avoided.

The backpackers picked me up and drove me out to Rosebank, a ritzy neighborhood famous for its mall. On Sundays, the mall's rooftop opens for a flea market, where treasures and cultural items from all over the continent can be found while one eats food from all over the world. On the streets outside the mall, men sell art and masks and other carvings. I found long, thin masks from Benin, full masks with hammered copper and beads from Congo, woven grass and seashell masks from Mozambique, folding chairs from Malawi carved with intricate designs and pictures, jewelry, necklaces, beads, bracelets, and countless other carvings from the countries of Africa.

I met Zindzi at an expensive coffee shop a few blocks from the Rosebank Mall. Despite her Zulu name, I found she spoke no Zulu and preferred English to any other language. She was tall with a stunning face and short dreadlocks, wearing stylish jeans and a black leather jacket. In the United States she could have easily been mistaken for a model.

After we had a drink, for which she paid, we got in a taxi. Zindzi was the first black South African I had ever seen in a meter taxi. It cost 20 rand to get to Melville (that is 8 more rand than it costs to go all the way from Pretoria to Johannesburg in a koombi). Throughout the taxi ride she told me where to send my guests. "Iyavaya is a nice African restaurant in Rosebank. Do you like Thai food?" Her urbanity took me by surprise. I had never seen black South Africans in a table-service restaurant in Pretoria, and the only restaurant I had ever been to in black South Africa was Southern Fried Chicken in eLukwatini.

I scribbled furiously in my notebook, asking exactly where the places were. "Rosebank's clubs are a lot of acid, house-type dance music," she continued. "Very Euro. I personally am a little more mellow, and Melville is a bit more low-key. Wait a minute," she said to the driver. "Could you please turn this up?"

On the radio the producer of a South African television drama was being interviewed. "Oh, that's my friend," said Zindzi. Everyone in Lochiel had been talking about this show. It took place in a township school and was controversial because of its violence and bad language. Because it centered on a school, it was the subject of much debate among my teachers. Along with most of the other young teachers, I thought it was a great show that forced people to think about what was really going on in township schools. The producer was saying much the same on the radio. When the interview ended, Zindzi picked up her cell phone. "Hey. I just heard the interview. Will you tell him I thought it was great.... OK, I'll talk to you later."

We arrived in Melville, a small set of streets and intersections lined with restaurants, bars, and shops. It looked like the hip section of any city in America. I spotted the Bass Line, which I had heard so much about, a tiny club with curtains in the window and a chalkboard out front indicating who was playing. As we walked into a small restaurant on a corner, Zindzi saw two of her roommates. We all said hello, and I was introduced to Khomotso and Lindy. The three black women spoke to each other in English, and Zindzi promised that we would meet them at an Italian restaurant around the corner after our meal.

Zindzi's lifestyle was an eye-opener. Though she was born in Atteridgeville, one of Pretoria's townships, she had gone to a white school and now lived in a highbrow neighborhood in Johannesburg, with the two other women I had just met. They all had professional jobs. Khomotso had gone to school in the United States and currently worked for an advertising company. Lindy was from Cape Town and worked for the South African Broadcasting Company (SABC). Zindzi had been a production assistant and had recently become a managing producer for several television shows.

She and I had some sort of chicken-spinach-pasta-fusion dish on the second-floor balcony of the restaurant. Looking over the railing, I saw that almost every table had people of different races eating together. Our table looked directly down onto a lounge area with white couches, white carpets and tables, and low lights. It was full of young black men and women, drinking and talking. Saturday night in Melville was not like Two Gs in eLukwatini. Here I felt underdressed and nervous. My Zulu and my Levi's made me the talk of the town in Lochiel, but neither got me very far in this crowd.

Besides the Peace Corps trainers, I had never talked to a black South African woman who acted like my equal. Zindzi and I talked and philosophized about the future of South Africa. I was so impressed by her that I said she needed to visit people living in the homelands. She and her friends would be terrific role models for thousands of young girls in Lochiel and Nhlazatje.

We left to make our après dinner rendezvous. Khomotso and Lindy were sitting with two white men and a black couple. We sat down, exchanged introductions, and shared a few bottles of wine. Talking about what black women could do to liberate black South Africa, I was excited.

The women, who were all my age, spoke Sotho or Tswana (two closely related languages, like Siswati and Zulu) as their mother tongue, but they all preferred English and spoke it even among themselves when no one else was around. At the lobola party in Potchefstroom, I had met exciting young black professionals, but I had remained firmly in black South Africa. Here, I could not tell which South Africa I was in.

I stood up to go to the bathroom. On my way back, I walked past two black men who worked in the restaurant.

"Heita," I said.

"*Ola.*"

"*Sho.*"

"*Shahp.*"

"*Moja.*"

"Hawu!" One of them finally said. "*Umtsotsi wena?*—Are you a tsotsi?"

"No," I said in Zulu. "But I live with black people, and they've taught me a little of their language."

They laughed, and we talked for a while in Zulu. One of them lived in Tembisa, a township outside Jo-burg where Boni sometimes went to stay with her brother. Both were Zulu, one from Piet Retief and the other from Natal near Durban. They asked me if I would come visit them in the location. Then they asked which one of the beautiful girls was my girlfriend.

"She's not there," I said. "But they are all beautiful, don't you think?"

"Over," one replied in agreement.

"But they don't like us," the other one said.

I looked at the table, suddenly confused. Zindzi and her friends sat drinking wine with several white men in a restaurant. Were these really role models for the little girls of Lochiel? I stood with two young black men who lived in the township near Gogo's cousins, and for the first time I saw blacks on both sides of the border between the two South Africas.

Zindzi and her friends suggested we go to reggae night at their favorite club in Johannesburg. The Rooftop quickly became my favorite club in Johannesburg as well. The neighborhood of Yeoville, once the Haight-Ashbury of South Africa, was today predominantly black. Zindzi and her friends were apparently comfortable crossing back into black South Africa. The club had two levels, one inside, and one on the roof of the building next door, looking over the trees and buildings of central Johannesburg. The three bars served everything from beer to mango smoothies. The music was incredible. Full of dreadlocks and dancing, the air was charged with all of the atmosphere you would expect from reggae night in urban Africa. I saw no other white people, but English was spoken all around and I recognized six or seven celebrities from South African television. This was clearly the place to be. Two weeks later there would be five white people: my four friends from home and me.

Saying good-bye to Zindzi and her friends, I got in a taxi around three and got out of bed at the backpackers 12 hours later. I wrote down all the names Zindzi had given me, with notes about the different neighborhoods: Rosebank, Melville, Yeoville, and the others she had mentioned. I felt like an expert. I had done my job both for the Diversity Committee and my visiting friends.

WHEN THEY ARRIVED, I MET THEM AT THE AIRPORT. THEY WERE GIDDY AS we rented a car from Hertz. Brad started punching Thomas in excitement. "Can you believe that there's a Hertz? Right here? In *Africa?*"

Still, they were nervous, anticipating problems that I had long since forgotten. "We don't have any South African money," Thomas said. "Is there a place to cash traveler's checks?"

"We could go to the bank," I answered. "But there's an ATM right there if you have your card."

"Wow. How much do we need to get out? How are we going to pay for the car or for dinner?"

"Well, guys, you can use your credit cards."

"Whoa! Are you serious?"

They were in for some surprises. We drove, on the left side of the road, to the backpackers in Pretoria. Lining the road, where they expected elephants and zebras, they saw the corporate headquarters for Hewlett-Packard, IBM, Nike, and Nokia. At the backpackers, they walked through the gate and saw the pool, the fine-looking home, and the trees perfectly shading the lawn.

"This is where you stay when you're in town?" they asked. "How can you afford this on a Peace Corps salary?"

"It's five bucks a night," I said. "Beers are seventy cents at the bar."

We walked to Hatfield and sat in a little Greek restaurant off the main road. Outside was a sitting area covered with a thatched roof and surrounded by brick arches. The restaurant is authentically Greek, sells ouzo, and will break a few plates if you ask. Five of us talked and caught up. I had lived with them during college, and we had been on plenty of spring breaks and road trips. I was excited to host them in my new country. I explained the history I had learned and told stories about my experiences. After appetizers, main courses, wine, and dessert, the owner brought us the check. Pat, who lived in New York City and was used to the prices there, said, "That's not that bad."

I looked at the bill. "Pat, that's not in dollars. Divide it by six."

The tone was set for the next two weeks.

We went out to Lochiel for two days, and they slept on my floor. This was the Africa they expected to see: women with buckets of water on their heads, mud houses. We cooked Gogo a big brunch with omelettes, potatoes, and fruit; it was the first time she ever had been waited on by five white men. I took them to Two Gs, and we played pool and looked out the windows at Nhlazatje's hills and homes. We ate at Southern Fried Chicken. They laughed at the name and stared at me when I unthinkingly broke my chicken into pieces to clean the meat off the bones. I pointed out how much meat they had left on their drumsticks. "Americans don't know how to eat," I said. "Y'all are wasteful and inefficient."

Hosting them in Lochiel was not easy, though. I had not anticipated the difficulties of the townspeople facing not one white man, but a group of five. When we walked around Lochiel, people were intimidated. We made people nervous, no matter how good our intentions. This made my own conversations stilted and hurried. I felt distant from my friends in Lochiel and was frustrated by the trouble my friends from home and I had crossing comfortably into black South Africa.

We went to Swaziland and took a walking safari through the country's largest game park. Our guide, a Swazi ranger, met us at our cabin at six o'clock. We had spent a restless night. At 3 a.m., two male rhinoceroses had dueled over a female, 30 yards behind our house. The grunting collisions of 5,000-pound horned, armored beasts can not only shake one from a deep sleep but also make it difficult to doze again.

We were nervous as we walked out into the park, past the electric fences that had provided us with such comfort in the middle of the previous night. But our guide was as nonchalant as could be. He carried only a walking stick. "And I never use it," he said.

The six of us walked through the gate and down a road marked by the ruts of cars. Unlike the game parks on the plains of Kenya and Tanzania, the parks of southern Africa contain a broad range of landscape. Dense thickets of thorn trees and scrub brush, forests of acacia or gum trees, and more tropical vines and ferns are almost as common as sweeping grassy meadows. In and out of the thickets or moving through the tall grass were impalas, kudus, waterbucks, zebras, and other game. Most of them remained yards away, too skittish to allow us to get closer, though we tried. Soon enough, I would be more concerned about how we would get away than with trying to get close.

We approached a sleeping white rhinoceros. The rhino occupied a mud hole in the middle of the road. Enormous and powerful even as it slept, it made us acutely aware of the difference between being on foot and being in a car. With no protection in sight, we felt tiny. We approached quietly until we stood, breathless, mere feet from the huge gray, hulking, heaving body. A horn more than two feet long rose from its snout, which rested on the ground. The sun was coming up, and dew hung from the leaves of bushes and from the countless spider webs spread over the trees.

Our guide, sensing some change, began to walk slowly backward. The rest of us were happy to do the same. At a safer distance—maybe 30 feet—we stopped again and watched as the rhino awoke and then balanced its enormous body on its four short legs. It was almost impossible to believe that rhinos can run at almost 35 miles an hour, but that fact kept our hearts racing. As the rhino stared down its horn at me, I asked our guide, "When are these really dangerous?"

"Oh, all the time," he answered.

We walked away slowly and continued with our safari. We saw giraffes, two more rhinos, and many impalas and zebras. At one point our guide stopped on the road and said, "Do you mind walking through the trees?"

"No, why?"

"Some elephants have gone that way," he said, pointing into a thicket of head-high bushes.

"Let's go," Pat said.

We tracked the elephants through thorns and thick brush for 25 minutes, almost running, trying to avoid ever fresher dung. The branches of the trees and bushes were bent and broken on both sides of their trail, but our arms were still covered with cuts and scrapes. We finally got close enough to see the group of 11, but the thick brush did not afford us any clear views. Still, the experience of tracking them, just knowing they were ahead, was thrilling.

As we drove out of the park that afternoon, we sped by ostriches, giraffes, and zebras, as if they could be found on every corner in America.

On the way back to South Africa, we stopped at the Royal Swazi Sun, a luxurious hotel in the Ezulwini Valley. "I have only spent 20 dollars in the last three days," Steve-o said. "I'm on vacation. Let's stay here."

We lounged near the pool, overlooking the golf course and the bowling green, the life-size chess set, and the white building that held the squash courts, backed by the blue-green mountain walls of the Ezulwini Valley. I cannot believe that another hotel in this world has a more beautiful setting than the Royal Swazi. We drank and gambled rand away in the casinos. In the morning, struggling to get out of bed, we discovered that massages in the spa—with its hot tub overlooking the mountains—were only 20 dollars. And aromatherapy was only 15. We left in the afternoon, late, and made it back to Johannesburg just in time to go to Yeoville for reggae night.

Two days later, in a backpackers in an old Johannesburg mansion, we read in the paper a review of the jazz concert we had seen the night before at the Bass Line. It was the best in years, the reviewer said. My friends were impressed with my leadership. But, no matter how hard I tried, there were aspects of South Africa I could not explain. I told them about matchbox houses, and as we drove by Chrissiesmeer on the way to Johannesburg, Brad pointed at the rows and rows of identical square houses on the hill behind the township. "That is absurd. Honestly, how could they not see the inhumanity of it? Look at that," he said, poking the car window. "It's ridiculous."

"Brad," I said sadly, "those houses were actually built by Mandela's Rural Development Project because the families had substandard housing."

"Oh, really? What are we supposed to think about that?"

I still do not have an answer.

As we drove from Johannesburg to Cape Town, I tried to point out a township. We drove for three days, crossing the entire breadth of South Africa, and never saw a township from the road. We passed hitchhikers and occasional koombis, but all other traces of black South Africa were wholly invisible from the highway.

On that trip we did see a good deal of the South African countryside. Through the Free State to Bloemfontein and then south we traveled in the Highveld. The land was lonely, with single trees or rock formations rising out of the monotonous windswept grassland. We didn't see a single car for more than six hours. It was Easter Sunday, and the religious people of the Free State, both white and black, were in church or at home with family.

From the Free State the land plunges down to the sea in a tumultuous mountain range. Perhaps our response was due in part to the contrast with the dry brown plains of the Highveld, but even so as we rounded the first of the mountains and emerged into the first valley, which extended to the horizon like a tropical Switzerland, we pulled our car over to the side of the road and stood in awed silence, staring into the distance.

These mountains of the Eastern Cape are what sustained the Boers in their early days. One spectacular valley follows another in a seemingly endless progression. When the son of an Afrikaner farmer in the 1700s wanted to set out on his own, he simply walked over a ridge of mountains and obtained an estate as impressive as his father's. As we traveled the route in the other direction, we were somewhat jealous. "I have never seen anything like this," Thomas said. "It goes on forever. Why doesn't everyone in the world want to come to South Africa?" I mentioned that my favorite South African book title was *Ah, But Your Land Is Beautiful*.

We spent the next two days driving down the coast on the Garden Route, the stretch of highway between Port Elizabeth and Cape Town. The towns along the way—Jeffreys Bay, George, Knysna, and Plettenbergbaai—cling to the mountains and overlook some of the most beautiful beaches in the world. We took our time, but still felt that we were leaving each place too soon.

In two days in Cape Town, the highlight was our visit to Robben Island. The island is six miles off the coast and provides a perfect vantage point for examining Cape Town's impressive skyline. The city spreads itself at the base of Table Mountain, a green mesa that rises 3,559 feet and stretches across the horizon for almost two miles, making Cape Town one of the most distinctive cities in the world.

On the ferry to the island, a video documented its history from its time as a colonial prison, through its years as a leper colony, and ending with its ascension as one of the most well-known political prisons in the world. At one point, Walter Sisulu, Nelson Mandela's best friend and one of the most famous political prisoners, appears on the screen and tells a story about a catchphrase prisoners shared with each other as they worked hard labor. They used to pass in the quarry where they mined limestone, shake their heads, and say, *"Umsebenzi wamlungu, angeke upelli amadnda*—Men, the white man's work is never done."

When my friends left for the United States, I was faced with a whirl of disturbing thoughts. I lived in a village in what used to be a South African homeland. I called the five black women at home my "family." Yet when I was traveling with my friends, I myself felt like a tourist all over again. What did I really understand about this country? Before I had time to think through the questions, I had another experience that further blurred the picture I'd formed of South Africa. Zindzi called to say she was having a birthday party, and I was invited.

Her house was as I thought it would be: an immaculate three-bedroom home surrounded by a large garden, a pool, and a wall. The three young women had a hundred friends, of which several were white. Everyone spoke English. They were ad executives and TV production assistants, marketing specialists, and writers for commercials, talk shows, or television dramas. Some were investment bankers, stock brokers, or foreign exchange traders for banks and insurance companies. Some were management consultants. I felt underdressed and out of my league. All of the women were beautiful and intelligent, the men witty and suave. Several had lived in the United States when they were younger, and several had gone to college there. Some had American accents that came and went.

The conversations were about finance policy, major cultural endeavors, the future of South African theatre, or jazz. These people went out for coffee and ate at the best restaurants in town. They worked out at health and racquet clubs. The next day a few women were taking the birthday girl to the spa for a facial, a pedicure, and a massage.

Most had not grown up in the townships, but in Mmabatho, the capital of Bophuthatswana, the Tswana homeland—or in Botswana, Zimbabwe, or Swaziland. None of them spoke Zulu. Before this, I thought every black person who lived in Jo-burg spoke both Zulu and Sotho. That was how we knew, in Lochiel, that someone was from Gauteng. Certainly everyone I had met before—even the Sotho-speaking people in Soshanguve—spoke Zulu. Even if their Zulu was not good, they still recognized the words. Here, English was the language of choice.

At one point just before dinner, as we were all standing in the kitchen, a young woman called me over, as charming as ever. "You're from America. You have Thanksgiving, right?"

"Sure," I said, still slightly unnerved by people who knew American customs so well. I was used to being asked if there were black people in America or if we had tribes there, or if we spoke Afrikaans.

She pointed to the pan. "Will you help us cut up this chicken?" she asked. "None of us know how to do it."

As fun as the party was, their culture was not black South Africa as I knew it. Yet they were the success stories of the New South Africa. I was confused. Was I going back to Lochiel to help the teachers transform their students into these people? What would Zakes or Tsimanga or Chiluga say about the way these people acted and their relationship to their culture?

In the morning, as I walked down the streets in Rosebank, I noticed that every single house was ringed with security fencing, concrete walls with razor wire on top. Many had signs warning about high voltage. These walls, Allister Sparks said, are a "cruel inversion of apartheid," imprisoning the people within.

I did not know if those people inside were white or black. It did not matter.

Here I was, trying to foster this change without any idea where the results were heading. Perhaps we were merely teaching so that the best and brightest could grow up and live behind these walls. And anyway, who was I to claim a role in this saga? My friends and I had eaten in one week the equivalent of Lochiel Primary School's yearly budget. I did not belong in Lochiel. Whom was I kidding?

At the backpackers in Pretoria the next morning, I sat outside on the porch at ten o'clock and calculated how long it would take to get to Lochiel: Take a meter taxi over to the taxi rank; get in a cramped koombi to sit for 45 minutes before it filled up for the one-hour ride to Witbank; wait in another cramped, smelly taxi at another taxi rank for another hour; ride for three more sweaty hours with my knees in my chest and my bag on my lap to Nhlazatje; and wait for 30 more minutes before the final taxi filled up and I could begin the last 30-minute trip up to Lochiel. I had not seen Gogo in almost two weeks. She would be cooking canned fish and pap, or phidvo. There was no milk because the grass was drying out; it was cold at Lochiel.

"Do you want to grab some breakfast?" someone asked. "I heard about this place that has eggs Benedict. Apparently it's pretty cheap."

"Yeah," I said. "My site is really far away. I don't think I can make it today anyway."

I WAS EMBARRASSED WHEN I HAD TO FACE THE PEOPLE IN LOCHIEL after wasting so much money, having blown the equivalents of monthly pensions on single dinners. Gogo was excited to see me, though, and she asked me all about my trip. Her excitement made me feel worse. I was not only a disgrace to myself but also doing a disservice to all of the people in Lochiel who had supported my work—work whose purpose was now unclear to me.

A few days after I returned, I went to Southern Fried Chicken in eLuk-watini. It was Andiswa's birthday, and I wanted to order a cake as a surprise. Behind the counter's glass front, they offer sandwiches, boiled eggs, cheese, cold meats, and all kinds of drinks. I focused on their *mageu*, a traditional sour sorghum drink that tastes vaguely like bananas. I had tasted the homemade, traditional variety at a funeral. The mageu had been passed around in a bucket, and I drank directly from it. This mageu behind the counter in Southern Fried was in a carton.

The bakery section of the restaurant sold loaves of bread and had a thriving birthday cake business. Southern Fried was the only place in town that would bake a cake, add icing, and decorate it. Everyone who had the money would buy one; they were delicious.

I was speaking in Zulu when two well-dressed black men I had never seen before walked in. They listened to me tell the woman behind the counter that I needed a cake because it was my sister Andiswa's birthday. *"Ngicela ubhala* 'Happy Birthday Andiswa.' *Uzobenaminyaka ay six. Ngiyabonga."*

One of the men asked, in English, "Where are you from?"

"I am from America, but right now I live in Lochiel."

"Hawu! That place on the way to Swaziland?"

"Yes."

"How long have you been there to speak Zulu or Siswati like this?"

"A year," I said.

"Hawu! What are you doing here?"

"I am working with teachers to help them with the implementation of the new curriculum. . . ."

"Curriculum 2005?" He interrupted.

"Yes," I said, thinking he might be a teacher, "and we also work with the community."

"Who sent you? Is it a church or something?"

"No," I said quickly. "I am with the United States Peace Corps." I had had this conversation a thousand times, in Siswati, Zulu, and

English, and could recite my lines on automatic pilot. "It is a part of the United States government that sends volunteers to work in maybe 90 countries around the world."

"Are they all teachers, like you?"

"No, they have different programs in different countries. In Mozambique, they do agriculture; in Zimbabwe, they do AIDS education. The government of South Africa invited the United States to send volunteers to help with rural education."

"So you come and live with the people?"

"Yes, we do our best to get to know the community."

"Wow," he said, and I felt a familiar flash of pride as he was getting to know the Peace Corps and buying into its ideals. "And you learn about our language and our culture? I mean, clearly you speak the language...." He motioned with his hand.

"We do our best to learn about how people live, their language, and their culture."

"So," he paused. "You are infiltrating us."

"No," I said, backtracking fast. "Uh, we don't think of it in that way. We...."

"We are so colonized already," he said, shaking his head and pointing at the glass counter, "that we now buy mageu that is processed and packaged in Johannesburg. And if we don't buy that, we drink Coca-Cola from Atlanta, Georgia."

I was flustered. I started talking about learning the local culture and all the great people I had met. He saw that I was upset.

"Don't get me wrong," he said, smiling sincerely. "Yours is the best way to colonize a people. Americans at least give you something in return."

The woman behind the counter, who had not been listening to the conversation, said, *"Musa, i-orda-yakho izolunga ngabo four. Hamba. Buya ngabo four, uyezwa?"* I was to come back at four to pick up my cake. I left and said good-bye to the man, feeling upset that he might be right.

Was I a part of the cultural stampede that I had decried before I left? Tupac "Thug Life" shirts, Snoop Dogg graffiti, and other bits and pieces of American hip-hop music dominated the Lochiel square. I had brought Sandile a *Source* magazine ("the Magazine of Hip-Hop Politics and Culture") when I came back from Washington, and the issue seemed to show up everywhere. "Musa, I have been reading that book you gave to Sandile. Thank you. Jay-Z is so cool." Boys wrote with pen on white T-shirts, "Cash Money" and "Puff Daddy" and "Tech-9." This cultural imperialism would have happened without me, but I could not escape the thought that I was contributing to it.

"Musa, how do you do this in America?" Conversations that I once thought were opportunities for education, I now regarded as opportunities for cultural destruction. Newly on guard, I noticed that teachers sometimes approached me and tried to impress me with statements like: "Musa, look at this. Can you believe how backward these people are?"

I knew that my job was on the front lines, but I did not know which way we were charging. I was helping the schools change their definition of success, but I did not know what it meant for them. Zindzi and her friends were successful, doing interesting, wide-ranging projects that affected South African society, but are they the goal of South African education? Now I no longer saw a clear goal, not only for me but also for the schools themselves.

One weekend shortly thereafter, at the backpackers in Nelspruit, a Dutch woman made a familiar argument: "Americans are so insensitive and so blind that they do not see anything that is happening outside their borders, and still their culture presses in everywhere. Even you, you come here to teach people how to be American."

"Look," I said, "I'm not trying to westernize anyone."

"No?" she said. "But it happens anyway. In Kenya, the Masai have stopped putting lip plates in their mouths because tourists thought it was disgusting. That is sad. They have done this for years, and now they stop because white people come to town with money."

Deep down, I agreed with her. The cultural stampede was moving right along, and something had to be done to preserve indigenous culture.

Another day I was taking a footpath to the secondary school. I was looking down, because I had walked this path a hundred times, when I almost walked right into a barbed-wire fence that cut across the path. The old path cut straight through the corner of this newly fenced-in yard.

Soon a grader came to town. The huge yellow machine with the American CAT logo plowed between the houses, forming a ten-foot-wide path from the highway through the middle of town up to the ridge. After a few weeks, it came back and graded the land again, making the road slightly wider and flatter. All of the people who lived near this new road erected fences, and all of the old footpaths had to change course. The town planner in the eLukwatini office, I was told, was officially parceling out the land. The people of Lochiel were being given plots of land on a grid so that the government could install sewers and electricity.

I spoke to Mr. Tshabalala, the secondary school principal, who supported the project. Shaking his head, he said, "It has taken them so long, Jason, to get this thing right. At first the people in Lochiel actually fought this thing. No one wanted to do it. You see, they thought they did not need plumbing or electricity. They had gone on well without it for all these years, and they said, 'Why should I be forced to move my home from the place where my father built it?' You see, they did not want to live in straight lines, everyone with fences. They were very poor, Jason, they have suffered. But they are so stubborn...." He trailed off.

I certainly thought sewers and electricity could improve the quality of life, but I had also celebrated the footpaths and the natural homesteads. During my time there, the number of fences increased perhaps 50 times, and I hated the thought that the outside world was muscling in on Lochiel. I had complained that white South Africa's power lines passed by without stopping, but now I was sad to see their tentacles reach into every home on the mountain.

DOUBTS ASSAILED ME EVEN AT WORK. EVERY POSITIVE ACHIEVEMENT

I made reinforced the idea that white people could do things black people could not. Teachers would come up to me after a Department of Education workshop and say, "This thing is impossible for us. That white woman at the workshop could do it, but us, Musa, never. I just don't understand. Musa, will you do it for me?"

"I wasn't even at the workshop."

"But you're white."

On another day I was sitting in the staff room at Masakhane talking to Mr. Nkambule. I respected him because he understood the beauty of his culture and yet was committed to helping the children in his English classes succeed. He always asked about new teaching strategies, and then he actually implemented them.

I had mentioned to him some weeks earlier that the teachers at Mlondozi made the students speak only in English so that they are forced to practice it. As we sat there, two students burst through the door. "Teacher, Teacher, Lenyoni was speaking Siswati in the classroom!" said the first student.

"No, you are lying. Bongani was speaking Siswati in the classroom," the other replied.

Mr. Nkambule, maybe to impress upon me that he was following my instructions, chastised the children. He hit each one on the hand with a ruler and sent them away. I was demoralized. Why should children be punished for speaking their own language? And at my suggestion!

The next morning, I was walking out of the high school at lunchtime to go to the primary school. I passed a boy on the road that went on up to the highway. He looked like he was just arriving.

"*Ubuyaphi?*" I asked. "Where are you coming from?"

"I'm from home right now," he answered.

"Why are you so late?"

"My grandfather says I must take care of the cows every day before I go to school."

"So you come to school every day at this time?"

"No, some days I arrive earlier."

For centuries, cows have been the most important measure of a person's worth in Lochiel. Education had never brought anything of value to anyone. Many people, however, were well respected because they had cows.

How was I, or how was anyone, for that matter, to change those priorities? Here I was, a year into my service, asking where to begin. Who was I to change hundreds of years of belief on anyone else's behalf?

South Africa's complexities were beginning to overwhelm me. My relationship, as an outsider, was strained when I became reacquainted with my American lifestyle. But these complexities, as difficult as they seemed to me at the time, merely clouded more fundamental truths. Once I uncovered them, the potential of both South Africa and my time in the Peace Corps became clear to me.

MASERU

CHAPTER SIXTEEN

THE TIME WAS RIPE TO SNAP OUT OF MY DOLDRUMS. ONE EXPERIENCE AT A time, I reconstructed my belief that South Africa's future is bright, and that fighting for that future is possible. One experience at a time, I decided, is also how South Africa itself will gain confidence in its success as a single, vibrant society.

As winter became spring in Lochiel, I cleaned my room one day, fed up with the mess. I cleaned all day, organizing and collating countless papers from school, from the circuit office, from the Peace Corps, and from home, as well as magazines that I wanted to save, and old calendars. I operated under the assumption that 18 well-thought-out piles of paper were better than two heaps, and I threw out a huge amount of trash. I recruited my three little sisters to help me. We burned hundreds of papers in the fireplace, and I gave them several bags of other trash to throw in the barrel in the square.

In the late afternoon, the girls came back to me with a trash bag I had given them. "Musa," Twana said to me, "you are crazy. Look what you did! You threw away all these things, but you did it by mistake!"

She held up the bag. In it were all of the things I had thought wrong to burn and had given to the girls to throw away. "Look, Musa!" Andiswa said, excited. She held up a black plastic tray with a mirror on it that had held an old version of a Gillette razor. Numbuso held up four batteries, smiling. Twana asked if she could have a tiny black box with the green and silver top that she was holding. It was a spent printer cartridge.

"You can have it all," I told them.

They screamed, "Ha! Musa!" and they ran off to play and brag to their friends about their new toys. These children, I thought, will not grow up to be bad people no matter what I do.

One night I went to tell Gogo for the umpteenth time that I was going to Nelspruit for the weekend. Every time, I felt I was telling her that Lochiel was not good enough for me. I always had excuses—Bill needs to meet with me about school, a friend is having a party, or whatever.

She was sitting in the kitchen watching a pot of bean soup steam. "Gogo," I said self-consciously, "I am really sorry, but I think I am going to Nelspruit tomorrow after school. I need to look at some books for Ma'am Ndlovu."

"No problem, Musa," she answered.

"Are you sure, Gogo? I'm really sorry."

"Ay, Musa. There's no problem. I know that life."

I was always surprised when pieces of language matched perfectly. Single words in Zulu often represent concepts that take six or seven English words and vice versa. Zulu has one word for both "blue" and "green," but it has three words for "grass." In Zulu there is an entire verb tense that indicates that an action is being performed for someone else. English and Zulu developed independently for thousands of years, and yet some idioms and constructions—that could not possibly have crossed from English to Zulu—remained identical. In Zulu, when someone is sad they speak of their heart hurting, especially if the pain involves a loved one. There is no logical reason for this, and yet the idiom is similar in both languages. Often phrases stuck with me only because I was surprised to hear the construction make so much sense in English. One of these was Gogo's statement, *"Ngiy'azi leimphilo*—I know that life."

She went on: "At the time when I lived in Pretoria with the white people, Musa, on Friday I was so happy to go and see my friend in Alexandra. Musa, we sat and talked and laughed. It was nice to see her because she had the same life. We talked. It was so nice. Go. Say hello to everyone for us."

Gogo understood what it was like to live in a foreign world minutes away from a familiar one. She had never said anything to me before about my life in Lochiel, or about South Africa's borders. Once I knew she understood that crossing back and forth was difficult, I never had another moment of discomfort with Gogo. She never had to say anything about it again.

IN JUNE, THE EXCITEMENT LEADING UP TO THE ELECTION REACHED ITS apex. The television news was dominated by coverage of the parties' campaigns, and electioneers in and around Lochiel were in full swing. The teachers at my schools were intimately involved in their unions' activities and in the ANC. The outcome of the election was not in doubt: The ANC was going to win handily. Thabo Mbeki would replace Nelson Mandela and become South Africa's second black president.

This election was not to be a transition to majority rule, but rather the first election in the new South Africa. The Democratic Party, led by the fiery and intelligent Tony Leon, was taking over as the primary voice of the white minority. The National Party, trying to distance itself from its apartheid days, recast itself as the "New National Party," but it was still trounced at the polls. Mangosuthu Buthelezi's Zulu nationalist Inkatha Freedom Party would poll well in KwaZulu-Natal, and the violence that had marked its past conflicts with the ANC was replaced by careful political maneuvers and manipulation of the media.

The ANC would win largely on the merits of its fight against apartheid and the legacy left by Nelson Mandela. But Thabo Mbeki's ascension to the presidency marked the end of the ANC's position as a party of freedom fighters and the beginning of its position as an incumbent government that was expected to deliver on its promises. Many of the liberation heroes would be replaced by career politicians. Mbeki had substantially run the government during Mandela's presidency, and he was well known and respected in Lochiel. But he was not Nelson Mandela and would not be afforded the latitude given a hero.

Still, the spirit of democracy remained strong, and people were excited about their election. In the valleys around Lochiel the ANC would poll over 90 percent, but others still campaigned. The telephone pole in front of the Lochiel garage was covered with posters from several parties. One day in downtown eLukwatini, I was surprised to see a white man standing in the bed of his pickup truck stapling a poster onto a pole near the complex. An NNP poster, no less. The *New* National Party, formerly the party of apartheid, was actually courting black votes. This man had driven miles from his home in white South Africa to put up posters for a party that would be lucky to get 10 votes out of 50,000 in the region. I had to admire his faith in democracy, and in the future of South Africa. I gave him a wave as I walked by.

In Lochiel, the polling station was in a classroom at Sisukumile Secondary School. The poll workers were friends of mine: Piet; Timothy, who was on the library committee; Louis from Gogo's church; and a few others excited to have a job for several days.

A few days before the election the schoolyard was crowded with *bogogo*—grandmothers and other elderly or handicapped people who were allowed to vote early. The old black men and women, most with canes, barefoot and wrapped in blankets, many blind or handicapped, lined up outside the polling center and waited patiently. They sat in school chairs in a line, standing up and moving to the next chair as each new person entered the classroom. These people, many of whom rarely left their yards, came from miles around, some walking all day just to vote in an election whose outcome was already decided. Seeing the effort it took to move from one chair in the line to the next, and seeing the children and grandchildren who accompanied them to help them walk—or even pushed them in a wheelbarrow—brought home to me the beauty of this election.

Election day was inspiring as well. All but 34 of the 1,375 people registered at Lochiel voted. The consensus among the election workers was that most of those nonvoters had died between the registration period and the election. When the polls opened at seven o'clock in the morning, more than 500 people stood in the line. When I got out of bed a short time later, frost still covered the ground. A long line of people (some shivering) stretched out of the Sisukumile schoolyard throughout the day. Almost everyone I talked to waited for more than an hour to cast a vote.

The atmosphere on Election Day, a national holiday in South Africa, was exuberant. During South Africa's last election, many in Lochiel had been nervous about violence, but not this year. The polling station was like a big democracy fest, and all of Lochiel was here. Women sold fruits and pies and steamed cornbread; people milled around outside, talking and drinking beer. Kids ran around kicking balls or just chasing each other. Cows and goats roamed in and out of the schoolyard. We hooked up my CD player to someone's car, and several of us sat on the ground playing chess, blaring reggae star Peter Tosh. People approached me constantly asking, "Did you vote?...Why not?"

My Election Day vocabulary was nonexistent, so I had to find a way to explain myself. Eventually, I assured people that we Americans would be voting the following year, in 2000. There was a sense of kinship between me, as an American, and my friends in Lochiel. It was as though we all belonged to the same democracy club, and they were proud of their membership. I had to hide my embarrassment at the reality of democracy at home in America. Through my work with the Carter Center and in South Africa, I had seen elections in five countries. Without a doubt, the ones in the United States are the least joyous.

I talked to one girl my age who was voting for the first time. She said she had practiced making X's all morning so that her first ballot would be perfect. The community was jubilant, and I went home at the end of the day excited and full of hope. I wrote an e-mail to everyone I knew saying that Election Day should be a national holiday and a celebration of democracy at home in the United States.

A few weeks later I found myself in Pretoria. Every year the United States ambassador hosts a Fourth of July party for Americans living in the country, held at the recreation center attached to the ambassadorial residence. Hundreds of people attend, including all of the diplomats and other staff at the embassy, their families, and other Americans who work in South Africa. My friend John and I had planned to go to the party and then continue on to Maseru, Lesotho, on the sixth to visit some other Peace Corps volunteers and to see a new country.

I left Lochiel on the third, hitched to Witbank, took a taxi to Pretoria, and then went to visit Gogo's family for a few hours in Soshanguve. That night I met up with John and a few other volunteers, and we spent the night at a backpackers in Pretoria. The embassy and the State Department issued travel warnings stating that Americans traveling in South Africa should never go to the townships, the former homelands, or to central Johannesburg because the areas were not safe. When I arrived for the party, I had passed through almost all of those places in the previous day. According to the embassy, Americans were never to travel by "minibus taxi." Three other volunteers and I stepped out of a koombi in front of the party. We walked past a long line of cars and snickered because "these folks get hardship bonuses on top of their regular salary because they have to live in the jungles of Africa."

I had attended the party the year before as a less jaded, more excited new volunteer who craved the food and the hint of luxury. This time I was prepared for the party to be just another First-World experience in South Africa. But I was soon won over. The recreation center has an enclosed yard with a playground, picnic areas, two gazebos, and tennis courts. It looked like a typical American park on the Fourth of July. There was a chili cook-off with prizes, a raffle sponsored by American businesses, grilled hamburgers and hot dogs, Domino's pizza, and McDonald's apple pies. People threw Frisbees; kids played on the playground and jumped around on a "Jungle Bounce" trampoline with the inflated walls and roof rented for the occasion; speakers blared Lee Greenwood's "God Bless the U.S.A." and other Americana; and the picnic tables and picnickers sported stars and stripes on their paper plates, napkins, and tablecloths. Red-white-and-blue bunting hung from the roof of the main picnic area where the winners of the chili cook-off and raffle would be announced. I loved it. I loved the ideal that my country represents, and as stereotypical as all theses paper symbols were, they were still symbols of home.

After the party, we went to a ritzy restaurant called Café Brazil in Brooklyn, Pretoria. A young American woman we met that day had invited us to meet one of her South African friends. John and I sat down with the two young women in a booth in the dark restaurant. Bamboo hung from the walls behind the booth, and a mural of Rio's skyline covered the far wall. We talked to the South African woman about her life, and she asked about our work. As it often does in white South Africa, the conversation turned to crime. She complained about how awful it was.

"So," I asked, "do you think things are worse now than they were during apartheid?"

"Oh, yes," she said. "Crime is terrible. We have to lock our car doors before we drive out our gate. We are constantly terrified."

"Do you think," John asked, with no attempt to disguise his irritation, "that things should have stayed like they were during apartheid?"

Clearly defensive, she explained what she meant. "Look, I am not a racist," she said. "I did not support apartheid. I just lived my life the way anyone would. I went to school every day at the best school my family could afford, just like anyone. Sure, apartheid was there the whole time, but it didn't affect my life. I saw the signs on the buses, but I didn't put them up."

John looked at me with wide eyes. We had been living in the homelands for a year and a half, seeing apartheid's legacy every day in every face. We had friends as close as family whose lives had been fundamentally disfigured by apartheid, and here, in this fancy all-white restaurant with pictures of Rio on the walls, this woman was telling us apartheid had meant no more to her than signs on the buses.

"Did apartheid affect you in any other way?" John asked.

"No, it really wasn't a part of my life. I never oppressed anyone," she said defiantly. "I like black people."

John had to go to the rest room to keep his tongue in check. While he was gone, she told me, "Yes, of course I felt bad for my maid, but what could I do?"

"Did you ever go to her house?"

"Our maid's house? Her family lived in the township," she said, as though it answered my question.

"Have you never been to the township?" I asked, knowing the answer.

"No, have you?" she asked, on guard against American hypocrisy.

"Yes."

John came back and I left for the bathroom.

Our other friends soon showed up and we ran out the door, exhausted by the uncomfortable social situation.

John and I got up early the next morning to begin our 300-mile hitchhiking trip to Lesotho. It was to be our first time there, and we were braced for cold weather. But at least we no longer had to worry about the violence. Earlier in the year we had met some other Peace Corps volunteers who had been evacuated from Lesotho after the elections in March 1999. After the elections, supporters of the king rioted in the streets, and the government of Lesotho called the South African military to assist them. It took the South Africa Defense Force weeks to gain control of the tiny country, and the foray into Lesotho was an embarrassment for the army. This incident was ammunition for right-wing racists and other opponents of the ANC government, who claimed that the once brilliant South African military was falling into disarray. It was also, interestingly, ammunition for supporters of the Swazi monarchy who viewed the violence in Lesotho as an example of the instability brought by democracy.

We hitched seven short lifts from exit to exit on the freeway in Gauteng, which took us four hours. Finally, at a tollbooth on the edge of the province, we convinced a white South African man our age to give us a lift to Bloemfontein, where we would then catch a taxi to Maseru.

In the car we talked for hours. He lived in a small apartment in Pretoria and was working for a software company. He played the new U2 CD and a few tapes of local bands that he enjoyed seeing live in certain bars in Gauteng.

He also told us when he first discovered the other side of apartheid. Growing up, he had known nothing about the way black people lived. "The first time I really thought about it," he said, "was when I was watching the cricket world cup this year, and they had these specials at the break about black cricketers. It hit me," he continued, "that I knew nothing at all about my own country." I thought about Nhlazatje and all of those townships from Jo-burg to Cape Town. The truth was just waiting there, but it was invisible from the road.

He asked us about our jobs. How were we received? What were the issues in the education process? What did we think was going to happen? He asked us if we knew any places in Pretoria where he could mingle with black people, and we gave him a few suggestions. He was liberated from his old world of lies, but like those people in Cantina Tequila, he still needed a bridge. I felt sorry for him, but I also admired him for his ability to see what so many people could not. He dropped us off in Bloemfontein and gave us his phone number "in case you are going back on Tuesday and need a ride."

Back in black South Africa, speaking no Sotho, it was clear how I had come to rely on my ability to speak Zulu. John and I received several different sets of directions and took 45 minutes to get to the correct place on the outskirts of Bloemfontein to get a ride to Maseru. By that time the sun was low in the sky and the wind was whipping across the plains. The Free State near Bloemfontein is desolate country. We stood for 30 minutes with two older people. We were bundled up in our expensive North Face jackets; they were wrapped in blankets and wearing stocking hats. A pickup truck stopped and the black driver told us that he would drop us off at a place on the way to Maseru where we could take a taxi "to the bridge." From our conversations in Bloemfontein, we had gleaned that a bridge of some kind was an important part of our trip. We hoped that from the bridge we would be able to get to 222 Kingsway in Maseru, our prearranged meeting place.

We climbed several hundred feet in elevation and pulled into a small community surrounding a factory. The sun was setting on a very South African scene. The wind was whipping dust through the small vendor stands made from wooden poles and scraps of plastic to protect the goods and the seller from the elements. The dirty brown plastic shredded and flapped in the wind. A few people walked across the dirt lot wearing the standard work coveralls with blankets wrapped around their shoulders. Most had stocking caps on their heads and tall rubber boots on their feet. The factory, a square building of brown brick surrounded by razor-wire fencing, stood in the dry, dusty grass, connected to the rest of South Africa by a wide belt of high-capacity power lines.

I had seen maps of the Sotho and Tswana homelands and knew that the government had created several small islands between Bloemfontein and Lesotho. I did not see any permanent houses, so I suspected that this factory had been a subsidized border industry, and that all the people lived in a former homeland settlement hidden somewhere in the plains.

Two koombis were parked in the swirling dust. A few people with large traveling bags congregated outside the taxis exhaling puffs of frost. I asked in Zulu if this was the taxi to Maseru. A woman answered in Sotho, nodding her head and pointing to a small hexagonal building with two barred windows. We walked over there and saw, through the dust and the twilight, the word "TICKETS." In English, we asked the woman behind the bars if we could get tickets to Maseru. She said they were 18 rand each and that we were lucky to get the last koombi. John and I looked at each other. What would we have done in this place in the dark?

We piled into the koombi, thankful for the warmth. It started off, scraping and clicking and popping its way up into the mountains. I read for five minutes before complete darkness fell. I had never ridden in a koombi so late at night, and certainly not in a strange country where I did not speak the language. As we rode, I realized the koombi's lights were so dim that we could not see more than 20 feet ahead. The driver hunched over as though driving in a snowstorm. We climbed at an excruciatingly slow pace, with one tire almost in the grass to the left of the road.

At a crossroads at the top of a mountain pass, the koombi finally stopped completely. I could almost never tell if koombis halted because they were supposed to or because they had broken down. The wind rattled the koombi's windows, and cold shot through the cracks in the door. I saw lights dotting the valley below us, making me wonder if the city below was Maseru. A car came from behind, and in its lights I could read the sign at the crossroads. Straight ahead was Landybrand, Maseru Bridge to the right. "Excuse me," I said to the woman in front of me. "How far from the bridge to the town of Maseru?"

"It is very close," she said. "If you cross the bridge, you are there, in Maseru."

"How far is that from here?"

"Some minutes," she said. "This taxi, his lights are too weak so he must wait for another to take us to the bridge."

Koombi lights soon appeared on the road coming from the bridge. Our driver got out and flagged the man down. They spoke for a minute—apparently negotiating a price—and we were told that everyone going to the bridge needed to get in the other taxi. John and I took our bags and our baseball caps and our fancy jackets across the road and got in the other koombi. Only six of the original fourteen passengers were going to Maseru. The new driver, after getting his money from our first driver, made a U-turn and drove us the ten minutes to the bridge.

I had crossed the Swazi border many times, and the Lesotho border was a much simpler process. Lesotho is completely surrounded by South Africa, so there is little reason to have the stolen car checks and drug searches that they have at the border post by Lochiel. The South African immigration official duly stamped our passports. She looked confused, though, when we, a white man and a Coloured man, told her we had no car. She gave us a gate pass and pointed us on our way. We walked across the bridge to Lesotho, Maseru glowing on the other side. Old men walked with us on the bridge wearing blankets over their shoulders and the distinctive Sotho straw hats. Ubiquitous in Lesotho, the hats are reminiscent of those worn by farmers in Asian paddies, with a pointed top and a chin strap.

On the Lesotho side of the border they also stamped our passports and thought it was odd that we were traveling on foot. I was nervous entering an unfamiliar African capital on foot at night with bags and suitcases announcing we were tourists. We checked the address again: 222 Kingsway. We did not know how far that was, and we did not know what type of transport we would use. I gripped my credit card with my toes to make sure it was still safely stowed in my shoe. Cash was stuffed in our socks and shoes, in the front pockets of our jeans. My wallet was in the inside front pocket of my jacket, and I had nothing but clothes in my bag. We walked into a crowd of people milling around several koombis. As we approached, everyone started yelling: "Triple Two, Triple Two?" I thought it was a Sotho tsotsi code word for "Jump 'em, they're stupid tourists who have wandered into our midst!"

"What's going on? What are they saying?" I asked John.

"Triple two. That's where we are going, isn't it?"

I looked down at the address. "How did they know?"

John looked at me and smiled. I laughed, and we got in a taxi that was offered to us by three or four attendants. They charged us a couple of rand and drove us the five minutes over to the Peace Corps house where we met the other volunteers.

LESOTHO, LIKE SWAZILAND, WAS MADE A BRITISH PROTECTORATE

in the early 19th century. During apartheid, it received international attention and aid as a frontline state in the diplomatic battle against South Africa's racist regime. Still, it is overpopulated, the climate is harsh, and the AIDS rate is one of the highest in Africa.

The streets of Maseru, the commercial capital of the country, had been dominated by signs advertising movie theaters, electronics stores, video rentals, clothing stores, restaurants, and groceries. Because Lesotho's economy is dominated by South Africa, the stores were familiar to me: Patrick Daniel, Jet, KFC, OK, ShopRite, CNA. But during the postelection riots, looters had rampaged through the town. A few months later, when I was there in July, many of the stores had not been repaired. Windows were missing and glass still lay scattered on some of the floors. Black scorch marks climbed the walls from the tops of broken windows. Entire blocks contained nothing but hollow remnants of trashed stores. Most of the larger shops had been cleaned up but not restored, leaving expansive rooms open to the street. These walls, gray and black from smoke, had housed racks of clothes and lines of shoppers. Then, during the riots, they housed looters, destroyed merchandise, broken shelves, and ravaged cash registers. The smoke damage rimming these cavernous, blackened shells often outlined the pattern of an old sign on a blank wall, showing that a store had been an "OK" grocery, or a "Something Fishy" restaurant. Lesotho is a poor country whose reputation as a safe place was greatly damaged by the unrest.

In the morning, we hitched out to the countryside with three volunteers to go to a mountain resort/hostel in northern Lesotho. The dead of winter, I thought, must be the worst time to visit Lesotho. Just east of Maseru, the land is desolate. Huge erosion canyons, symptomatic of the massive deforestation and the toll that the population has taken on the land, crisscrossed the brown, dry valleys on either side of the road, and the mountains that dominated the horizon deepened the bleak gray of the sky. Lesotho is a few thousand feet higher than Lochiel, and it is bitterly cold.

As we turned north, however, the sky brightened a bit. We drove almost straight into the mountains, and they began to sparkle in the sunlight, taking on various shades of blue. Small groups of thatched roofs took the place of the gray concrete blocks and rusty corrugated iron that had dominated the villages farther below. Children rode horses in the distance. Entire villages spread vertically up the mountainside. People wearing blankets on their shoulders and cone-shaped hats on their heads walked on the road, leading laden horses. John and I soon agreed; it was a charming place.

We arrived at the small resort—several farmhouses and a host of rondavels for tourists—perched on the top of a mountain between two other massive ranges. We stayed in the hostel for a few days, relaxing and marveling at the tremendous breadth of the purple mountains and the brown valleys. From the front of the hostel we could watch people crossing the vista on horseback or on foot, heading to some quaint village in the highest mountains of Africa.

An older woman and her daughter who had been staying at the resort offered to drive us to Johannesburg in their rented car. They were from South Carolina, and John and I talked to them about the Peace Corps for a good portion of the six-hour ride. When she returned to the United States, the older woman—in her 60s—volunteered and left for Ghana a few months after John and I ended our Peace Corps service.

I called Gogo from Pretoria and told her I would be home the next day. In the morning, John and I left early to take the first taxi to Witbank and then to Ermelo. John was going on to Mayflower, but I had some time and decided to stop in on Gogo's daughter who worked in town.

I left the taxi rank, walked past the Sanlam Sentrum, and entered white South Africa. Up ahead, I saw the sign for KFC, the familiar white letters shaped like a chicken bucket with Colonel Sanders and his bow tie. Down the street to the left, mannequins and clothes stood in the windows of the Jet and the Patrick Daniel. These signs and windows were not taped together. The walls of Ermelo's stores were not streaked with smoke stains, and the floors were not littered with bent racks or broken cash registers destroyed by looting. Families walked in and out of the stores, white and black, buying clothes, shoes, or fried chicken and cole slaw. At the end of apartheid, Ermelo had every reason to end up like Maseru, or worse, but it did not. This realization fueled a renewed optimism that South Africa's peaceful transformation was an enduring gift from the oppressed to the new nation and to the world. The source of that gift is the unshakable core of black South African humanity, the same humanity that underpins the community of Lochiel and cannot be left behind no matter how Western their lifestyles become. That realization allowed me to attack my job with a renewed belief that I had a role to play in South Africa's important transformation.

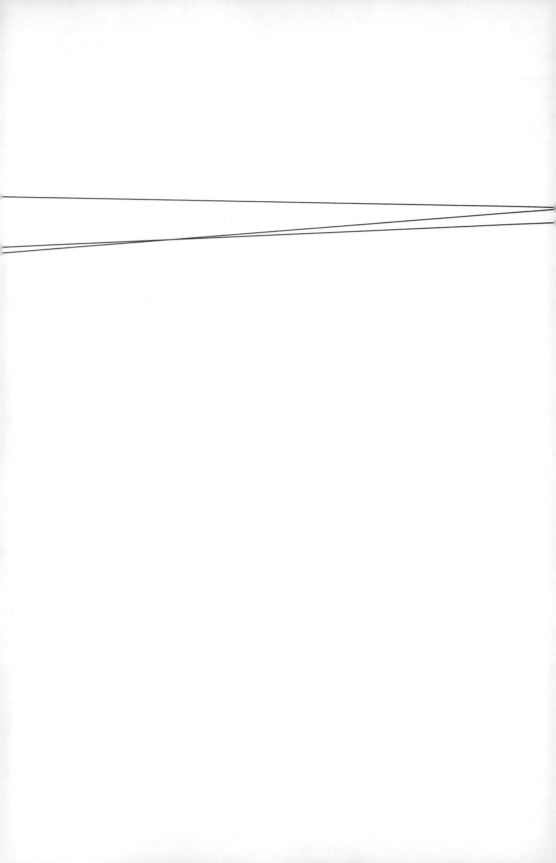

UBUNTU
CHAPTER SEVENTEEN

THE BOOKS OF STEVE BIKO AND DESMOND TUTU CELEBRATE THE fundamental aspects of African culture. I remember sitting in the back seat of a taxi between Witbank and Nhlzatshe as a little girl of five or six lay sleeping across our laps. Because she was the mandatory fourth person in the back seat, the rest of us had some extra room. Reading a sermon from Tutu's *The Rainbow People of God*, I was entranced. He explained the concept of Ubuntu clearly, and the idea hit home for the first time.

In my first week at Lochiel, Twana had recited a saying for me:

Umuntu,
Ubuntu,
Nabanye Bantu.

It translates well into English: "A person is a person through other people."

In South Africa much is made of Ubuntu. Our teachers told us about it during training. The preschool teaches the saying to all the little children, and the children learn about it at home. The television uses the word all the time, and most television shows and contests publicly strive to achieve their goals "in the spirit of Ubuntu." Even the new, complex curriculum contains a Specific Outcome that asks learners to demonstrate an understanding of the concept of Ubuntu. There are Assessment Criteria and Performance Indicators that will be used to measure a learner's progress in this regard.

Tutu explains that Ubuntu means "that you are bound up with others in the bundle of life, for a person is only a person through other persons." That which defines our humanity is other people. When one person suffers, the whole of humanity suffers. Other people define our own worth. If we do not value those other people and their lives, then the value of our own humanity and our own lives is diminished. Ubuntu, as Tutu said, is about being "truly human." "It refers to gentleness, to compassion, to hospitality, to openness to others, to vulnerability, to being available to others.... And so we search for this ultimate attribute and reject ethnicity and other such qualities as irrelevancies. A person is a person because he recognizes others as persons."

I went to turn the page, and a brown, callused hand pressed it back down. The little girl's mother, sitting next to me, had not finished reading. She lives this way, I thought. Ubuntu permeates her life and all of her interactions with others. In words, it sounds beautiful; in reality, it is even more stunning.

One afternoon Gogo and I were in the kitchen talking about Nombuso when someone knocked on the thin metal of the screen door, making it click and rattle.

"Come in!"

It was a boy perhaps 14 years old. He lowered his head, as all young people do to show respect, and he spoke so softly that I had to strain to hear him. Most children talked like this. He was very matter-of-fact and plainspoken as he explained his problem. His father worked in Johannesburg. His mother had not heard from him in months, so several weeks ago she went to Johannesburg to find him because the family needed money. She left the kids in the house because they were in school. This boy was the oldest. The mother had left them with a 40-kilogram bag of maize meal, and now it was gone. "The principal sent me to you," the boy finished. "We have no food at home."

There was no shame in his voice. He was not coming to beg for pity. He was merely telling Gogo the facts of the situation. *"Aish,"* Gogo said shaking her head. "Go back to school. We will find a way."

The boy left. Gogo never said anything more about it to me. She found a way to help, and she went on with her life. Later that day she made dinner. She set out an extra plate for Rabbit, Mr. Magagula's grandson, who had been staying with us for more than a month while his mother worked, and another plate for Mthembu, just like every night. These people and their lives were bound up in her own.

MRS. NDLOVU AND HER HUSBAND, A FORMER POLICE OFFICER AND successful businessman, built a beautiful house in Ermelo. They built in the Indian location, Cassim Park, a step up from the black location of Wesselton. The house had four bedrooms and a large garage, with at least five cars parked outside (most of the cars did not run, but still had value).

Behind the house were two small houses dedicated to the ancestors. Mrs. Ndlovu could not have a house party to honor the completion of the house until those smaller houses were finished and animals were sacrificed to thank the ancestors for allowing the current residents to have such a beautiful home. This was simply a matter of respect for those who came before her, and she saw no inconsistency with her Methodist beliefs.

Nhlanhla and I went to visit her so that I could see her new house. When we arrived, an old man in work coveralls was working on one of the cars. I asked about him, and Ma'am Ndlovu said, "Oh, that's Mkhulu. He's a godsend."

Mkhulu means "grandfather," and I suspected that she had misused the word "godsend." "Where is he from?" I asked.

"Dundonald."

"How do you know him?"

"He's a godsend, Musa. On the first day we owned this house, he came by and said he saw some black people moving into this beautiful home and wondered if we could give him some food. He was a beggar. I thought that God must have sent him to us so we could give thanks for this new house, and I invited him in. We let him take a bath in our bathroom, and gave him some food. Now he lives with us here, works around the house, and he eats with us at night. Hey, Mkhulu!"

"Yebo," said the old man.

"*NgaMusa, mfanawami lo buya emelika. Umbingelela nge sizulu uyasikhuluma kahle kakhulu.*—This is Musa from America. You can speak to him in Zulu."

Mkhulu and I exchanged greetings, and from then on, I saw him every time I visited Mrs. Ndlovu. He has no other family, and now lives with hers. Mkhulu is not a check written to a charity. He is a part of Ma'am Ndlovu's everyday life.

Ubuntu is so fundamental to the culture that it appears everywhere. Some time after she moved into her new house, Mrs. Ndlovu's car broke down on her way back from school. She hitchhiked home and called Nhlanhla. He soon came to my door and asked me to come with him to help tow the car. He needed me to sit in Mrs. Ndlovu's car to steer or hit the brakes as necessary to prevent it from slamming into the back of Nhlanhla's car when he slowed down or turned. First of all, though, we needed to find a chain or a bar, he explained.

Nhlanhla and I went off to look for a chain. We asked Mr. Magagula if he had one. He said yes and went off to find it. We waited in the courtyard for ten minutes and then decided to ask someone else. We found

Mr. Ncongwane tinkering under the hood of his trunk and asked him. "Yes, I have a chain," he said. "Come with me."

We followed him around the back of the store. He rummaged through a pile of junk and then looked through the small shelter where they park the tractor. "Babe, we're in a hurry," Nhlanhla said.

"OK," Mr. Ncongwane answered. "Go ask Shongwe. I will look a little more."

We circled back around to the garage, and I decided that we needed to tell Gogo where we were going. When we came out, we spotted Shongwe walking to his shop. We caught him and explained our problem. "Come on," he said, and we crossed the courtyard past the dead cars outside his place.

Inside, Mr. Magagula and Mr. Ncongwane stood talking. "Hey," Shongwe said, "where's the chain?"

Nhlanhla and I laughed. All three men had promised us the very same chain. (We eventually found one across the road at the Xabas' and towed the car to Ermelo.)

THE CHILDREN AT THE PRESCHOOL ATTEND CLASSES EVEN WHEN THE primary and secondary schools are on break, so some months the preschoolers were the only schoolkids I saw. And because their school was attached to my house, I saw quite a lot of them.

I understood their Siswati better than most, and I enjoyed their company. They ran around with tires, rolling them with their hands to see how long they could go. As four-year-old children, they all had bucktoothed, snaggled smiles a little too big for their faces. They would find pretty rocks or caterpillars on leaves and bring them around for my inspection. They would grab me by the hand and lead me to a place on the road where they pointed at a flattened frog.

When I first met them, all they could do was stare. Most had never been this close to a white person. Almost none had ever touched a white person's skin or hair. They sometimes crowded around, touched my arm with a finger, and then ran away screaming and talking about what it felt like.

On the whole, these little kids were just like my four- and five-year-old cousins in Georgia. Sometimes they would bring to school a shoom or a two-bob that their parents had given them to buy "sweets" during playtime. Soon after I arrived, after they had begun calling me Musa instead of *mlungu* (white man), I went to Doris's store and met S'fiso walking out. He had a huge gap-toothed smile, and he always wore a stocking cap with a ball on top. "Musa! *Bheka!*" Look here!

He held out his hand to show me two Flaky-Nut candies. Flaky-Nuts are shaped like peanuts and are crunchy like a Butterfinger. They are pretty good little candies, and the store sold them for ten cents each. S'fiso must have given them a two-bob, because he had two. My cousin Jamie would hold out candy in the same way. I would pretend to take one, and Jamie would scream, close his fist on the candy as tight as he could, put it behind his back, and run away. With S'fiso, I pretended that I was going to take his candy and, sure enough, he snapped his hand shut and put it behind his back. "Ha! Musa!"

Then he pulled his hand out, took one of the Flaky Nuts, and said, "*Ngaisweeti yakho, Musa. Thatha, idla*—Here is a sweet for you, Musa. Take it and eat it."

I had never seen a kid give away a piece of candy in my entire life. I certainly don't remember ever doing it myself. I took it in total disbelief. He couldn't have had any more money in his pocket. Just how early did these people learn about Ubuntu?

As I walked down the road near Badplaas in the early spring, not hitchhiking, I was surprised when a light-blue Volkswagen Polo stopped to give me a ride. I saw a beautiful young woman sitting in the passenger seat and a man in a purple silk shirt driving. "Hello," he said. "Do you remember me?"

It was the man from Southern Fried Chicken whose speech about American colonization had so unnerved me. He was on his way to Barberton, he said, and would have to drop me off at the crossroads. He introduced me to his girlfriend in Siswati, and she and I had a short "hello-how-are-you-oh-my!-Your-Swazi-is-so-good-for-a-white-person" exchange. In their tape deck was R. Kelly, an American R&B singer.

The crossroads was close by, and it took only a few seconds. "Here, take my card," he said. "Give me a call if you are ever in Barberton."

I got out and walked across the road to find a good place to hitch to Nhlazatje. I looked at his card: "Traditional Leader." He was the Swazi chief for the Barberton area.

A man committed to his culture, who had lamented to me about colonization, was at that very moment driving a Volkswagen while wearing a silk shirt and listening to American R&B. Perhaps, as Steve Biko says, the trappings of the culture are unimportant compared to the deeper understanding of how to relate to the world. This chief might have been upset that the minor manifestations of his culture were being overrun, but he was not worried about losing the essence of his heritage.

After I decided to write this book, a photographer came to visit and take the pictures that are included here. A few days before I was to leave, a local friend informed me that the chief was holding a ceremony to celebrate the end of summer. I wanted to say good-bye to the people in the community and suggested that the photographer come with me. When we arrived, I introduced her to some of my friends and to the chief. Dressed in his normal work clothes, he insisted that if we wanted to take pictures, we should wait for him to go home and change into his traditional attire. We waited patiently for him to return, and we took some great pictures. But it seemed a little ridiculous: Did his clothes make him African? Or a chief?

I had been upset with the trappings—with Lochiel teenagers and their Snoop Dogg graffiti, with Zindzi's facials, and even with the chief the first time I saw him listening to Dolly Parton in his pickup truck and his rain pants. But the true roots and worldview were never going to change. As Biko says, it is this mode of life, this human-centered idea of community, that outsiders and Africans alike need to learn to respect as important to world culture:

> (T)he cornerstone of society is man himself—not just his welfare, not his material wellbeing but just man himself with all his ramifications. We reject the power-based society of the Westerner that seems to be ever concerned with perfecting their technological know-how while losing out on their spiritual dimension. We believe that in the long run the special contribution to the world by Africa will be in this field of human relationship. The great powers of the world may have done wonders in giving the world an industrial and military look, but the great gift still has to come from Africa—giving the world a more human face.

I have no doubt that those like Zindzi, successful South Africans who were born in townships or homelands, are grounded in this same spirit. And I have no doubt that the world will be a better place if more children from Lochiel grow up to participate in it as fully as they can.

To say to the Masai, "Get those lip plates back in your mouth or you'll lose your culture," is absurd.

GO WELL

CHAPTER EIGHTEEN

BY MY LAST DAYS IN LOCHIEL I BEGAN TO FEEL I COULD STAY THERE
forever. I understood how my life would proceed, where I would want my
house, to which school I would send my children. I could have gotten a job
at the circuit office, a car, and a membership at the Royal Swazi Health
Club. And at the same time, I would feel that I was helping in the battle
against the pervasive poverty that was the legacy of apartheid.

But in truth, these fantasies ran free in my mind because I knew my
time was up. I knew that I would not call my family in the United States
to tell them I was staying. I would go home.

In my final weeks in Lochiel, the breakthroughs for which I had been
waiting throughout my Peace Corps service happened one after the other.
"Great," I thought, as I am sure other volunteers have thought before
me. "Just as I am getting ready to leave, everything gets easy."

I brought a lesson-planning form that I had slaved over to my last
grade-one-and-two teachers' meeting. It had 12 lines with spaces for the
Specific Outcomes and the Performance Indicators, and a place to describe

the lesson in detail and in summary. The top of the sheet allowed a teacher to indicate the other subjects that had been integrated, plus the overall Program Organizer under which the lesson fell. The bottom of the sheet left room for summary and continuous evaluation, as well as a place for a teacher to make notes about the lesson's effectiveness.

I had to use tiny type, but as I saw it, I had grasped the Holy Grail of Curriculum 2005 lesson planning: one sheet of paper that included everything. If the teachers used this every day, they would be implementing OBE. This was to be my lasting contribution, something concrete like the library project John spearheaded in Mayflower or the basketball court Bill had helped build in Nhlazatje. We met in a first-grade classroom. The teachers from the four schools sat in tiny chairs at the students' desks. I stood at the front of the classroom and explained how I envisioned them planning their lessons using this new form.

Ms. Mdluli, an exceptional young teacher, raised her hand and asked a question. I didn't get exactly what she was saying, so she stood up and took the chalk from my hand, as the other teachers giggled. She began writing on the board.

"Why don't you do it like this...?" She drew some lines and a potential lesson plan. It was much simpler and more elegant than my form. "You see, this is how I do it."

She talked for five more minutes, writing on the board and answering questions. Her writing and speaking became faster as different aspects of her ideas became clearer to her even as she explained them.

I sat down in one of the little chairs and watched. Another teacher asked her a question, and she answered. They began to talk among themselves. Suddenly she looked over at me, embarrassed. She put the chalk down with a nervous laugh and sat down in her chair.

In two years, despite my best efforts, no one had questioned me about lesson planning or anything else, and no one had stepped forward with a creative way to attack the problem of implementing this curriculum in Lochiel. But now, days before I was to leave, someone had come up with a much better lesson-planning system than mine, and she had explained it to her peers. The teachers were excited. As they were planning their next meeting, I said good-bye and slipped out.

My last task before the school term ended was to organize the AIDS-education workshops to be conducted with the students from the AIDS committees during the upcoming school break. I called the hospital's education coordinator every day for a week. I went to the hospital in eLukwatini on two occasions, but I just missed her both times.

I was so busy saying good-bye and preparing to leave that I never got through. These children had worked hard on the committee and were going to be in charge of leading discussions with their classmates. Yet now, in the end, I failed to organize the key workshops.

On the last day of school I hitched a ride on the Litje Lembube teachers' bus. When I saw Mr. Mashubane, I felt terrible.

"I am very sorry," I said, "but I never got through to the AIDS workers at the hospital, and I am leaving in a few days. I know this is terrible, but maybe the kids can do the workshops during the next school break.... I am very sorry.... I think I have the number here somewhere...." My feeling of failure showed on my face as I dug through my bag.

"Musa, what are you talking about?" Mashubane said. "That coordinator from the hospital is my neighbor, and I organized the workshop a week ago. The students start on Monday. You told us that we had to learn to do things without you."

As I prepared to leave, my friends began telling me about new encounters with white people. Eddie Msithini bought a car in Nelspruit, and the next Monday at school he related the process. "Jason, I walked in and I walked right up to the white man and said *'Sanibonani, ninjani? Bengifuna kubona letinye timoto tenu.'*

"Oh, that man, Jason, he said, 'Excuse me?' in Afrikaans. And I said to him, 'Oh, you don't speak Siswati? We can speak English if that's OK.'"

"Are you serious?" I said to Eddie.

"Oh, yes. And I would have never done that if I did not know you. I was always a bit intimidated. But I decided before I walked in there that I would do it correctly. And you know what? He respected me so much more. He was a nice man."

"That's great," I told Eddie. I had been the first white person in 50 homes, and I had been the only white friend that a hundred different people had ever had. When I saw Eddie in the staff room later, with four other teachers listening to him recount his experience at the car dealership, I was as proud as I could be.

That is one of the beauties of the Peace Corps. Later, I went to visit Nikki in Kromdraai. It was to be my last time in the little town where I had been introduced to South Africa. Nikki went with me to say good-bye to my home-stay family, the Khozas.

As we walked down the dirt street, passing the small square concrete houses that had been built to house the mine workers, someone called out to Nikki. We stopped and a teenage girl in an old, too-small, graying dress walked over to the fence in front of her yard. She balanced a toddler on her hip as she spoke to Nikki. Nikki leaned with one foot on the fence and listened intently.

They spoke for a minute while I stood in the road, unable to hear.

Nikki thanked the girl and walked slowly back over to me. We continued our walk down the road. "Who was that?" I asked.

"I don't know. I'd never met her before," Nikki said. "But do you know what she said?"

"What?"

"She wanted to thank me and Nicole for being here. She said she loved seeing black women walk around with their heads up, talking to whoever they wanted and looking everyone in the eye."

"Wow," I said.

"Wow is right," said Nikki.

ON MY LAST DAY AT LOCHIEL PRIMARY, I SAT IN THE STAFF ROOM.

From the plastic skeleton in the corner hung the outdated maps the geography teachers still used. The big gray metal cabinets were opened, showing stacks of brown paper exercise books filled with the writing of Lochiel's children. The walls varied from white to dark brown in splotches, and sun came in the window a dusty yellow. There was still no electricity, but the circuit office had promised us that plans were in the works.

Sam Malaza was sitting, impeccably dressed in a burgundy suit and perfectly polished shoes, at the table grading papers. Sam, the perennial MC for the numerous school events and beauty pageants, was everyone's favorite teacher. My sister Twana was excited about fourth grade and often came home at night talking about Mr. Malaza's class.

Eddie and I had gone to visit him over the weekend (in Eddie's new car). As we drove up, he was standing on his porch watching as a nephew fixed his front gate. Sam had planted his yard with grass, and his lush lawn stood in stark contrast to the red, dusty lots surrounding him. He was laughing and making fun of the teenage nephew who was apparently doing the job rather slowly. Eddie and I had joked about Sam being the master of his castle.

Next to him in the staff room on my last day was Muzi Shongwe, a history teacher. Muzi had a wife and a child in Tjakastad and was proud to provide for them with his teaching salary. He was very athletic—the best soccer player around—and was charismatic and intelligent.

What would these men and women have done, I thought. What would they be, if not for apartheid?

Eddie Msithini, Nhlanhla Ndlovu, Zwelethu "Chiluga" Mthethwa, Bongani Manyisa, M. E. Nkosi, Tholakele Mhlangu, Motha, Nkambule, Zodwa Msithini, Mrs. Mashinini, Busi Ndlovu, Norma Ngwenya, I. J. Nkabindze, R. S. Sibanyoni, Mr. Tshabalala—the list is endless. All of these teachers were held back, their lives distorted, and yet today they are all proud of their heritage and culture and of the communities they serve.

What could they have done with their lives if their fathers were doctors in Cincinnati? What if their mothers were bankers in New York City, or real estate agents in San Francisco? How many people would they have touched if their moms were the mayors of their little towns in Iowa, or if a grandfather was President of the United States? What if they had simply been born in America instead of South Africa? What if they had simply been born white?

And then I came to the question that really worried me: What if *I* had been born black in South Africa? I was going home soon, to a place where people take every opportunity, every advantage that they have over Eddie Msithini, for granted.

"Hey, Jay-seen! Are you OK?" Sam asked.

"He's just thinking of home," Tholakele said from the other side of the room.

A FEW MONTHS BEFORE I LEFT SOUTH AFRICA, MR. BOSCHOFF, THE WHITE principal of the Diepgezet Mine School who had invited us into his home in Kromdraai, reentered my life as well. The mine owners, noting that all of the children at his school were black and that the original purpose of the school had been to educate the white children of the mine administrators, told Mr. Boschoff that he would have to leave the premises or pay all of the back rent the school owed the mine. Undeterred, he moved his operation to eLukwatini. The number of children at his school almost doubled as the teachers, principals, and other professionals in the community flooded it with their own children.

Boschoff's is a public school and part of the same circuit as Lochiel Primary. But all of the teachers are white, and the students pay hundreds of times more to go there. The budget is much larger; the expectations of the teachers are much higher. And the students, who are all black, receive a wonderful education.

At one time I would have been disheartened by the fact that the white teachers were the ones who were successful. But as I was preparing to leave the country, Mr. Boschoff and his staff were reaching out to the other schools in the circuit. I went with several of the teachers from our mountain schools to observe the teachers at his school and pick up some advice. "Please, Jason," he said to me one day. "Help us with the other teachers in the region. We, here, need to prove that these kids can do just as much as any others."

He continues to struggle with South Africa's borders. But when faced with the choice of packing up their school and leaving the area—a decision that would have been very easy to make—he and his staff all chose to stay, to rebuild and expand their school instead of being run out by racists. Their high expectations for the kids will surely rub off to some extent on the adults.

Boschoff's school has many resources and a huge store of knowledge that could greatly benefit the other schools in the area. These other schools know this. But Mr. Boschoff came to me with much more urgency in trying to facilitate links. Like much of white South Africa he desperately wants to reach out, but often he just doesn't know how. But if he and his staff can match their willingness to teach the other educators in the area with a sincere desire to learn about the culture, language, and families of the other teachers, then there is no doubt that the circuit of schools can succeed mightily. "Please, Jason," he said to me on my last visit to his new school in eLukwatini. "I believe what we are doing is so important. We want to help everyone succeed, and we are really trying so hard. You must let people out there know about what we are trying to do to include everyone. Tell them we want to help in any way we can."

My final good-byes were filled with sadness and hope. I remember vividly the last time I saw Mtunzi. We were sitting in the square, on the small wall in front of the hotel.

People were coming and going in the late afternoon as they did every other day. The public cell phone booth, which had been installed because it is much cheaper than a phone line, was becoming a darker green as the sun lowered, and the Petrol sign was beginning to silhouette the primary school and the left side of Lochiel's amphitheater hills. The sun was just approaching the tips of the trees standing on the old border. Barefoot children sent by their parents were buying onions or bread or soup packets from Doris, who was getting ready to close up her shop. Rabbit was running by with Andiswa. Boni and Mama waSwazi were talking in front of the bottle store. Six boys stood in a circle playing a game of keep-away with a soccer ball, with one person in the middle of their circle trying to get a foot on the ball. The taxis were pulling into the garage empty; their only trip would be taking the driver home.

Mtunzi had just returned from a job near Graskop. I had not seen him in almost a year, and I was excited to have a chance to talk to him before I left. Piet and Shongwe and Bongani, with his Jimi Hendrix Afro, were sitting behind us in the garden, passing around a bottle of beer.

"Mtunzi," I said, "I love this time of day. Lochiel becomes so beautiful. Everyone is done with work and going home. The light is great, and the place is just beautiful."

"You know, Musa," He said. "In the past, we would never be here like this. In the eighties, no way we would be sitting here like this at this time. We would be running around to get home because we were scared."

"Of what?" I asked.

"Of the police, Musa."

"They would come out here?"

"Oh yes, Musa. I remember one time in the eighties we were sitting just like this. Everyone around in this place." He motioned with his hand. "And the hippo came crashing through. Boom, boom. Police shouting in Afrikaans and *sjamboking* people." He slapped his hands. "The people scattered. It was crazy."

"Hippo" was the name that black people gave the apartheid government's troop transports. The tall round body of the vehicle resembles the huge African animal, and hippos were famous for carrying brutal policemen and occupying townships. I could not imagine that the people in Lochiel posed any threat that would have necessitated a troop transport. Yet the states of emergency that governed South Africa for so many years brought plenty of violence to otherwise peaceful places.

"Did the police come here often?" I asked.

"Sometimes, Musa. But anyway, we were always afraid."

"Did anything ever happen to you?" I asked.

"They came one time for my grandfather. Two white policemen. I was at home. They broke down the door with their feet. Bang bang bang, and they took my grandfather, and they went all over the house." He stood up to demonstrate. He spoke like a reporter, very matter-of-factly, but his body movements became animated. "They reached up on top of the cabinets in the kitchen, and they found an *assegai*, like a long spear." With his hands he showed that it was about four feet long. "And they asked why my grandfather had this. I was standing in the corner of the room." He drew his elbows in tight to his body to show that he had been standing at attention. "They searched everything. My mother was screaming, Musa. *Ayish.* They found this thing, you know that thing that my grandfather used to shoot squirrels and birds and monkeys. You put rocks in it? Um, what do you call it? It is that thing that David used to kill Goliath?"

"A slingshot?"

"Yes. My grandfather had a slingshot, and they took it and they arrested him. They came back the next day, and they asked me to sign a paper. I looked at the paper. I did not know Afrikaans, but I was taking it at school. I saw the words for 'rifle' and 'bullets.' I said to the man, 'Look, this says bullets. There were no bullets. I cannot sign your paper.'"

"You said that to the policeman?" I asked, shocked. "What did he do?"

"He yelled at me, but said it did not matter. They left again and did not bring my grandfather back for three weeks!"

"Wow." I said.

"Yeah, Musa, the eighties were bad."

"It's getting better, though, don't you think?"

"Yeah, a little better, but it is still the same."

"Why do you say that?"

"It's like my job in Graskop. This white man, he was crazy, Musa. Some days I worked from seven in the morning, sometimes until three at night. And Musa, I looked at my paycheck, and he did not pay me from five until three." He sat back down next to me. "I had to get money for my family here, Musa, for my son. I worked so hard. You know, this guy takes oranges and he puts them onto trucks. I worked in with the trucks, loading and unloading.

"You remember, Musa, when I left, I was so happy to have a job...." I nodded. "...and then I go and it is like this....

"I ate only maize meal for three months, Musa. For *three months*. I was working until twelve every night, and sometimes until three. I walked for 30 minutes to get to work. I was so tired!

"On Saturday he comes to me, and he says, come work in my garden at home. At home, Musa! At his house. No, that is not right. I said to him, 'It is not right to make us work so much if you only pay us for a few hours.' He said to me, if I didn't want the job, I could go, because he could find 20 people who want the job. I worked in his garden, Musa, and I hated him. I hated him so much, Musa. I thought to myself, 'No, this man is oppressing me too much. He is oppressing me to the point where I will be forced to hit him.'"

He paused. I looked out over the square, thinking about how many would have taken that job, would have jumped at the opportunity to work at all.

"And I thought, Musa," Mtunzi continued, "that is illegal and I will be in trouble if I hit him. So I left. One day I just walked home,

I collected my clothes and things, put them in my bag, and I left. I did not even tell him I was going to leave. I was supposed to be paid on Monday, Musa, and I did not even go and get my money. I did not want him to see me ask him for money. No, I wanted to go. I do not need money that bad. I know how to be poor, Musa. I did not need the money that bad."

In Mandela's autobiography he talks about a moment of triumph: "I could walk upright like a man and look everyone in the eye with the dignity that comes from not having succumbed to oppression and fear." Mtunzi was certainly triumphant, but his triumph also put him out of a job.

ON MY LAST MORNING IN LOCHIEL, I TOOK MY THINGS AND LOADED THEM into Nhlanhla's car. He was going to drive me to Pretoria.

Gogo was attending a Methodist women's conference, and we waited for her to get back. She and I had spent hours a day together every day for two years. She had been my mother, my colleague, and one of my closest friends, and I had helped her with every single one of her projects. I was nervous about saying good-bye. Boni had almost cried earlier in the day, and I would not be able to handle a tearful Gogo.

She came into the kitchen wearing her white collar and hat and her red suit that all the women in the Methodist group wear. "Musa," she said, "are you leaving?"

"Yebo, Gogo."

"OK," she said. "Go well."

"OK, Gogo. Bye."

"Bye, Musa." And she watched us walk out the door, dry-eyed as she could be. Gogo, I thought, has dealt with much more difficult issues than my departure.

The African liberation hero Sekou Toure said:

> To take part in the African revolution, it is not enough to write
> a revolutionary song; you must first fashion the revolution with

the people. And if you fashion it with the people, the songs will come by themselves and of themselves.

The people of Lochiel are participating in a revolution. Their society is intercut with borders but founded on Ubuntu. In even the poorest parts of the country, new revolutionary songs are beginning to be heard. As I left Lochiel for my own country, which is also laced with borders, I thought about a letter that Gogo received from an African-American grandmother.

Jackie Robinson, a friend of my mother's, grew up in Cabrini Green, one of the most notorious housing projects in Chicago. In high school we had been told that a murder occurred there daily. In college some friends and I made a wrong turn driving to Wrigley Field, and when we passed a sign for Cabrini Green, we panicked—not unlike the woman whose car broke down in front of the Lochiel garage. Shouting in fear, we made a U-turn and sped away. When we got back to a better neighborhood, we had to stop the car to catch our breath.

Jackie's life has taken all the turns that one reads about in the newspaper. One of her sons is in prison for killing someone in a drug deal that went bad. Another is on parole. Her husband is unemployed. Jackie was hit in the leg by a stray bullet on the way home from work. She became a grandmother when my mother's children were still in elementary school, and she has worked for barely more than minimum wage most of her life. Yet she has managed to buy her own house away from Cabrini Green, and when she can afford it, she takes classes toward a bachelor's degree from a local college. She is a leader in her community; Jackie served as an elected member of her local school council, making policy for the elementary school that her youngest son attended. Children in her neighborhood know that her house is a refuge and source of help when they need it.

Before I left South Africa, a package arrived in Lochiel addressed to Gogo. Inside were two photos and a note that explained the pictures:

One was of Head Start families holding a banner, about to board a bus for Washington, D.C., to attend a march for children—a group Jackie helped organize. The other picture was of Jackie and 15 other people in their state representative's office in Springfield, Illinois. Jackie had organized the trip to introduce others in her community to the person who represented them. "I want you to know," her letter to Gogo said, "that people who look like you and me can make a difference."

Enclosed in the note was also a $100 bill for the preschool. I know that Jackie was working temporary jobs at that time, making barely enough to pay her mortgage with nothing left for anything else. She had heard about the Lochiel Preschool from my mother and wanted to make a contribution. I had to look away to keep from crying as I read the letter to Gogo. "With this," she wrote, "I am throwing hope like a boomerang. I know that if I can give it to you, it will eventually make it back here to me."

IN GOGO'S MIND, SHE TRANSLATED THE WORD "HOPE" TO THE ZULU word *themba*. "Themba" means not only "hope" but also "believe." For Gogo, "hope" is not a possibility but a certainty.

Too often, perhaps, we lose hope because we fail to look for it where we least expect it—among poor black people in a South African homeland or an American inner city, or poor white farmers in clapboard shacks in south Georgia. But there it is.

SOUTH AFRICA HAS PUT A FEW MORE YEARS OF THE POST-APARTHEID struggle behind it, but many more are to come. The government continues to make changes in the structure of its bureaucracy. Mr. Boschoff and other white South Africans continue their quest for a meaningful relationship with their black brethren. Politicians, CEOs, and central bank administrators struggle with the slow economy. Black and white teachers both work to inspire the next generation of South African leaders as they remove apartheid's constraints from their own lives. Health care workers continue their battle to educate the society about AIDS and to stop the misinformation spread by too many in South Africa. The virus continues to take lives.

In Lochiel, they bury their dead every Saturday. But the community continues. Mtunzi, I am sure, is still looking for a job good enough to match his spirit. The teachers at the three schools on that mountain ridge continue to teach every day, and students continue to learn. The families who moved their homes to the plots on the grid have electricity and may soon have water. There will be fewer children without candles to study by. The power lines now stop in Lochiel, and I am hopeful.

How could I not be? I received a letter from Gogo the other day. *"Siyaphila,"* she said. "We're still alive." And doing just fine.

ACKNOWLEDGMENTS

THERE ARE MANY WHOM I WOULD LIKE TO THANK FOR THE HELP THEY
have given me in the preparation of this book. First and foremost, Terry
Adamson, as connected to me and my family as any other could possibly be, thought of this as a book before anyone else. Nina Hoffman, Kevin
Mulroy, Johnna Rizzo, Lisa Thomas, Dale Herring, and the rest of the
people at National Geographic books made this possible. It is almost
embarrassing how much better the book is after John Paine and Kevin
Mulroy's outstanding edits.

I would like to give special thanks to John Coyne for all that he has
done for so many Peace Corps writers. And I would also like to note that
so many Peace Corps volunteers who came before me, and the countless
that will follow, all deserve a chance to write a book like this. Many of
the experiences herein are unique not to me, but to the Peace Corps experience. This applies with more force to those who served with me in
South Africa. This is my story only because I am telling it. All of us had
these experiences.

Beverly Brettman helped with the early stages of the book more than any other, but many of my best friends read and edited and made suggestions. Thank you to Joe Clair, Chris Shultz, Pat Thomasma, Keith Cossrow, Dave Marek, Matt Price, Shana Gallentine, Brad Vigrass, and Thomas Bates (who sneaked in to this list at the very end). Doug McClary would have helped as well, but I am proud to say he had already left for the Peace Corps in Uganda to work for real.

My brilliant wife Kate has helped me through every part of this process, both with her journalist ear to the language of the book and her enormous heart to every other aspect of our lives together. My mother and Bob, my grandmother, and my grandfather, accomplished authors all, gave valuable input on the writing process. My dad and Elizabeth read every draft and supported me from the very beginning. Audrey Lewis gave extensive input on the grammar, and is a great mother-in-law. Without my family, the support they have given me, the times they turned me toward Africa or toward Georgia, and the examples they have offered, I would not be who I am, and this book would never have happened. I single out my grandfather Carter, who has given me so many opportunities, and inspired so many other people, for giving the best advice possible. When I left for Africa, he told me simply to keep a journal.

Power Lines is a tribute to the people I lived with in South Africa, Gogo, Boni, Sandile, the girls, the teachers, and the students. They are acknowledged by the book itself. I hope they get a chance to read it and understand how much they meant to me. Ngiyabonga kakhulu. Ngizonikhumbula njalo njalo.